Acting Out in Groups

Contents

The Jargon of Inauthenticity

AN INTRODUCTION TO *ACTING OUT IN GROUPS*

John Mowitt

In Theory

I am tempted to begin by relating how I came to have the unenviable task of "introducing" the following essays, but, in the end, it is not a terribly interesting story. More interesting, and perhaps even remarkable, is why someone in my position would begin by characterizing his task as "unenviable." Setting aside, for the moment, what precisely my position is, I invite you to consider the resemblance (no doubt familial) between the vaguely diplomatic labor of introducing scholars and audiences to one another, and the exercise of commentary. As is well known, this last has been the object of academic derision and contempt at least since *The Archaeology of Knowledge*, if not well before. However, the general problem with commentary, namely, the delusion it promotes concerning its detachment from both the work and the world, is aggravated here by the simple fact that these essays—both individually and as a group—have anticipated, if not in fact solicited, my position. They are, in effect, lying in wait for the act of introduction, an act that Catherine Liu's opening salvo associates—through the implicit chain "introduce," "introject," "incorporate"—with the practice of cannibalism. At the risk of seeming melodramatic, what then constitutes the unenviable character of this act is the fact that in carrying it out one confronts the possibility—nay, the likelihood—of being eaten alive.

In the "publish and perish" world in which contemporary academic intellectuals work, "being eaten alive" has lost its denotative link to the event of public, though rarely conscious, humiliation (one thinks here, I suppose, of the graduate seminar presided over by either the novice or the incompetent). Connotatively, of course, this association endures, and for this reason it is important to emphasize that academia has reduced to nil the pragmatic value of fearing such humiliation. After all, is anyone other than your friends paying attention? This fact notwithstanding, the essays grouped together here render such humiliation virtually impossible by establishing, in advance, that one is destined to misread them. In short, they are not intended for popular consumption (emphasis on *consumption*). Thus, in the absence of even the possibility of "misrepresentation," the discomfort of being eaten alive is, for all intents and purposes, eliminated. However, precisely to the degree that here the impossibility of misrepresentation is openly divorced from the delusions of exegetical voluntarism—in other words, from the belief that "anything goes"—these essays confront someone in my position with the more serious problem of compromise; that is, can they be introduced, can they be made public, without their either devouring—and thereby incorporating—the act of introduction (rendering it at once unnecessary and unhelpful), or their becoming, through that very act, what they are not, namely, just more examples of psychoanalytically inflected cultural criticism? Perhaps I *am* relating the story of this task after all . . .

My wager, obviously, is that they can be so introduced, but not without a certain tact. And, if I have begun by overemphasizing the problem of an introduction as such, it is because tact requires that one acknowledge that this very problem is an avatar of one of the persistent theoretical preoccupations of this volume, namely, the act of grouping. The detachment earlier associated with commentary allows one not only to group his or her forces, but to group that which constitutes their object. To the extent that this activity prompts reflection on the logic of compromise, it reminds one that grouping is never far removed from the polis and its politics, even when the groups involved are merely stables of authors. For this reason, *Acting Out in Groups* finds itself entangled in precisely the conundrum delineated by Adorno when he addressed himself to the etymological hybrid of "cultural criticism." Though the contributors to this volume may not be in the habit of "thinking with their ears," they are, in different ways, struggling with and against the crosscurrents Adorno channeled in the following formulation: "The culture critic is not happy with civilization, to which alone he owes his discontent." And although none of the essays grouped here openly embraces the antiphilistinism that Adorno renders synonymous with the twisted happiness of the cultural critic, several of them (notably, those of Laurence A. Rickels, the editor), both stylistically and thematically, address themselves to the distinctly Freudian resonance of Adorno's dialectical formulation. The theoretical constellation at stake here might be diagrammed this way: just as a certain irreducible and therefore constitutive guilt represents the price of admission to that "great get-together" we call civilization, a certain, equally constitutive, unhappiness bonds the critic to culture. However, because the latter is not simply a reiteration of the former, the constellation tells us something in particular about critique when articulated in the cultural realm, namely, that it effectively drafts the contract that groups together critics, culture, and the civilization that lets everyone down, but certainly not off.

The act of criticism, of course, is divided by the very divisions that it discerns, including of course the ambivalent, if not unlivable, division between the critic and culture. It is along this unstable front that precisely what separates this volume from garden-variety psychoanalytically inflected cultural criticism can be characterized. Although my insistence on the affinity between the concerns and the procedures of the critics grouped together here may well have already clarified the point for some, for others a bit of context might be useful. Where to begin? For the sake of argument, let us just say that this volume belongs to the "new world order," or at least to the version of that order that, at the international level, has declared that the end of history is at hand, that globalism (corporate multinationalism) is triumphant, and that in the precincts of academia, "excellence" has replaced "culture" as the tithe paid by the university to the state. Under such circumstances scholars, particularly in the humanities (where, after all, academic cultural criticism tends to be practiced), have been obliged to regroup, not only to defend their jobs, but, in rare yet telling instances, to reconstitute themselves as "public intellectuals." At the risk of adopting an "apocalyptic tone," this is a situation through which humanities educators may well now be glimpsing their own obsolescence. As books such as *Will Teach for Food* make abundantly clear, the most vicious, and perhaps therefore politically important, form that this illusion of a future has taken is in the organized attacks on graduate student training and professionalization, attacks that, in addition to rendering the lives of many talented individuals absolutely miserable (and yes, I recognize the "atypical" character of graduate students at Yale), also undermine any regrouping of the faculty by restricting its temporal range to the generations currently protected by the obviously fragile provisions of the tenure code. Equally nefarious, of course, is the controversial but deplorable trend toward hiring more and more part-time or even full-time "adjuncts"—those who, even if not seeking tenure, will never have it to lose. Faced with such developments, that is, developments within professional institutions and organizations more typically inclined to regard, say, the North American Free Trade Agreement as someone else's problem, "cultural criticism" has acquired a new urgency even as it remains ensnared within familiar double binds.

Again, for the sake of argument, one might reasonably claim that this revitalization of academic "cultural criticism" has prompted, among other things, a theoretical crisis. This is a crisis that has led to significant regroupings within and among academic partisans of various theoretical persuasions, but it has also instigated a full-scale attack on Theory regardless of persuasion. Psychoanalytic theory has figured centrally here—not because psychoanalysis has assumed the predictably phallic function of a lightning rod, but because its reputed "ahistoricism" uncannily coincides with the perceived deficiency of Theory—and certainly one of the things at stake in this volume is what its own prepositional preoccupations would urge one in my position to call in-crowd infighting.

Perhaps it would make sense here to point to the fairly recent establishment of the *Journal of the Psychoanalysis of Culture and Society (JPCS)*, a journal inaugurated in 1996 with the expressed intention not simply of revitalizing psychoanalysis as a theoretical activity in the Anglophone world, but also of linking this revitalization to a resurgence of cultural criticism. This is a development that, for various reasons, ought to be seen in conjunction with Slavoj Zizek's effort to "return to Lacan" through Hitchcock, or Teresa Brennan's and Joan Copjec's interventions on behalf of psychoanalysis within the discipline of history—all instances of regrouping that acknowledge some of the defeats of psychoanalysis while stubbornly insisting that Freud's family romance may yet have the last word. I refer to this as "in-crowd infighting" because not only does it bear witness to the struggle among Theory partisans (that is, all those who insist that it has consequences and that one really cannot leave home without it) over the legacy of the posthumanist paradigm, but it underscores the fact that psychoanalysis itself has double-crossed (at the very least) its own path.

Those committed to the project of *JPCS* (here reduced to a symptom) believe that psychoanalysis has something vital to contribute to the contemporary practice of cultural criticism, because culture is incomprehensible without a theory of the human subject. From such a perspective, what much of contemporary cultural politics misses is the fact that the polis is an intersubjective field mediated by language and what Jacques Lacan once called "the dialectic of desire." Against those who reduce psychoanalysis to the status of an ahistorical, class-specific theory of sexuality, the *JPCS* partisans insist that this is only the latest avatar of a long-standing social resistance to psychoanalysis, a resistance that is now putting the very practice of cultural criticism at risk. The in-crowd thus being rivalrously challenged here is what, for lack of a better term, I will call the cultural studies in-crowd, the new (?) discipline on the (historical) block. One aim of the *JPCS* partisans is to take up the gauntlet thrown down by cultural studies, and to reassert the importance of psychoanalytic theory, but to articulate a discursive practice of psychoanalysis that effectively realigns it with the traumatic preoccupations of the present.

The positions staked out in *Acting Out in Groups* represent an alternative articulation of the importance of psychoanalysis for cultural criticism—in fact, an articulation that challenges what its partisans might characterize as the "compromise" effected by Zizek and others. Virtually every piece contained here not only addresses itself to one of those characteristic offerings of the culture industry from which audiences are insatiably repelled—the *Jerry Springer Show*, the late Kathy Acker's onanistic writing techniques, a fairy-tale precursor to *Carrie*, a made-for-television "documentary" on troubled children, the cacophonics of Cecil Taylor, the German national symbol after "reunification," various queer and feminist advocacy groups, documentaries of comic book authors, etc., etc.—but does so in order to use Sigmund Freud (and typically the Freud of Jacques Derrida, *not* Lacan) as a way to establish what resists theorization in cultural-studies approaches to such material. The aim here—and the infighting is unmistakable—is not simply to establish how cultural "resistance" (a cultural-studies fetish if there ever was one) resists itself (whereby "progressive" projects collapse into their pre-Freudian, and therefore conservative, assumptions), but to insist, against those who place credence in the pedagogical rigors of First World cinemas, that cultural criticism must be both more and less faithful to psychoanalysis. At least, in theory.

Inaction

Obviously, much hangs on how one unpacks this "more" and this "less." Let's take "more." Throughout *Acting Out in Groups*, and perhaps most insistently in Rickels's own contributions, effort is made to construct a genealogy of "deviation"; that is, how, when, and by whom "acting out" (Freud's *Agieren*) was converted into authentic psychoanalytic jargon is something detailed with considerable patience. The price of this conversion is not simply a pop-psychological reduction of the concept ("acting out" as behaving—typically conspic-uously—in response to the workings of some obscure, if not uncon-scious, motive), but a betrayal of Freud, who is valued, conversely, for the provocative irreducibility he folded into the concept. The aim is not, of course, to whine about the act of betrayal. This is understood to be inevitable. Rather, the aim is to resuscitate the Freudian corpus, to make its incommensurable discussions of acting out come to life inside our contemporary preoccupations with agency and action. Peter Canning, who—at least here—cleaves to the most Lacanian line of the collection, diagrams the uncanny character of this resuscitation by setting up a dis-tinction between acting out (an act that remains readable as a symp-tom) and "passing to the act" (Lacan's *passage à l'acte*, which passes through readability in order to antagonize the signifying chain as such). Precisely because he accepts that Lacan's return is indeed simply a read-ing of the Freudian text, Canning is able to mobilize this distinction as a properly Freudian component of our relation to action itself. This represents, in the context of the in-crowd infighting I am addressing here, a commitment to psychoanalytic theory that strikes out both at cultural-studies partisans who want to "fight the power" by finding their way *back* into action, *and* at, for lack of a less reductive term, the partisans of *JPCS*, who are implicitly perceived as having gone too far in the direction of rethinking the agenda of psychoanalytic theory in light of the crisis of cultural criticism. In other words, if everything you wanted to know about Lacan is really *in* Hitchcock, then cultural criti-cism can indeed find its theoretical footing precisely where all matters of discernment become merely academic, that is, where academic criticism matters least. In this sense, the writers grouped together here (to varying degrees, to be sure) appear more faithful to psychoanalysis and would never indulge in the irritating apologetics that mar Stephen Crook's otherwise probing introduction to *Adorno: The Stars Down to Earth*.

This matters, not because it allows contending in-groups to delineate the fronts of their infighting (though I am, of course, arguing that this is—at a certain institutional level—of capital importance), but because it confronts the contemporary activity of cultural criticism with a theoretical question, namely, how are we to link the conditions of such criticism to an account of the psychosociogenesis of subjects? Is cultural criticism viable in the absence of such an account, and do the dire straits within which such criticism currently finds itself legitimately warrant the bracketing of such a question? In the end, the issue is not about Freud or Lacan or Theodor Adorno. It is about criticism. What makes it possible and what makes it matter? The writers grouped here have the temerity to insist—in spite of everything theoretical, political, clinical, neurobiological, and so on, that has significantly called the Freudian breakthrough into question (and there can be no serious doubt about this)—that psychoanalysis is not only still pertinent, but of urgent importance precisely for those most committed, here and now, to "passing to the act," to dispensing with theory and getting on with the proverbial business at hand.

The degree to which the positions sketched out here are, to the same degree, *less* faithful to psychoanalysis can be illuminated by returning briefly to my earlier evocation of the "prepositional preoccupations" of these texts. There, my aim was to stress the need for hearing both "in GROUPS" and "IN groups" in the title of this volume. Here, I want to expand this point to, among other things, provide some small justification for the title of these introductory remarks. Those familiar with the work of Rickels know the extent to which his style, the very texture of his writing, has developed as an exercise in the paronomastic baroque. Because of its proximity to the cryptographics of Derrida and others, it is characteristically perceived as an expression of a commitment to the deconstructive tangent of the so-called linguistic turn. It is certainly that, but it is also more. Specifically, what is so striking about Rickels's style is the way he deploys it in order to, as it were, argue "in stereo," that is, to write with a forked tongue. Just to take a small, but telling, example, consider his persistent use of the substantive "midlife criticism." Premised or perched on Paul de Man's hinging of crisis and criticism, this substantive loops the reader through an etymological convergence that reconstitutes it as "midlife crisis," something we think we readily understand. However, once formed, this understanding gives way to the corrosive effects of the word *criticism* on "midlife crisis." Although, ultimately, comprehension may depend here on an engagement with Rickels's notion of the Teen Age, it is clear that the substantive speaks at least twice: once about psychology and once about criticism. When placed in a theoretical formulation addressing critical practice, "midlife criticism" semantically reiterates the duplicity, the doubleness, it allows Rickels to discern in critical practice that envies the lawlessness it condemns in those who have displaced it within the scheme of intellectual generations.

At the risk of overstating the sway held by Rickels over the essays grouped here, a third statement performed by the substantive "midlife criticism" is nevertheless worth considering. It is the one that states directly in what sense these essays are less faithful to psychoanalysis. Thus, in addition to speaking about both psychology and criticism, "midlife criticism" also speaks about mass culture and the discourse of the jingle, the slogan, the pitch. Or better, it *speaks* mass culture (in the case at hand, the inauthentic jargon of *Psychology Today*). In fact, many of the writers grouped here, through recourse to precisely those linguistic elements that Ferdinand de Saussure originally denied the existence of, namely, willfully fashioned signs, let their arguments advance through the sound bites or discursive "ready-mades" of the culture industry. Against those who believed in the supreme agency of language, the contributors to *Acting Out in Groups* proceed according to the notion that cultural criticism forges the links in its signifying chain out of a discourse that, unlike language, no one (perhaps not even those paid to synthesize it) is inclined to claim responsibility for. Otherwise, cultural criticism's twisted raving against the anti-intellectualism of the masses is merely the tortuous exposition of a critique destined to miss its mark. If one of the hallmarks of the international emergence of psychoanalysis as a disciplinary and professional field was its elaboration of an authentic, Latinate jargon ("parapraxis" for *Fehlleistung*, or "ego" for *Ich*), then the strategy pursued by the contributors to this volume represents a betrayal. It is a turning away from the despotic core of the field, toward the same rich indecisiveness that Rickels teases out of Freud's *Agieren*, and toward the jolt of the jingle, that is, the current avatar of "the concept."

The aim here is not to discover psychoanalytic theory in the abbreviated rigor of a headline, nor to assume that Woody Allen has even the remotest familiarity with *Of Grammatology*, but rather to deploy the "ready-made" texture of mass cultural discourse on behalf of theory, that is, on behalf of an approach to cultural criticism that refuses to abandon theory while nevertheless repudiating its metalinguistic pretensions. Although such a repudiation typically involves an epistemological modification wherein statements about other statements are stripped of any authority, technical or otherwise, here this repudiation produces not only the self-defeating phenomenon of an inauthentic jargon, but also—as suggested earlier—an alternative style of argumentation (if it can even be called that). Here is not the place to delineate this style in detail, but—to take the earlier example of "midlife criticism"—clearly one of its features is the stereophonic spreading that occurs when a point about criticism is run through two separate disciplinary channels. The reader is thus confronted with a prompt, a signal, that obliges him or her not just to finish the point, but to construct the logic implied by the associations twisted together within it. Not exactly "sillygisms," but close, and Rickels may be right to suggest that this addictive ambivalence is a perfectly effective way to rearticulate the constitutive discontent of the cultural critic without lapsing into either self-loathing or cynical clowning.

Here, of course, we are confronted with perhaps the boldest aspect of the gamble taken by *Acting Out in Groups*. I say this because the "sillygism" is, among other things, a sorting device; it forms ingroups. It can't help it. There are those "in the know," that is, those who recognize and respond (even if errantly) to the prompts, and those who can't, won't, or don't. By working so intimately with the discourse of "ready-mades" and "found thoughts," many more people than usual are solicited by the prompts, and the potential for group formation is thus heightened. Because the matter of the group weighs heavily on every page—it is there in the poetics of the prose—as one proceeds from essay to essay, the group formations reread in light of Freud's *Agieren* (the horde, the audience, the nation, etc.) converge to underscore a strategic omission. Unlike the provocatively reflexive distinction between "acting out" and "passing to the act," there is no similar formulation concerning a distinction between *Massenpsychologie* (group psychology) and something like "in-group" psychology. And one might reasonably argue that even establishing the self-defeating character of such a distinction would—as a reflexive gesture—nevertheless illuminate the shadows where this grouping of authors and the actions of those groups they analyze crowd against one another. By characterizing this as a strategic omission, I am of course signaling that the collection puts an analytic value on placing such matters on the inactive list. Precisely how this places cultural criticism and psychoanalysis in action— that is, at the service of those acting in concert against those seeking to make the writing of such books impossible—will have to be teased out of the readings that follow. In theory, in action, indeed.

On the Genealogy of a Concept; or, Turning up the Volume

Laurence A. Rickels

"Acting out" is one of those still current pop-sociopsychological terms that's a mouthful. If it's been fitting in your mouth, not in your hands, then that's because there's been way too little thinking-writing on the concept or on its outer-concept activities or on the tension between the letter of the law, of the concept, and the recycling spread of its diagnostic fill-in-the-blank function. The blanks to be fired up are, of course, delinquency and deviance in the Teen Age — in other words, *in* groups. As derogation, acting out cuts us a wide birth — the birth of a context that's really a contest between political correctness and therapeutic correctness. The polymorphous publicity that characterizes acting out to this day can be tracked back, then, to the ongoing falling out with — the fall out from — those century-long merger attempts between a Marxistoid sociology and an eclectic but still psychoanalysis-based psychology that, all violence and denial notwithstanding, just never really went through.

A series of *Dasein*-rhymes would seem to confirm all the reservations about acting out in theory and in act. The "official" psychoanalytic dossier on acting out, largely in the service of the concept's containment for greater analytic and therapeutic efficacy, appears in 1968, in the *International Journal of Psychoanalysis*, just in time for political activity. In 1965, a volume edited by Lawrence Abt and Stuart Weissman, *Acting Out*, which represented an earlier interdisciplinary attempt to functionalize and subspecialize the eclecticism of the concept, was dedicated to President Kennedy, whose assassination coincided with the conception of the volume: "To John Fitzgerald Kennedy ... who stood for reason and intelligence in human affairs and became the victim of acting out destructiveness." Now, in time for the millennium, we have *Acting Out in Groups*. But current events will not prove an ironic commentary on this "collection." Our in-group of authors will have given thought to a whole spin of the dial, of the denial, of all the settings and channels of acting out, without, however, ever getting phobic about whatever contaminations and combinations come our way. No guidance counseling is being offered this time around, at least none that could be distinguished once and for all from the performance. What the different contributions share is a sense of complicity with the charge of acting out.

In what follows, we will be introduced to many of the forms and forums of acting out—nonencounter, imposture, and improvisation, among all the other venues—on the one hand (in shorthand) in writing shot straight from the quip, with the cathexis commanded by headline events, in pun-filled metabolizations of timely and thus dated media events, on the other hand (in longhand) in writing that plays the syntax of argument for the music it's time to face. Although individual authors may seem so far away in their respective styles of presentation, they are so often so close in the way their texts attempt to theorize, to see acting out from both sides now—as constative and as performative activity. Either you land on the side—or the inside—of the constative where criticism that appears to uphold Enlightenment standards is also already performing or acting out its own survival of the ends of its criticism, or you get deeper and deeper into the performance, into the performative side of the unbalancing act. At the same time, the performer ends up excavating in outer spaces between what's already representable or repressible certain sliding but nameable coordinates of improvisation that could, at one point, stand still for constative restatement. But then the performance would be over.

In each case, the spot of opinion we are all in—the journalistic condition—just doesn't simply come out. The essays address "acting out" in various contexts, down various corridors, like those shared by psychoanalysis and literary theory, but also dress down to focus on media cultures of acting out that grow up in front of television or, behind the scenes, inside the live taping of talk and game shows. It's just one culture after all—just one, one culture.

Given their origin in the AIDS crisis, the new, politicized reappropriations of "acting out" (Act Up et al.) haunt a place of improper closure or burial. A certain murderous pop discourse in which homosexuality gets framed as teenager-forever, group-psychopathological, borderline-psychotic, you name it, required the split-leveling of all that's left open at Freud's end, for example, at the end of his Dora case. It is on location with this contamination of terms and interests that Andrew Hewitt and Julie Carlson enter our group exploration of the meanings and settings of acting out. As is the case throughout this group-theory session, the encounter with acting out does not forego the powerful frame or apparatus in which the dis-order has been theorized, administered, contained, but rather really gets into it. Hello! Hello! Like, it's not like pop psychology and social studies—the lip services whereby we prey on the other—could ever be stopped, once and for all. And joining in also has its attractions (critical ones, too).

Hewitt analyzes a headline scandal from the recent past—a past that always is, according to Adorno, as remote, primal, and catastrophic as any prehistory. It's Arlene Croce's all-out critique of so-called victim art on the occasion of not attending but having heard all about Bill T. Jones's *Still/Here*, which put on stage the recognizably living and those recognizably dying of AIDS (and, because the relay and delay of video was also involved, the already dead). Hewitt dismantles the whole trafficking in journalistic texts that jammed with this charge of acting out, one that was, as so often happens only to recur, itself always just another example of acting out. Hewitt comes to some powerful conclusions that stand out from the journalistic jam everyone else was in at that time. Acting out, as a disguised form of inactivity, characterizes the actions or acts of art. This is where that old unrepresentable, Death, makes an entrance just the same: "Death threatens criticism because it threatens the fiction of alterity and distance upon which Enlightenment critique would be grounded." But then there's survival: not only in Jones's performance, but even, or especially, in Croce's critique, which overstepped its own Enlightenment frame and thus also entered the center stage of performativity. Because performance is always only admitted to preclude the practice of criticism, when criticism nevertheless gets performed, it is its survival—its survival of the demise of traditional paradigms—that catches the show. All parties to this context or contest, therefore, could not but blast apart the boundaries between performance and critique, two ends of representation that have enjoyed "a somewhat strained relationship" throughout the historical emergence of our public sphere. Hewitt strums and listens to the strains that cannot simply be picked apart.

Julie Carlson presents the case of Master Betty, whose marginal sexual and gender identifications were given shelter up in the bright lights of the group's short attention span. In 1804, this child star dominated the London theater scene, booked high and low as everyone's culture hero. While more established or grown-up actors-out quit their companies in protest rancor when Betty won all the major Shakespeare roles for that year, the men and women in the sold-out audiences were really getting off. In the manner of repression of early childhood masturbation, Master Betty was at the same time desexualized as the "I" of a discursive storm that described and enacted teen passion. The manic half-life of his career completed itself by 1805, and the sacrificial star of early mass culture withdrew into the missing-persons report filled out on the margin of mainstream cathexis. Carlson's reservations regarding an entirely upbeat turn to theatrical analogies for promotion of current notions of gender performativity are thus confirmed by this study in career theory. Where there's theater, there's still the consumerist metabolization—short-span, fast-object—of any subjects up, out, and away there. At the historical opening of this All Rise to a critical attention newly awarded the arts, we are struck, thanks to Carlson's careful reconstruction, by the emergence of a group psychology of stardom and fandom that preempts any stable differentiation between criticism and performance or, for that matter, between high and low cultures.

Fred Moten addresses and performs an ensemble of diversity discourses that settles down ultimately to think the links and limits of a certain brand of queer nostalgia. Above all, however—or rather, at the same time—Moten's essay is about facing the music while making it all resound. All associations and connections proceed along recognizable in-group-only philosophical lines. Moten riffs on the critical discourses we can identify, the same ones with which we have already identified, from the split shares of Marxo-Freudianism, utopian dialectics, to 1980s deconstruction, and, finally, queer studies. The last two provide the bulk of Moten's materialized tension between the former's syntactic blasting apart or derepression of opposition and closure and the latter-day retrenchment of certain metaphysical, metaphorical comforts within a perspective that's all about acting out. But one legitimate critique can be another symptomatic disconnection. What Moten manages to allude to and perform—to improvise—is a basic disownership of psychoanalysis. Moten's approach shares with the public text of queer affirmation a desire to engage in autoanalysis without engaging in the transference work of and on the institution of Freud's discoveries. But

Moten makes this move and takes this risk consciously, and thus he also raises the stakes of the queer affirmation to consciousness. Changing the world is still really out there. Moten thus restores some sense of justice—in support of all the other forms of resistance that are out and about—by making acting out open up to improvisation and the ensemble.

Once upon a time, Freud rejected Jung's rediagnosis of a patient, Otto Gross, who had just split treatment. First he was obsessional-compulsive, now that he's gone he's psychotic. That just cannot be happening, not after the fact, not after first contact has already been made with the patient in session. Jung, in other words, had been unwilling to interpret for the resistance, the transference, and the countertransference. The rediagnosis as psychotic meets a certain prejudice or prediagnosis that's all the rage—the one putting it all on the psychopaths or sociopaths out there—somewhere over an unexamined transferential setting. Already within the immediate following or understanding of Freud, we can observe, then, that the all-out psycholabeling of every disconnection from the social contract always refers back to a resistance or repression going down and acted out in the misfiring interchange between transference and countertransference. This spreading it on sick of the acting-out label is everywhere in evidence, right at the beginning, already in the first station-identification, which remains, however, so singularly difficult to locate. The dis-location of the onset of the instant spread doubly books the itinerary of the concept of acting out, right from the start, as site-specific installation (within psychoanalysis) *and* outer-corpus experience. It's by no means certain that Freud's use of *Agieren* in fact translates into any of the many associations with acting out that are so out there.

When the International Psychoanalytical Congress in 1967 organized its proceedings around the topic of acting out, Anna Freud led the way in calling for clarification of a concept that by that time bore little resemblance to the original contexts into which Freud was seen to have first introduced it. Leo Rangell from Los Angeles, another 1967 conference-goer, seconded the admonition:

> Menninger (1958) has described the history of nosologies as consisting of successive waves of differentiation, followed by contractions, and then by differentiation again. Similar alternation has been the case with the phenomenon of acting out. After an initial specific coinage and use, there followed a phase of diffuse

expansion of our understanding and usage of the term, from
which our challenge today, I believe, is to contract it again to a
more narrow and precise form. (1968: 195)

Prior to the beginning of contractions, the widest expansionism of the
concept was already playing on the psychopathy and sociopathy channels of our reception of adolescence or perpetual adolescence. The use
of acting out as near synonym of or placeholder for a mix and medley
of teenage delinquency and deviance is largely a World War II development, one that thus parallels the first rearticulations of Freud's group
psychology into terms of group therapy by Anglo-American and German psychodynamic therapists and analysts during that same wartime.
Without going into the military-psychological details of this mobilization of a diagnosis that would be so liberally applied in the postwar
era to all those rebels without causes, but even already with this much
mentioned in passing, it can be proposed that the first pop application
of acting out started out a stranger to Freud's use of *Agieren*. The
alleged first use of "the" concept of acting out would then have been
adopted only after the fact as model or mascot for something Freud had
not directly inspired, at least not under that name. In Freud, *Agieren*,
much like repetition, was covered and cornered by the transference
contest with remembering: what is enacted or repeated remains inaccessible to the in-session work of remembering. In the after-the-fact
"Freudian" view, acting out can therefore be seen as an upsurge of the
transference, in the transference, that locks the transferential lines of
communciation between selves and others onto the beam of unstoppable unconscious behavior, keeping them all sealed off from the work
of analysis, which *is*, bottom line, the working-through—without ever
completely passing through—all that unexamined transferences can
set in the way of understanding or experience. In turn, once a transferential relationship or frame has been established, the whole dimension
of "action" never leaves the setting of analysis, even when it hits the
streets or goes suicidal home alone.

After the fact, according to the two-timing going into the alleged
tradition of reflections on acting out, Freud's case study of Dora looks
real good, just like an example of acting out, one that, moreover, seems
to belong to both conceptual contexts, the immediate one attributed to
Freud, and the other, outer one of attention to group or adolescent psychology, one that's also analysis-compatible (at least up to the point

where it gets lost in the mix-up with social studies). For the 1967–68 group effort, Margarete Mitscherlich-Nielsen explored Freud's Dora as the original test case of acting out. Dora's rapid termination of treatment just when Freud felt their analytic relationship was beginning to get to work, acted out a traumatic scene of rejection that she thus repeated and reversed (no longer dumpee, now she did the dumping) but did not remember, in other words, re-member, reorganize for consciousness raising (ibid., 190). The Dora case was, significantly, also the one in which Freud first recognized the force of transference, but not before it was too late. The backfiring and misfiring side effects that were the static at the end of the line for Dora and Freud belonged to a transference that had been left unattended. Freud concluded that, if he had interpreted the transference, he should have been able to counteract Dora's revenge-like reenactment of a scene that had her behaviorism under its remote control. In a footnote, the one that drags behind the case study proper like Dora's one bona fide hysterical symptom, her swollen foot or "Oedipus," Freud admits that the transferential connection he failed to make in Dora's case was addressed in the first place to her mother and mother substitutes. Freud's admission thus brought the analytic setting of Dora's acting out full circle by opening up prospects for the analyst's no-longer-captive participation in the scene of splitting he now shared in—through his own unexamined countertransference. Dora's homosexual (maternal-transferential) bond with Frau K. (and not her disappointment with Herr K., her own father, or Freud) was the transference resource that both Freud and Dora, for their different resistance reasons, had failed to open up for exploration and treatment. Acting out, therefore, as an after-the-fact construction or conceptualization, links and separates transference and countertransference. What's more, this example of acting out reclaimed by a later analytic—indeed, "Freudian"—reception as precedent includes in its medley of resistant conditions for Dora's nonencounter with analysis (and with the father of psychoanalysis) both adolescence (Dora was, after all, a teenager) and homosexuality (the bond with Frau K., which was in the analyst's court, in the countertransference, and because left unattended led to the patient's premature rejection of analysis).

Analysts who filed their claim to follow Freud closely, and therefore subscribed, by implication or exclusion, to the construction that all research conducted on acting out followed, interpreted, or resisted Freud, openly recognized acting out as responding all over the place to the pressures of being in analysis. "Acting out in the psychoanalytic situation may be observed both in the analytic session itself, where it is an expression of transference directed towards the analyst, and in situations outside the consulting-room, as a reflection of the analytic process" (ibid., 188).

From where we write, the transferential circuit covers corridors of writing: from journalism to academic criticism and back again, from theory to literature and back again. Thus, in the specific setting of this group session, the aristocritical encounter with journalism (in or as writing for journalism) can represent the "Freudian" intake of all that's going on out there within one medium of legibility, conflict, transference, and treatment. Journalism is the most resistant patient: like a group formation in its own writing, journalism is able to contain instability through a surplus of the same instability or self-reflexivity. Thus, the media could take the blame for Princess Di's accident (or imperative) by absorbing it all within a spectacle of commemoration that delivered everyone from their own in-session dynamics of mourning and transference. But to describe this short circuit from demonization to idealization is to locate at least—at last—the blinders and batteries of a mass medium getting organized around acting out.

In the tradition of Karl Kraus, then, Gary Indiana and Rhonda Lieberman keep up with another Jones, Jenny, the talk-show hostess with the most acting-out side effects, in the first case with an example of toxic dumping in the reception area, in the second with an inside feature of being donor part of the live audience at the taping together of one of the shows. The off-camera murder of a young gay man by the object of his interest, an unidentified desiring object, following the public broadcasting of that interest right out there on the air, in group, with both subject and object attending (and with Jenny Jones facilitating), represents a special occasion for analysis: the media event leaks toxic spillover into the medicolegal precincts of murder investigation (a change of scene, therefore, from the pre-Oedipal to the Oedipal stages), where it all has to follow a different beat in the borderline zone thus opened up inside as-live show time, where zoning out is reordered to admit greater legibility, accountability, treatability. Indiana keeps open, if only for a few more heartbeats, the wide-I wounding of TV's self-containment. The blood that flows outward marks a beginning of healing or congealing, a scab that cannot go back inside the forget-together of screen and screed time. He reconvenes the Jenny Jones group-therapy session and reintroduces the group-level conflict as a series of one-on-one encounters, not only between the dead-or-alive parties to the trial rundown of the fatal show, but also between the intelligent life that has its moment in the clearing, the all-clearing, if only for a moment, and the mass-media sensurround that's really just so pre-fab-you-less.

Lieberman takes up the "I Was There" challenge of journalism and goes there, on an academic field trip to an exotic talk-show space that ends up being, of course, just a room away down the same corridor. The group formation she describes places recovery at the top of its agenda in the sacrificial form of the host or hostess. Getting into the following of this leader is for the as-live audience member too already part of a program of recovery or rewiring. Behind the scenes, Lieberman undergoes the prep-workout. At one point, she takes a break for a word from our sponsor of such encounters: Can the talk show be the fulfillment of Walter Benjamin's prophecy (or of that other aura-queen's forecast, I mean the one made by Andy Warhol) that all of us would become actors or agents in the newly media-mutated field of representation? But between or behind the lines, Lieberman discovers that we're all just actors-out, whose unconscious behavior, however, is kept on a short control-release. We are left, then, in the primal journalistic mode of "Dear Diary," with the same existentialist first contact with one's death that middlebrow guardians of high culture reserve for their separatist claims. Unjournalism can remake such a difference and keep it there for only so long. So long! It's "Hi-Low" out there, again.

If, with a look to the ancestors of "Freudian" unjournalism, Lieberman holds the place of Adorno, it's with or within a more reality-checked-out attention span. The ignited fuse that could keep apart the happy medium or fusion of life in the sensurround is short, even shorter once the critical language comes into contact with its mass cultural object or objection. For Indiana, the disdain in spades falls largely under the reign of Kraus or Benjamin: another sense of audience keeps the reception area open for a show of resistance or revaluation that's not already the side effect or prep work of unstoppable TV. As in a Benjaminian typology, Indiana recasts the "psychiatric expert" who today orbits between courtroom and talk show as a reader of the pulse of what goes down as group-therapeutic volatility under the strains of eclecticism, novelty, and consumer choice. In this relay of interior spaces subservient to one sensurround, a certain delay keeps one outer space safe for rereading. While in TV's inner circle the infantile dyadic

crisis rules—according to the short terms of this one and only relationship you never had, you're either double or nothing, you're either
famous or you're a loser—at the psychiatric end of the corridors of
intervention there's a new room for accountability, which, however,
soon enough opens and shuts on the notion of "diminished capacity,"
the catchall giving us ultimate consumer protection or projection. But
sometimes a created notion, for all its protectiveness, rings in responsibility. Where all involved in the Jenny Jones trial can check in and
out as running on diminished capacity, it's still all up to someone like
Indiana, like you, dear reader: it's your call.

The Rickels dossier presents the resurrected versions of two of his
ghost appearances in *Artforum International*. The opening attraction,
which is also in the meantime, as always in the meantime, a commemoration, is the full-length document of the interview I conducted with
Kathy Acker in Santa Barbara in the summer of 1993.[1] The in-house
reception of this interview led to my enlistment to give the pro to the
contra of some piece of resentment the magazine just had to publish.
The original version of my contribution, which appears here for the
first time, charts, inside itself, the origin of current receptions of acting
out back to the lineup during the world wars of war neurosis and
homosexuality as the interchangeable targets of cure-all along a new
borderline that had just been opened up between neurosis and psychosis.[2] But this original article is not alone; it must also, beside itself,
register the more real-time acting-out effects of its original journalistic
setting. Because there's always one response too many, and then because
there can also always be the slip of unintended fax transmission, all the
behind-the-screen prep work of copyediting—of damage preparedness
or control—is brought to the naught, the zero, the nihilism it all
amounts to anyway. The inclusion of *Artforum*'s slipup, as a ready-
made context or preface given to the article, means, thanks once again
to the ones too many, that we can settle with the package deal. The
inclusion of the anonymous response to my original version, which I
received by faxident, reanimates and releases the complete aversion for
a more fully closed encounter. But, on the sliding scale of interminable
analysis, the therapeutic closure we are thus given also figures as an
intervention, one that admits the future, the other, what's just got to
happen next. On the upbeat, then, it's always possible to be grateful to
your enemies, even the least worthy ones.

Rangell's 1967 call for better boundaries around "acting out" further argued for a move beyond the diffuse spread of the concept in order that psychoanalysis could finally stake its claim on what also ultimately belongs inside the session—action itself. "This tacit spread of meaning, by common usage rather than by it being explicitly advocated, has, in my opinion, led not only to a reduction in the original usefulness of the specific concept of acting out but also to a delay in the achievement of a wider cohesive and unified psychoanalytic theory of action" (1968: 195). This is where the Lacanian interventions in the conceptualization of acting out, with consequences not so far off from the "Freudian" understanding of the concept, begin. According to Peter Canning, the breakthrough to action in theory follows Lacan's turn to the "passage to the act." The libidinal refrain and restraint of not getting no satisfaction addresses the problem of justice, which, as Nietzsche pointed out, is hard repressed to shake the stammer that makes it part and past participle of "seeking vengeance" (*gerecht* and *gerächt*). Lacan's understanding of the "passage to the act" raises the question of the law: the law alone can curb its own dogma, that is, its sense of justice, its superego, its violence. In the name of this law, the father must contain his violation of the family; it's the father's self-repression that says no to the act. The acting-out "child" is therefore inside the very order he is just testing—to the point or to get the point of provoking the father's order, the order that someone get lost. Where acting out pops up, then, it is the paternal function that has failed to control the situation, the violence inside the situation. The unbounded act, which aims to get satisfaction and have it too, must lift every prohibition that *jouissance* otherwise encounters: the act presses toward total satisfaction in the demolition of the signifier, memory, and the language of the law. In 1990 Derrida thus brought the *passage à l'acte* to bear on the erasure of the patronymic, as in the forced removal of his own name from the title of one of the other contributions to the conference, at which Derrida was also given his turn to speak out on Lacan's influence in philosophy. But Derrida could also recognize this acting out as the symptomatic expression of a problem he had all along been analyzing closely throughout his work of deconstruction.

Elisabeth Weber unpacks the Grimm fable "Willfulness" to replay its unstoppable violence as a special feature of dyadic merger or murder attempts in the absence of father. The mother's own law must guarantee the absence of the third agency once and for all, even, or especially, in death. Weber thus grounds the willful fist that rises up from a child's grave only forever to be beaten back down in a series of Lacanian-Oedipal footnotes. The p-unitive relationship that persists even in death does away with whatever comes between us, toward us, whether empty or full: language, the law, and desire. Weber's running contrast is elegantly poised between the Grimm story of eternal or internal instruction and the cultural phenomenon of Jewish humor, which in Freud's interpretation was hoisted by its own regard of itself as inferior ego in identification with the superego, figure of the ego's triangulation, substitution, and mourning. The volatile alternations between the happy interface of German-Jewish assimilation—the great Enlightenment experiment—and the face-off between Aryans and subhumans in the Holocaust are accorded a tentative frame through Weber's interpretation.

Canning's elaboration of the Lacanian theory of the act also issues in a series of historical, or even topical, diagnoses. The tension between "just say no" and "just do it" continues to withdraw before the rise of maternal bureaucracies of micromanagement. For structural reasons, these institutions of welfare cannot say no to—and protect us from—the impulses to control, discipline, and punish (which they themselves continue to represent and administer). Along these lines of historical and political diagnosis, it's the murder and cannibalization of the primal dad or dead that offer a point of entry for Catherine Liu's report back from the corridor wars between psychoanalytic or deconstructive theories and all the name brands acting out there of cultural studies. It's only back in the primal time of the brothers in the band murdering father and then opening wide for his mourning reception that so-called social change can be admitted or introduced as psychoanalysis-compatible, as more than just more small change.

Cannibalism and, in particular, autocannibalism would in turn represent the psychoanalytic system as closed or, rather, as open *and* shut. When the superego gets erected or thrown up, we have finally had our fill: we've eaten our own mouths, which, as superegos, unstoppably chew us over and out. The phantasm of the mouth eating itself is the backdrop or staging against which superego, as figure of thirdness, sets itself (even though originally a part of the same setting) apart. This place of tension is, then, according to psychoanalysis, the only so-called social context for change. In turn, cannibalism figures in the reception of psychoanalytic theory as the proof that's missing from the plodding encounter with empiricism. In other words, cannibalism provides the paradoxical grounding for all theoretical speculation in psychoanalysis.

Acting out and outside analytic theory, conspiracy theories (like those the JFK assassination attracted) demonstrate the kind of self-affirmation or staying power (in spite of countless disproofs) that also suggests the take on truth at stake here to be on the mythic or endopsychic side of evidence. Conspiracy's rapport with truth is more than remotely related to the one thus evidenced by psychoanalytic mythmaking, the primal kind and kindred that enabled Freud to introduce his inside viewing of the psychology of groups and psychos (who can be conceived, moreover, one by one, as groups of one). The psychoanalytic theory of conspiracy—group psychology by any other name—is internally or eternally organized around the primal father murder mystery, the youdunit, which provokes the disbelief and resistance that only prove Freud right.

Liu identifies these popular conspiracy theories as the syndication of the marriage that failed, the Big One proposed over and again between psychoanalysis and Marxism. But, more specifically, Liu addresses the "feminist fantasy" exhibited by the group called Women's Action Coalition (WAC), which formulated and applied an agenda of "directed action" that acted out ambivalent relations with the cannibalization of the primal father from which the girl brides, the incest-is-best sisters and daughters, had been excluded or had excluded themselves. If the boys come into a relation of ambivalence and mourning in the activity of eating up the dad, the girls couldn't kill, eat, or mourn the father they had also, in spite of it all, cherished. Out of this relationship of unfinished illness with the primal father, we see the importance of the father figure in the development of girl psychology, a significance that extends to the wife as defender of the reproductive couple and thus of the law of the father against the group's matricentric or other-womanly hold on the husband (see the film *Fatal Attraction*). WAC organized its group cohesion around the rapist, a protective, projective move that, loud as denial, reversed and preserved the significance of the father. A reversal of this tall order belongs therefore to the feminist side effects of acting out's primal scene. According to Liu's case study, the rise and fall of the Women's Action Coalition belatedly repeated (and rehearsed) the murder of the father, who was all along the one figured (out) by the group's construction of the rapist as scapegoat. In this case, the acting out found in groups is autoanalytic breakthrough material. Even if the father was not put to test or rest, the group, like the monster in Shelley's *Frankenstein*, always manages to put itself to rest.

The 1968 collection of conference papers awarded a prominent second place (right after Anna Freud's opener) to Leon Grinberg's object-relations take on acting out, which resituates extra-analytic activities squarely within the circular relations between transference and countertransference. If it takes two to act out, as in the "Freudian" insistence that acting out refers only to dynamics internal to the analytic session, those two were always ultimately mother and baby bonded across the abyss of their separation. According to Grinberg's representation of the object-relations approach, the actor-out is looking for what early on the mother provides and models, namely, in Wilfred Bion's terms, a container (which is in turn the service the analyst must provide in session, a kind of holding pattern at the patient's disposal):

> A clue to the understanding of the dynamics and vicissitudes of acting out can also be found in the model for the early and conflictful mother-child relationship. According to Bion, when the infant feels very acute anxiety (for example, fear of dying), he needs to project it into a container (his mother) capable of holding it and giving it back in such a way that the anxiety is lessened. If the mother fails to metabolize this anxiety and even deprives it of its specific quality (the fear of dying), the infant will receive back a "nameless dread" which he cannot tolerate. According to this model, the patient's need to find an object in the external world that could take on his pain and separation anxiety is a significant element in acting out. (Ibid., 171–72)

When it comes to acting out, then, the work on transference must lead to the work of mourning: "Experience in acting out has taught me that one of its essential roots is often associated with experiences of object loss and separation that determined earlier mournings which were not worked through" (ibid., 171). That's putting it materially or maternally: in session, another literalization corresponds to this unfinished work. In one of the case studies Grinberg presents, he shows how he was able to set the timer of all his patient's other mournings to the termination of the session in the here and now (ibid., 176). To address the session in the session can contain or enliven the encounter with the transference. Transferred to the test case study of Dora, to the dream reported in Dora's final session with Freud, which Freud, after the fact, rereads as signaling the break that Dora had to act out also because Freud hadn't interpreted it in time, the object-relations focus on the site-specificity of whatever happens in session would find in Dora's recounting of her dream reference to the tight spot she and Freud are cornered in right then and there, in session. Quite simply, it's a matter of timing: her indecision about the time frame in the dream, either fifteen minutes or more than two hours, averages out to be the analytic hour, the calculation of which is always up for grabs while still in progress.

The all-out attempt at the 1967 conference to address or redress the "diffuse expansionism" of the term as the disconnection between Freud's setting of acting out on the transference and those applied psychosocial meanings that are still with us never left the transference contest between remembering and acting out that pervades even—or especially—the greater context of the concept's history. Not only is acting out a performative conceptualization, *nachträglich*, after the fact, but it also serves as placeholder and pressure point within theorizations of in-session materiality. It thus takes up a place of distinction from transference or countertransference, one that must be thought, even though it most likely cannot be upheld. The object-relations redefinition or refinding of splitting, together with the school's brand-new notion of projective identification, came to share the place of this untenable but necessary distinction:

> When confronted with loss and frustration experiences (perceived as intolerable mournings), the precarious psychic balance that existed breaks down. Persecutory anxiety increases and a tyrannical intrapsychic relationship between the two split parts of the self is then established.... This originates an intolerable increase of tension that leads the patients to evacuate violent projective identifications which massively break through into the external object. The patients thus project the tyrannical relationship into the object, inducing it, in turn, to act out. (Ibid., 177)

This extension or refinement of acting out, as I show and tell in my contribution, was accompanied, in the work of Bion, W. Ronald D. Fairbairn, and D. W. Winnicott, by the group-formatting, during World War II, of analytic interventions that could now collaborate, on their own terms, with the eclecticization or extension of analysis into psychotherapy. Bion would, in fact, bracket out the transference as a rate of exchange available only to couples or to individual therapy; in groups, the act that bonds, the enactment of bonding, was of another order. Treatment of groups, which was originally reserved for severe cases of regression, became, in a more literal sense, all about containment, and could no longer pass as work on the more personalized states of transference. In this way, a focus on the in-session relationship (without the splitting or cutting back and forth between the theoretical and the therapeutic) opens up, along group lines, to prospects for more grounded psychohistorical diagnosis.

Klaus Theweleit explores Elias Canetti's notion of the national mass symbol, which, when given in examples, goes like this: to the British goes the sea, but the forest belongs to Germany. Theweleit can still see this forest for all the dying trees going down in the German headlines. Reading between the lines, Theweleit sees the symptomatic poisoning of the literal embodiments of the German national mass symbol as carrying with it—via the splitting off of its share—the sparing of the army. What had thus been all along on one analogical lineup with the rows of tall trees could now close ranks as the uncontaminated container of what's truly, purely German. From there Theweleit follows the dotted line of splitting right up against the wall, and all the walls that had to go up once the Big One came tumbling down. Theweleit examines extended senses of an object-relations approach to all cultural phenomena: ever since the outpouring of *Male Fantasies*, Theweleit's major contribution to the psychohistorical study of artifacts and contexts has been less the inclusion of all the multiples and way more the granting of greater spans of time or attention to the material before him, before shortcutting to the jargonic refrains of analytic interpretation. In sync with the shift of emphasis in object-relations analysis from a separate theory to a theory always coextensive with the in-session dynamics of therapy in motion, Theweleit doesn't contradict the classical interpretations but insists instead on their timing: interpretation turns into jargon when given in no time, at the wrong time, too soon. This hovering attentiveness to the materials as they come his way also treats the critical conditions of psychohistory. In the early midst of the object-relations approach, D. W. Winnicott was moved, in 1969, to make a transitional objection out of the recent history of political events, one that's still fitting or befitting the span of in-session attention. What seems so close or local is also so far and away global and intrapsychic. This encounter with what's out there took Winnicott right up to the same wall that Theweleit is up against:

> It will be observed that in the depressed state which is probably part of the normal or psychiatrically healthy individual's personality structure, there is a toleration of the potential state of war. It is as if there is a Berlin Wall, or what is at present being called the army's peace line in Belfast. These are parochial matters, and by

the time this paper has found a reader they may have been
forgotten because of some other and better example of a dividing
line, which at its worst postpones conflict and at its best holds
opposing forces away from each other for long periods of time so
that people may play and pursue the arts of peace. The arts of
peace belong to the temporary success of a dividing line between
opposing forces; the lull between times when the wall has ceased
to segregate good and bad. (224)

The wall is symbol both of the container of toxic or volatile elements
and of the splitting that turns the bad against the good, the good
around the bad, and leaves what's excessive but no longer accessible on
the other side:

> In the inner psychic reality which I am describing, there is not
> always war simply because of the line and the segregation of
> benign and persecutory elements. Help is afforded by the fact that
> benign elements can be exported, or projected, and so also may
> persecutory elements. In this way human beings are always
> inventing God and are always organizing disposal of dangerous
> or waste products. (223)

Always the good German, who can thus act as a container for the splitting images of his fellow citizens, Theweleit goes against the upsurge of
jubilation attending reunification, and cuts to the mourning work that
will never be begun as long as these primitive defenses give way only to
another round of displacements, from the historical wall to the more
current electronic defense shield to the cone of immortality in which
television gets watched watching.

But you only die twice. The first death only counts down to the
second death, the only death that counts as conclusive and metaboliz-
able. According to Theweleit, there's so much in Germany that has not
died twice. In closing, therefore, by way of forecast, and from within
the same lab space in which Nietzsche's superman experiments failed
long time ago, Theweleit gives us notice: Wagner just hasn't died the
second time around yet. (Richard Wagner is dead. Undead! Undead!)

Susan Derwin rereads Terry Zwigoff's film *Crumb* via the reactive
reception to its screening displayed by academics convened around
their shared specialized interest in psychoanalysis. She discovers and
then unpacks the stressed or crumbling containers and boundaries of
identification and splitting to be found even in professional groups.
Derwin thereby establishes one continuity shot after another: for

example, Zwigoff's cinematic text is in control of the split ends of a reception it generates, isolates, undermines precisely by splitting off the controlling interest in the case and leaving that one with the critics interviewed. These perspectives on screen are parts and portraits of the reactive reception that Zwigoff puts down in advance. In the process, then, of entering or resisting entry into Robert Crumb's world—a passage that requires that we be beside ourselves, filling up with all the feelings Robert just can't hold on his own—we have stumbled across one of the conditions or conditionings of all acting out. It all begins with a certain Michael Eaton, a film critic, and his newspaper-thin view of the film, which Derwin quotes early on. Eaton says the movie is so in control of all the responses in group that it can count as being without any unconscious. Now, that's an inside view, caught in a quote, that in turn rides or writes out the unknown current of an unexamined transference.

Derwin performs the control measure introduced by the journalist inside her quote by entering fully into the discourse of the object-relations school. Object relations, the only analytic school recognized as an option, alongside, say, family systems, by California's Board of Behavioral Science Examiners, was also the community lip service of the group of professionals whose acting out prompted Derwin's own hypermimetic act of rereading (and rewriting). Derwin thus joins the object-relations group perspective or discourse on its own terms, giving a corrective reading of the acting-out reactions of her colleagues on the terms they have already, at some level, accepted. Thus performed or acted out by Derwin's text, again in the mode of total control, is the notion implicit in the work of certain object relationists that the relationship in question, in session, is without an unconscious precisely because, taken so interpersonally, it is fully developing and fully graspable in sessions (hence the importance of working with the very young, as though to catch the unconscious where it breeds). Derwin performs Zwigoff who performs Crumb whose performance is one of a kind of vacancy through which all the container walls out there in a work or world without any unconscious get tested for their vitality or crumbling degenerescence. Thus, Derwin reduces several times over, and without end, the object-relations focus down to the same relations of splitting and acting out that it is fixed or fixated on (and that it acts out). The uncontainment or unconscious is thus sent away, down the endless relay of recycling containers and control releases.

Notes

1. The *Artforum* version appeared in the February 1994 issue, pp. 60–63, 103, 104.
2. The *Artforum* version of "Act Out/Turn On" can be found in the April 1994 issue, 70–73, 127.

Bibliography

Abt, Lawrence E., and Stuart L. Weissman, eds. *Acting Out: Theoretical and Clinical Aspects*. New York and London: Grune and Stratton, 1965.

Derrida, Jacques. Pour l'amour de Lacan," in Bibliothèque du Collège international de philosophie, *Lacan avec les philosophes*. Paris: Albin Michel, 1991: 397–420.

Hurwitz, Emanuel. *Otto Gross. Paradies-Sucher zwischen Freud und Jung*. Frankfurt am Main: Suhrkamp Verlag, 1988 [1979].

International Journal of Psychoanalysis. Vol. 49 (1968). This dossier on acting out includes an introduction by Anna Freud and presentations and responses by (in the order of their appearance) Leon Grinberg, Hedwig Schwarz, Burness E. Moore, Julien Rouart, Margarete Mitscherlich-Nielsen, Hector Garbarino, Leo Rangell, S. Lebovici, Thorkil Vanggaard, Phyllis Greenacre, Laura Achard de Demaria, and Norman B. Atkins.

Winnicott, D. W. *Home Is Where We Start From: Essays by a Psychoanalyst*. New York and London: W. W. Norton, 1986.

Forget Theory

ACTING OUT OR PSYCHOANALYSIS AND SOCIAL CHANGE

Catherine Liu

Allegories of Deception

The lessons of Freud's *Moses and Monotheism* can be understood as having to do with the fate of psychoanalytic theory and a truth that is easy to swallow, but hard to digest. The story of the delayed reception of monotheism by the tribes of the Old Testament alludes to the difficulty of swallowing the bitter pill of a truth that demands a rather dramatic act of renunciation. Let us recall that, according to Freud, it took the murder of Moses and two generations of wandering around in regressed polytheism before the Jews finally identified monotheism as a "precious treasure" at all. What happened to Moses' special delivery of the "message" of monotheism? It got lost in the mail for two generations because it was refused by the addressee and returned to the sender. The refusal took place as a murder, the murder of the messenger — Moses himself. The belated reception of the message as the most precious of missives demanded that the assassination of the messenger be assiduously covered up. Hence the biblical rewriting of Moses' assassination as a "disappearance." Monotheism was a sort of letter, then, addressed by Akhenaton, carried by Moses to the Jews, who returned it to the sender, or perhaps merely forwarded it to the future. The rhythm of this delay in reception is formed by a movement between light resistance, violent repudiation, regression, and subsequent cover-up.

In the intellectual climate of the academy today, we see that the result of our eating-disordered reception of two theoretical discourses, psychoanalysis and deconstruction, has produced a sort of monster child with a very big appetite — cultural studies. The incorporation of psychoanalytic and deconstructive terms in cultural studies allows for a kind of terminal forgetting or strategic nonreading and reflexive gagging on (psychoanalytic and deconstructive) theory itself. This forgetting is justified by the accusations that pure theory has been discovered to be politically irresponsible and ineffective. But let us not throw too much blame in the way of the Anglo-American Marxists running cultural studies with organs such as *Social Text*. Theory, psychoanalytic and deconstructive, seems to contain in itself the threat of its total destruction, or we could say, theory is that which most effectively produces the most tenacious forms of resistance to itself. Theory, once swallowed too quickly, becomes thereafter resistance to theory. There are carnivorous, all-devouring apprenticeships the very zealousness of which leads to the indigestion of amnesia.

This essay is perhaps one protracted attempt to eat and digest more slowly the problem of self-citation, or what one might call autocannibalism. It is a commonplace that citation can be compared with textual incorporation and discursive ingestion: What happens, then, when one cites oneself and in so doing rewrites one's own work? Would this gesture be comparable to autocannibalism then? In the course of what follows, I will perform the unpleasant task of paraphrasing myself, that is, I will steal my own ideas and rewrite or digest them out of context. In the fall of 1996, I participated in a conference organized by the newly established Association for the Psychoanalysis of Culture and Society. I found the title of the conference—"Psychoanalysis and Social Change"—disturbing, until I understood that those four words begged to be read as a kind of epistle, posted to a persecutory addressee. It seemed to me that the proper name of psychoanalysis was heretofore going to promise to repair a certain haunting failure on its part, to engage or conjoin with the problem of the social changing. In the context of the American academy, a discussion of social change and "psychoanalysis" would have to rest on two primary assumptions that will be subject to a certain amount of interrogation: (1) psychoanalysis is on the side of *change for the better*, that is, it would be or could be a promulgator of the teleological force behind change, and (2) social change is incontrovertibly and without doubt change for the better. Of the four words of the title, "Psychoanalysis and Social Change," the conjunction "and" is probably the most problematic, for what does psychoanalysis really have to do with social change? And is this a rhetorical question? A month later, I was participating in a conference on the topic "Anthropophagie und Literatur," a title that begs a similar sort of inquiry: What are the functions of such conjunctions?

To theorize social changes from a psychoanalytic point of view throws some light on the role of cannibalism and the figure of the cannibal whose intervention in Freud's second system opens one path to interpreting changes in the formation of social groups. In Géza Róheim's 1956 article, "The Individual, the Group, and Mankind," progress is described ironically: "Progress as it is usually understood means increased mastery over the forces of nature, prolonged life, increasing numbers, and much unhappiness." Róheim implies that our unhappiness has to do with the increasing distance that civilization puts between its subjects and undisturbed oral satisfaction or the imagined happiness of cannibals. From the point of view of psychoanalytic theory, history is not necessarily the story of progress and the logic of progress is not necessarily the condition of history.

If we are to rethink the question of the social and the question of change in the context of psychoanalytic theory, we should return to Freud's second system, and especially to *Moses and Monotheism* and *Civilization and Its Discontents*. I will refer to an analysis that I have done elsewhere of the foundations of a feminist fantasy of political action, "Edible Dad: Psychoanalysis as Conspiracy Theory or One Aspect of the Feminist Fantasy," in order to reflect on the question of psychoanalytic theory and the telos of social change. I will then raise the question of allegory in reading history: it is in seizing the allegorical moment of reading that a disjunctive temporality is best represented. The cannibal or the moment of cannibalism is one of the privileged moments in the allegory of history. The role he or she is given is one that must participate in both our ontogenetic and phylogenetic organization.

If conscience can gnaw away at me and guilt eats away at my entrails, then superego is always introjected as a mouth that chews me over, eats me alive from within at the same time that it does not stop talking about what I'm doing wrong. The introjection of superego, however, takes place along the lines of the sensory orifices—eyes, ears, nose, skin—which are perhaps nothing more than metonymical sites for the mouth: the primary orifice whose first contact with the breast not only sustains me, but is not differentiated from me. Autocannibalism, then, is not quite as outrageous as it first appeared. The infant's first fantasy, the infant's first mistake and first misapprehension of the world, happens around the prehensile muscles of the mouth: sucking allows the infant to survive, but in sucking the world into its mouth, the infant mis-takes nourishment and the source of nourishment for itself. Infants do not differentiate between self and nipple, because the prospect of weaning is too unbearable and must be denied. ("The infant imagines the nipple to be part of itself because it cannot tolerate the frustration that arises from weaning. Since no wish can be satisfied the moment it arises, the desired object is frustrating as well as gratifying" [Róheim[3]]). Every infant is an autocannibal, or is at least for a time, phantasmatically autophagous: the breast is imagined as part of the infant's body. Oral frustration as the result of weaning destroys this fantasy forever, but it haunts us in one form or another, in fantasies of absolute self-sufficiency. When the child has successfully introjected or internalized superego, whose taste for cruelty is matched only by the id's appetite for pleasure, he or she has, in a sense, eaten its own mouth, which from now on will chew us out, from within. To have internalized the big mouth of infantile drives is to prepare the way for being devoured by one's own appetites.

To Theorize Cannibalism and Social Change

Cannibalism has something to do with conspiracy and unsubstantiated rumors (see W. Arens's *The Man-Eating Myth: Anthropology and Anthropopagy*): the failure to establish empirical proof of the act of cannibalism for anthropology and psychoanalysis is homologous with the missed encounter with empiricism that is constitutive of the structure of theoretical speculation itself. There is, for example, little empirical proof of conspiracy theories around John F. Kennedy's assassination, but the paucity of what might constitute actual evidence does nothing to mitigate the enthusiasm of conspiracy theorists. If we are to follow the scientific axiom that the simplest theory of any event is the one that is truest, conspiracy theories around the assassination would have to be dismissed because of their baroque complexity. Disproved, much as Ernst Sellin's theories of Moses' murder can be disproved, conspiracy theories, like rumors of cannibalism, have a way of staying on our minds. The primal conspiracy is the conspiracy that destroyed the structure of the horde: so rumors of conspiracy will continue to both fascinate and haunt us. Conspiracy theory, then, does not need to be based on facts: it draws its power from its relationship to a structure of rumormongering and hearsay, a structure derived precisely from the dissemination of the mark of the theoretical.

Conspiracy theory is important, then, not only because of its relation to conspiracy, but also because of its relationship to *theory*. Conspiracy theories around John F. Kennedy's assassination can be read as popular or mass-media attempts at theoretical production in following Frankfurt School imperatives: the conspiracy theories themselves include vulgar Marxist interpretation (JFK is a victim of a Mafia conspiracy with anti-Castro paramilitary forces, the Mafia representing an extreme capitalist hegemony in relationship to Cuba), vulgar Freudian analysis (which from one point of view would account for the acting out of intense Oedipal jealousy on the part of Lyndon B. Johnson and J. Edgar Hoover, who, as representatives of a conspiracy of sexual and class resentment, must engineer the death of JFK to accede to greater power). It seems that the only affectively satisfying attempts to "understand" or assimilate the trauma of the JFK assassination have led to the production of conspiracy theories in which popular culture tries to make up for failed attempts on the part of intellectuals and academics to arrange a marriage of convenience between Marxism and psychoanalytic theory. Interpretation always already falls into overinterpretation, and if, as in English, one can always be accused of "reading too much into something," then the theorist, as a mutation of the philosopher, might take a kind of perverse pleasure in the fact that, at least according to Freud, "the delusions of paranoiacs have an unpalatable external similarity and internal kinship to the systems of our philosophers" (1955: 17:261). Every text is a conspiracy.

In *Civilization and Its Discontents*, the constitutive aggressive instincts of the human subject make for the most ambivalent sorts of relations in social or intersubjective life, but in psychoanalytic terms, intrapsychic life is also conditioned by instincts of aggression and destruction that one part of the psychic apparatus directs at another. Psychoanalytic theory, then, is about the thinking through of intersubjective aggressiveness in terms of or alongside intrapsychic aggressiveness.

WAC Is Watching

I observed with great interest the rise of a women's group, the Women's Action Coalition (WAC), formed in New York City in 1991. The founders of WAC were outraged by recent events in politics and the media. The group's slogan was "WAC is Watching" and I watched WAC emerge into a particular form of vigilance. In the words of WAC itself, it promised to mount a "visible and remarkable resistance."

Resistance implies a subversive posture to an oppressive order, but resistance that is remarkable can function on many levels, in and outside of the register of the socius, on and off of the couch. In psychoanalytic terms, we might be tempted to read in direct action a kind of directed acting out, acting out in commemoration and rememoration of repressed events. That we can call direct action "directed acting out" should not be read as being in any way derogatory: if all actions are susceptible to being called "acting out," the act of political engagement for social change is neither specifically privileged nor denigrated.

The women's group, like most American organizations on the left, was obsessively careful about not falling into behaviors that would replicate oppressive, "patriarchal" structures. This devaluation of the leader position and the generalized imperative for horizontal identification among group members were one of the features of American civilization that Freud identified as a cause of the "psychological poverty of groups" (*Civilization and Its Discontents*). In a certain sense, the American group is united in its identification of strong leaders with patriarchal and therefore bad group formations. This kind of leader phobia, I would argue, is based precisely on the denial of the memory of a charismatic and all-powerful leader of the primal horde who was, for better or worse, a male; for, if we follow Freud's theory that "the group appears to us a revival of the primal horde" (1955: 18:123), every group, including WAC, has to deal with the legacy of horde formation: "the psychology of groups is the oldest human psychology" (ibid.). And this is the legacy that WAC precisely hoped to fend off and this is the history that WAC wanted to "correct." (It is necessary, however, to point out that the adulation and admiration of a male figure are acceptable in groupie formations, which feminists usually view with some horror.)

An analysis of the psychology of groups or "masses" leads Freud back to the horde, which was dominated by one powerful male. The strong male of the horde had access to all the females. If a son posed a challenge to the power of the strong male and if "they roused their father's jealousy they were killed or castrated or driven out [of the horde]" (ibid., 23:81). This social organization was changed only when the brothers who had been driven out banded together and killed the father. They ate him in order to share the guilt and incorporate his attributes that they admired. The "band of brothers" might be considered the first "direct-action group;" the first "direct action" is the murder of the father of the horde. In psychoanalytic theory, this coup d'état inaugurates history. A murder in the name of what we can call anachronistically "social change" inaugurates psychoanalytic history. The primal father's sacrifice produces a particularly nourishing meal, one whose ingestion allows for the subsequent introjection of the incest taboo and the superegoic interdictions that will allow for the deferral of all sorts of gratification. The identificatory aspect of all acts of cannibalism cannot be ignored here, because consuming the body of the father is also an expression of the desire to be like him. Once the body has been entirely consumed, all traces of its existence and the act of murder will also have been erased. As Freud observes, murders are easy to commit and texts easy to censor; the difficulty lies in the cover-up. The corpse in pieces becomes the object of the oral drive where love and aggression meet in the mouth of the cannibal as murderer and/or lover.

The primal father ruled by force and banished, killed, and/or castrated the sons whom he found threatening. He had sexual access to all the women of the horde. It is easy to imagine that the father of the primal horde did not refrain from taking a woman by force and against her will whenever he so desired. In extrapolating from Freud's description of the primal father's treatment of his sons (exile, murder, castration), we can safely draw the following conclusion: the primal father is the primal rapist. His omnipotence and hypervirility were founded on his refusal of sexual deferral or sublimation. In the horde, the difference between the father and everyone else would seem to override all other differences. A submissive posture must be assumed vis-à-vis this powerful figure, or else. Memories of the omnipotence of the father of the primal horde are reconstructed and the father commemorated in the formation of cults (Charles Manson, David Koresh) and in the behavior of Third World despots, whose absolute rule is reminiscent of the charismatic rule of the primal father. The undeniable charm of totalitarian leaders in weak nation-states is a function of a certain nostalgia for this primeval state of affairs, when father not only knew best, but did what he damn well pleased.

It was only when the brothers decided to move out of the one-on-one with the primal father that a group evolved out of the horde in the form of a conspiracy. According to Freud, "His [the primal father's] jealousy and intolerance became in the last resort the causes of group psychology" (1955, 18:124). In this act of coming together as a group to take down the father, the brothers also "come out" to demarcate the lines of sexual difference: it is they who kill and eat the father. Freud makes no mention of women at this crucial get-together. The sexes thus found themselves sundered in the absence of the primal father and in an ambivalent relation to each other. The women of the horde had obviously been complicit with the primal father during his lifetime in one way or another, but they were not punished along with him. Their intimacy with the primal father made them more charismatic and attractive in the brothers' eyes, but their passive complicity with the father's violent regime cast a pall of ambivalence on the new state of affairs.

We can imagine that a kind of resentment sprang up on both sides of the sexual divide: on the one hand, the brothers resented the women for their closeness to the father and their unwillingness or inability to rebel against the father's harsh rule. The women, on the other hand, were ambivalent not about the social changes that had been instituted without their consent or participation; but rather because of: (1) their attachment to the dead father and (2) the fact that they were denied access to direct action against him.

Following Freud it is possible to show that WAC focused on the issue of sexual violence against women as a symptom of its group psychological formation: "Inclined as it itself [the group] is to all extremes, a group can only be excited by an excess of stimulus. Anyone who wishes to produce an effect upon it needs no logical adjustment in his arguments; he must paint in the most forcible colors, he must exaggerate and he must repeat the same thing again and again" (SE 18:78). The question of rape provided this group with the necessary excess of stimulus. Rape inspired an intense and immediate affectual response that, at the same time, demanded immediate affectual satisfaction. I am in no way suggesting that rape is not a violent crime, unworthy of our concern: its importance for WAC, however, was overwhelming, and I could not help but compare the strong reaction of the group to the problem of sexual violence and its much more subdued reaction to the problem of economic inequities between the sexes.

What stabilizes groups and produces a repression of the irreconcilable contradictions within them that threaten to tear them apart at any time is the selection/persecution of a scapegoat. WAC produced a few significant ones, the most important of which was probably the rapist. In the culture of WAC, the phobia about leaders is related to the group's ambivalence to the primal leader, the father of the horde. The rapist is a figure that marks one place where the memory of the father of the primal horde is buried. The rapist is certainly guilty of an act of violence against women: but he is not responsible for all the injustices that are a consequence of the vicissitudes of sexual difference and its representation in the social sphere. The scapegoat as rapist allowed WAC access to a temporary and fragile cohesion despite its internal tensions. The structure of the women's "direct-action" group commemorates the conspiracy of the banding together of the exiled brothers. This commemoration can be seen in the group's strict exclusion of men, its goal of "direct action," and its preoccupations with the question of sexual violence.

Both Derrida and Rickels have shown that those who renounce the eating of flesh renounce responsibility and the necessity of sacrifice, which would be an act of violence necessary to culture itself. Vegetarians are those who hope that by actively renouncing their places at the meal of the father's body they can avoid the guilt of this primal murder. This is why vegetarianism always has a moralizing aspect of avoidance — whether in the Buddhist vegetarian's referral to an economy of karma or in the politicized ecological vegetarian's condemnation of animal abuse. The abused and slaughtered animal is always the totem animal, but for vegetarians there are no special feast days when the eating of the animal is permitted. It is no accident that there is a privileged relationship between vegetarians and feminists. The feminist group that we have examined refuses responsibility for the murder of the primal father by repudiating strong leaders in favor of a consensus-driven decision-making structure for direct action. The fantasy of the group is that it is not a group, or a mass, or a horde, but rather a gathering of reasonable individuals seeking justice for women. Unfortunately, it is difficult to measure whether the group's activities (such as demonstrations during rape trials, picketing media events) produced more justice for women.

In the context of the primal horde, justice for women has to do with the question of exclusion. If women did not partake of and were not nourished by the primal father's body, then their guilt and their responsibility for resisting and producing social change would be much more ambiguous. Both above and below the ethical standard set by the conspiracy of civilization, women have to confront as uninvited guests the question of sexual difference and injustice. The problem, of course, is that once the corpse of the father is consumed, it is maternalized, and nourishment and superego are introjected as part paternal injunction and maternal frustration. To celebrate such a case of superegoic trans-sexualism as sexual liberation, however, would be very misguided. One aspect of the feminist fantasy is that to kill and eat the primal father again, a renewed incest taboo—this time, by and for women—would be enacted, inaugurating a different kind of civilizing process with per-haps more enlightened and more refined table manners.

What the women of the horde have been excluded from is a meal of ritualized, totemic cannibalism—which in turn has inspired a sharp appetite for justice. Cannibalism is related not only to the adoption of the incest taboo and the deferral of instinctual gratification, it is also now an important feature in the formation of sexual difference and the notion of sex segregation. Misogyny, the exclusion and sequestration of women, could be based on the identification of women with the totemic father: hence the proliferation of cultural taboos around contact with women, during, before, and after menses, pregnancy, and so on. What feminist theory has identified as conspiratorial homosocial bonding between men is always perceived as being inimical to women.

Civilization and Its Discontents seems to be turning over a ques-tion, "Why have we conceived such a hostility toward the notion of civilization?" We can update this question in a certain sense: "Why have we conceived such a hostility toward Western civilization on the left when we address the notion of politics today?" Even to ask the question, however, seems to leave us open to accusations of complicity with the oppressive forces that be; let us run that risk, however, and insist that psychoanalysis is dependent on certain political and social conditions to flourish, especially a secular government and the social and political enfranchisement of women. I am not suggesting that we overlook the crimes committed in the name of Western civilization, nor that we exonerate those guilty of the exploitation of others, but merely that we reflect more carefully on what this leftist hostility might be about, especially given the fact that it is in the West that secular govern-ment and the simultaneous protection of the rights of women have been most firmly established. Since the Renaissance, a secular, social space in which men and women could interact without fear of violence has been protected by elite groups; and initiation into the more sophisticated codes of civility in such groups took place by means of an apprentice-ship to vernacular, worldly literature.

As technological progress and the material well-being of a certain part of the world's population continue to fail to alleviate suffering for the great majority, we will see an increased hostility toward practices and discourses. It is under these conditions that we must be cautious in embracing any supposedly transparent notion of "social change." In my understanding of the practice and theory of psychoanalysis, there is never the promise of a monumental alleviation of suffering on a grand social scale. A theorization of such promises, however, is made possible by psychoanalytic inquiry (especially in the later Freud) and by the practices of deconstruction. In "Analysis Terminable and Interminable" and elsewhere, Freud outlines enormous resistances to change during the analytic process: social changes would have to be as difficult to come by—because in modifying intersubjective relations, intrasubjective relations cannot be neglected. Engineering social change would have something to do with transforming our relation to the cannibal within, the elusive personification of oral gratification and oral aggression, a figure who is both especially innocent and especially guilty of civilization itself. The figure of the cannibal is one who is nourished by the fantasies of civilization's discontents.

Note

This essay was given in slightly altered form at two conferences during the winter of 1996: first at the second annual conference of the Association for the Psychoanalysis of Culture and Society titled "Psychoanalysis and Social Change" and second at a colloquium organized by the Graduiertenkolleg of the University of Konstanz, "Anthropophagie und Literatur." The paper for the later conference is forthcoming and will appear as "Edible Dad" *Verschlungene Grenzen, Anthropophagie in Literatur und Kulturwissenschaften*, ed. Annette Keck, Inka Kording, Anja Prochaska, Tübingen (Narr-Verlag).

Bibliography

Arens, W. *The Man-Eating Myth: Anthropology and Anthropophagy*. New York: Oxford University Press, 1979.

Freud, Sigmund. *The Standard Edition of the Complete Psychological Works of Sigmund Freud*. Trans. and ed. James Strachey in collaboration with Anna Freud. London: Hogarth Press, 1955.

Lacan, Jacques. *L'Envers de la psychanalyse*. Paris: Seuil, 1991.

Liu, Catherine. "Psychoanalysis as Conspiracy Theory or One Aspect of the Feminist Fantasy." *International Journal for Clinical Psychoanalysis*. 2:2 (1996): 87–102.

Pommier, Gérard. *Du bon usage érotique de la colère*. Paris: Aubier, 1994.

Rickels, Laurence A. *The Case of California*. Baltimore: Johns Hopkins University Press, 1991.

Róheim, Géza. "The Individual, the Group, and Mankind." *Psychoanalytic Quarterly* (January 1956): 1–10.

Ronell, Avital. *The Telephone Book*. Lincoln: University of Nebraska Press, 1989.
Roudinesco, Elisabeth. *Jacques Lacan and Co.* Trans. Jeffrey Mehlman. Chicago: University of Chicago Press, 1990.
Saper, Craig. "Scandalography." *Lusitania* Vol. 1:4 (1993): 87–99.
Tausk, Victor. *Sexuality, War, Schizophrenia*. Trans. Paul Roazen. New Brunswick, N.J.: Transaction Publishers, 1991.

Victim Art

CRITIQUE AND/OF THE FAMILY BUSINESS

Andrew Hewitt

In a now (in)famous article in the December 26, 1994–January 2, 1995, edition of the *New Yorker*, "Discussing the Undiscussable," Arlene Croce, one of the most respected dance critics in the country, took the performance of a new work by the Bill T. Jones and Arnie Zane Dance Company at the Brooklyn Academy of Music as the occasion for a renewed attack on what has come to be known as "victim art."[1] Such art, she contends, unmans criticism by presenting artists not as performers but as martyrs—usually members of minority groups—who supposedly use performance as a way of rehearsing rather than transcending their grievances with society. In the case of Jones's new piece, *Still/Here*, the would-be critic is confronted with "people ... who are terminally ill and talk about it" (54). "By working dying people into his act," Croce claims, "Jones is putting himself beyond the reach of criticism" (ibid.). Two issues would dominate debates concerning Croce's article: her decision not to view—and hence not to review—the piece; and the possibilities for art's response to—or incorporation of—death. I wish to address both these questions in terms of an acting out or acting up, thereby raising two fundamental and parallel issues. First, what does it mean for a "victim" to perform? Does the "performance" of death—assuming, for the moment, that Jones's piece was, in fact about this—transcend or merely aestheticize the fact of death? Can a victim, in fact, perform, or does victimization consist instead in an alienation from the media of performance? Linked to this is the metadiscursive question: What does it mean for the critic to act up, to refuse to perform her duty within the public sphere? At this level, I will seek to understand the practice of criticism as a performative rather than a denotative or judgmental function.

It is necessary to recapitulate briefly the issues raised by Croce's article. First, she attacks Jones for antagonizing any and all critical response (it should be noted that she has not seen *Still/Here*). Jones, she claims, has "crossed the line between theatre and reality" and "thinks that victimhood in and of itself is sufficient to the creation of an art spectacle" (ibid.). Specifically, then—despite the broader aesthetic questions it raises—the article attacks the introduction of identity politics into the realm of performance; for once identity, in the form of victimhood, has been foregrounded, so criticism cannot fail to be ad hominem and thereby fail its broader cause. Accordingly, though Croce will claim a lack of interest in Jones's own persona (which the *New Yorker* itself profiled in its November 28, 1994, edition), she cannot— as bell hooks would observe in a response to the article—but be obsessed with it.[2]

Jones's piece uses as a backdrop to the dance video footage— taken in survival and self-empowerment workshops—of people living with AIDS. In Croce's words, "Jones presents people (as he has in the past) who are terminally ill and talk about it" (ibid.). The problem is perhaps most clearly articulated in a letter to the *New York Times* of March 5, 1995, written in response to Joyce Carol Oates's defense of Jones the previous week. It reads as follows: "Mr. Jones has crossed a line. He is not presenting art about victims. He is presenting victims as art. These victims are not just subjects of a documentary film, photographic insight, choreographic vision; they are the performing artists."[3] If the terminology is not rigorously philosophical, the sense of the critique is clear: the problem is that victimhood and death are not the "subjects" (that is, the objects) of the art. Strictly speaking, the problem is that the "victims" *are*, in fact, the subjects of this art. Now, this raises problems all around. First, if we must place "victim" between quotation marks, it is because one defense of Jones's piece—the one offered by his publicist, Ellen Jacobs, in a letter to the *New Yorker*—is that "the show's cast members are professional, international-class dancers, members of Mr. Jones's own modern-dance troupe—not 'sick people.'" We can but note the implied antithesis—marked, indeed, by a line of segregation—between the "professional dancers" and the "sick people." What if Mr. Jones's cast members were both?[4] Even if Jacobs's position can be read as acknowledging the coexistence of "sickness" and art, it implies by the negation—"not 'sick people'"—a transcendence of sickness through art. To this extent, I think Arlene Croce's piece might do us greater service: it acknowledges what we might call the materiality of the signifier, the "sick" body.

Second, *Still/Here*—with or without Croce's noncritique—seems to cross a line, the line, perhaps that marks the title of Jones's piece, a line separating temporal from spatial shifters, presence from iteration; for the piece suggests a lack of presence in the spatial present and a disruption of sequential narrative form. The disruption thematized in the work will itself be reiterated at the metadiscursive level of critique. For example, the editors of the *New York Times* title Susan Sontag's letter of March 5 "Philistinism All Over Again," suggesting—and, indeed, instigating—a repetition at the heart of the present. We are left with a sense, in Croce's terms, of a cyclical rather than a progressive movement and a fatalistic sense of being "condemned to repeat history" (56). This "still-ness" of Jones's piece, what is it? A silence? Or a lingering, a drawing out of temporality into an omnipresence that denies the immanence of presence? Or, in terms outlined by Jean-François Lyotard, "How is one to understand the sublime, or let us say provisionally, the object of a sublime experience, as a 'here and now'? Quite to the contrary, isn't it essential to this feeling that it alludes to something which can't be shown, or presented (as Kant said, *dargestellt*)?"[5] What Jones's piece seems to question for Croce are the aesthetic and critical presumptions of a modernism depending on notions of the sublime as the unrepresentable. What it seems to enact is the recognition, instead, of the sublime—in the form of death—as the *condition* of representation. The still-ness that should be a silence becomes a spatial marker, the mark of an event, an occurrence, a performance—which, in Lyotard's paraphrase of Martin Heidegger, would be "infinitely simple, but this simplicity can only be approached through a state of privation" (197).

Instead, then, of examining the possibility of representing death from the position of life—a position I would call vitalistic, and which Croce calls "transcendent"—I suggest we seek to understand the deathly logic of representation itself. Does death have the status of a speech act—a "phrase," in Lyotard's terms—or is it in fact the silence (the "still-ness") at the heart of *Still/Here*? Or is this question even well put? For still-ness—understood as silence, rather than as a temporal shifter—suggests the retention of death at the level of a thematic reading, in which, as Freud asserts, "dumbness represents death."[6] In the context of a performance, is silence to be understood as the (negative) "phrasing" of death or as its enactment? Or, is it not rather a question

—surely it is—of undecidability? What we confront is the performance of a representation—a real pretense.

It is further significant that such questions are raised in the specific context of a performance piece, for in question, at the virtual point, is the possibility of performing death: of death, that is, as a performative. Who can perform death if it can be performed at all? What residue of life and signifying possibility would death leave? Those who seek to legitimate Jones's project with reference to artists and writers of the past who treated of death as a central motif miss the point. What is specific here is the nature of *performance*, which—at least ideologically—performs the possible erasure of the parameters of referentiality that otherwise confine death at the level of the thematic. Performance is always the performance of its own possibility. Defending Jones with nineteenth-century Romantic precedent misses the point. What is at stake is something unprecedented: death itself. If death can, indeed, be performed, what is the function of that performance? Is it no more—or no less—than "a kind of messianic traveling medicine show, designed to do some good for sufferers of fatal illnesses," as Arlene Croce claims (54)?

Within our consideration of this question, it is important to note the iconography of race and sexuality in Croce's piece. Tropes of race and ethnicity pervade her article in a disturbing way. "I can live with the flabby, the feeble, the scoliotic," she writes, "But with the righteous I cannot function at all" (55). The aestheticized eugenicism of Croce's adumbration of what she can and cannot live with is more than disturbing and seems to break the boundaries of what is otherwise a reasoned—if heftily polemical—piece. It will subsequently lead her, in comparing Jones's work with that of another artist whose "cathartic" treatment of sickness and death suits her better, to muse on how its author, David Gordon, "one of the original radicals of postmodern dance, escaped being trapped by the logic of sixties permissiveness." She does not answer the question, offering and rejecting only one possible solution: "some presumed cultural advantage that Jews have over blacks" (60). What is being affirmed in this rejection? Why raise the specter of a racialized culture at all at this point? And, if the specter does present itself, is it somehow linked to the broader aesthetic argument of the article?

Reflecting on the impact of AIDS on aesthetic discourse and performance practice, Croce compares the putatively unmediated response of Jones to the Romantic tradition of death poetry in the nineteenth century. The self-transcendence of the suffering individual in such poetry now results—in performance—not in any transcendence of life in its limited physical form for a life of the eternal spirit, but only in the constitution of a collective. The AIDS quilt, Croce claims, would be emblematic of this aesthetic and spiritual deterioration: "the wistful desire to commemorate is converted into a pathetic lumping together, the individual absorbed by the group, the group by the disease" (ibid.). Finally, Croce places her reflections in the context of broader social, political, and ethical concerns that marked the twentieth century. "After two world wars," she writes, "and the other unspeakable terrors of our century, death is no longer the nameless one; we have unmasked death. But we have also created an art with no power of transcendence, no way of assuring us that the grandeur of the individual spirit is more worth celebrating than the political clout of the group" (59). After this rather remarkable trivialization of the specific horrors of World War II— Auschwitz as a missed aesthetic opportunity—Croce concludes with a comparison of Jones's work to other works that seem to hold greater promise of the transcendent aesthetic she mourns.

I will argue that, for Croce, heterosexuality and the power of *production* or *generation* is what not only *figures* but also *performs* transcendence. "The morbidity of so much romantic art is bearable," Croce argues, "because it has a spiritual dimension. The immolation of the body leaves something behind" (60). Organizing the debate around questions of literality and figurality, I will seek to ask what it is, this soul that *remains* in Romantic art, as opposed to the simple, literal, physical "remains" of Jones's piece. Croce astutely refers to Romanticism as offering us "a life beyond life—not the 'afterlife'" (ibid.), and I would like to use Jacques Derrida's notion of living on to explore just what it is that Jones might be doing to this Romantic tradition.[7]

Croce's final sally, however, will be against those who threaten *critics*. Citing Oscar Wilde—a notable point of reference and one that will also be invoked by Camille Paglia in a letter to the *New Yorker*— Croce reiterates "that the Greeks had no art critics because they were a nation of art critics." To Wilde she adds:

> But the critic who wished to restore the old connection between
> the artist and his audience appeals in vain to readers who have
> been brought up on the idea of art as something that's beneficial
> and arcane at the same time. People for whom art is too fine, too

high, too educational, too complicated may find themselves
turning with relief to the new tribe of victim artists parading their
wounds. (60)

Ultimately, Croce seeks to redeem the function of the critic not just as
a player within the public sphere, but—in the tradition of the depoliticized public sphere of the Enlightenment—as the public sphere's creator. Her criticism serves to preserve the rights of a minority—the
minority of those equipped to criticize sophisticated works of art—
against the incursion of extra-aesthetic criteria that seek to simplify aesthetic consumption. Rather than a salvo within a fairly circumscribed—
if disturbing—cultural and political attack, Croce's piece should be
taken seriously as a reflection on the role of criticism within the postmodern public sphere.

　　This brings us to the third issue raised by Croce's article. Much
debate would turn on Croce's decision not to view the work and yet to
write something other than a piece of criticism (to this extent, it should
be noted that her aesthetic critique therefore transgresses the limits
she sets herself for a reflection on the status of criticism itself). What
would it mean to read criticism as performance—that is, as a performative rather than a denotative speech act? The commonsensical reproach
leveled at Croce—namely, that she should not presume to write on a
piece she has not viewed—assumes that the function of criticism
remains denotative, when in fact even the defenders of traditional
critical values (such as Robert Brustein and even Susan Sontag, who, in
a letter to the *New York Times*, supports Croce's position while deplor-
ing her decision not to view the piece)[8] constantly cite those tasks
that criticism is meant to perform: most notably, the redemption of
American art.

　　Croce's very title—"Discussing the Undiscussable"—brings together two central issues in this debate: on the one hand, the importance of discussion and criticism in a postmodern public sphere, the
status of Enlightenment models of aesthetic community in an age of
apparent social and cultural fragmentation; and, on the other hand, the
question of the "undiscussable" itself, which I take as a question about
the status of the sublime. I would now like to look at the question of
presenting something as unpresentable, discussing the undiscussable in
order to question just what is being transcended in this art that we have
supposedly now lost. If the performance—"literally undiscussable"

(54) — is, in fact, to be discussed, what language does it oblige the critic to speak in? What remains when the language of the literal has been foreclosed by the "literality" of a death that is not merely referenced, but "acted out"?

What I am proposing, then, is a reading of criticism as performance. After considering the function of the article as an attempt to re-create a public sphere of critical debate, I will take up the extraordinary implications of the article's subtitle, "When players in a production aren't just acting out death but are really dying—as in Bill T. Jones's *Still/Here*—is it really art?" (ibid.), to examine the relationship of the aesthetic to the phenomenon of "acting out" and performativity in general. How might one "act out" death? And what is the significance of the performers' failure—or refusal, or inability—to do so in this case? What survival of death is presupposed by the repetition involved in all acting out? And what is the nature of this repetition—a rehearsal or *répétition* perhaps—when thought in terms of performance? In brief, the issue will be one of the representation of death—or, rather, the short-circuiting of representation through performance. If Jones's piece is presented as a therapeutic "traveling medicine show," how are we to imagine a work of art that works through death? Is there a modality of working through that implies not working through and *out of death*—as the traditional call for transcendence would suppose—but that thinks the "through" instrumentally: death as the tool *through which* the aesthetic might perform its work on life? This discussion will focus on the idea of "victimhood" and the possibility of its performance.

Because I would like to move closer to Jones's work in the course of this essay, I begin with a brief consideration of this final question—the role of critique within the bourgeois public sphere. It should come as no surprise that Croce's article was interpreted by friend and foe alike as an inflammatory political polemic (it is!), but of greater import is the way in which the fundamental political questions the article poses were overlooked. Critics and defenders discussed the rights and wrongs of Croce's aesthetic pronouncements, but very little was said of the *performativity* of the piece itself. I wish to argue that a critic so steeped in formal analysis herself deserves a formal critique; for, in the context of the present book, Croce's article raises the question of the relationship of "acting out" and performance to the constitution of the public sphere. Reading this critical debate (or polemic) as a performance, we are obliged to ask ourselves to what extent criticism operates not within the parameters of the public sphere, but rather as the modality of its definition. Before we even address the question of "acting out" as a pathologization of art, we need to address the respective roles of performance and critique in the constitution of the public sphere.

As Jürgen Habermas has pointed out in his analysis of *The Structural Transformation of the Public Sphere*, literary and aesthetic criticism was precisely the means by which the emerging bourgeoisie forged for itself a sphere of critical exchange—explicitly depoliticized—that would subsequently serve as the space of a political class formation.[9] The formalism of the Kantian aesthetic—as exemplified in the Third Critique—reflects the politicized depoliticization of critical discourse in the eighteenth century. I argue that Croce's article serves as a catalyst for investigating the function of that discourse in the declining twentieth century. In other words, her piece needs to be read not only as the critique of a performance, but as the performance of a critique. Of course, performance and critique have enjoyed a somewhat strained relationship in the historical emergence of the bourgeois public sphere; and, if the clinical term was never invoked, one might nevertheless ascribe this uneasy relationship to the suspicion in critical thought that all performance is an "acting out." Indeed, Habermas's presentation of the shift from "representative" to "bourgeois" public spheres explicitly marks a shift from notions of social performance to social literacy. Theatricality, for Habermas, characterized precisely that prebourgeois "representative" public sphere in which "lordship was something publicly represented. This *publicness* (or *publicity*) of *representation* was not constituted as a social realm, that is, as a public sphere; rather, it was something like a status attribute" (7). If the lord *performs a function*, his function, we might say, was, precisely, performance: the embodiment of power "not for, but 'before' the people" (8). In other words, the notion of subjectivity as performance offends both the bourgeois ideology of unique individuality and the political imperative of deliberative community.

The notion of the bourgeois public sphere seems inextricably linked to a shift from the theatricality and performativity of the "representative" public sphere to a new insistence on *literacy* and *critique* as the fundaments of publicity. Whereas Croce's article takes Jones to task for the specific subject positions he performs, the fundamental issue is with the very possibility of performing one's identity at all: "If we consider that the experience, open to the public, as it is, may also be intolerably voyeuristic, the remedy is also obvious: Don't go" (54). The "representative' nature of performance forces upon the critic the role of "voyeur"—takes her from the realm of linguistic into the realm of immanent, visual experience. Thus, she is torn between "a cozy kind of complicity"—the passivity of the enthralled spectator—and a feeling of having been excluded as a critic; for what performance would seem to preclude is, indeed, the practice of criticism.

When Joyce Carol Oates—attacking Croce—or any number of her supporters cite works from the Western canon and beyond that transcend death in a way that Jones's piece supposedly did not, distinctions of genre are necessarily blurred.[10] None of the participants address the status of performance itself in the debate. Croce, at least, indicates the importance of these distinctions when she observes of emerging postmodern dance forms in the 1960s that "it seemed to many that this kind of dance had a built-in resistance to criticism—not to writing but to criticism. There were critics who specialized in this art, or anti-art, but few of them went beyond description" (56). Her presentation, however, acknowledges a problem: from the 1960s on, writing and criticism can no longer be used as synonyms as they are by Habermas. What is the implicit opposition of writing and criticism that is being suggested here? And what would a writing be if it were "mere description"? Croce's oppositions seem at first to pit criticism against writing, but when that writing is itself reduced to "description"—or de-scription, an undoing of writing—the opposition collapses. Is she claiming some more radical form of writing for criticism, a writing that would not undo itself? And what happens to the concept of literacy when writing and critique are uncoupled? In fact, a descriptive writing would be a reiterative writing, but because what it reiterates in this case is only the everyday actions of postmodern dance, there seems to be some danger of its falling back into the everyday itself. In other words, criticism would be a writing that retains a notion of difference, whereas "mere" writing would be a writing that inscribes itself into the reiterative process of the everyday. Thus, whereas postmodern dance blurs the distinction between art and the everyday, "writing" about this dance—for Croce—blurs the distinction between art and criticism. In other words, what Croce wishes to hold at bay is the acknowledgment of the "event of narration"—the performativity that is criticism.

The questions of performance raised in this debate about Bill T.

Jones force us to remember that bourgeois literacy is grounded in forms of prebourgeois performance. Could Croce's unease at Jones's tactics of "intimidation" arise from precisely this sense of the performative—by which I do not mean the mimetic—in the practice of critique? Indeed, if her piece offers a critique, it cannot be read as criticism in the everyday sense of the word. "I have not seen Bill T. Jones's *Still/Here*," she announces in the opening line of the article, "and have no plans to review it" (54). This, I think, rather than the specifics of the polemic, is the key issue in Croce's piece. Even Croce's supporters—indeed, *particularly* her supporters—regret her decision not to view the piece and yet to offer a critique. But, as a performance in its own right, Croce's article in fact operates beyond the critical parameters designated by her allies: in a hyperbolic exaggeration of the Kantian aesthetic imperative, this critique is, indeed, disinterested. In the most radical sense, it has no interest in the existence of the performance that is its moment. If supporters feel let down by Croce's eschewing of traditional critical etiquette (and they have a right to feel let down, because Croce's article ultimately seeks to reinstate those standards), they ignore the ethical reconfiguration that Croce asserts. "A critic has three options," she writes: "(1) to see and review; (2) to see and not review; (3) not to see. A fourth option—to write about what one has not seen—becomes possible on strange occasions like *Still/Here* from which one feels excluded by reason of its express intentions, which are unintelligible as theatre" (ibid).

In fact, as Homi Bhabha points out in his article "Dance This Diss Around":

> Pious pleas that Croce should have seen *Still/Here* before writing
> her piece entirely miss the radical point of her polemic. By
> creating a defiant hole at the very heart of her essay, in the space
> where, customarily, the experience or analysis of the work would
> have appeared, Croce makes it clear that hers is no simple act of
> critical interpretation and evaluation, not even a meditation on
> the arts, it is a frankly ideological maneuver.[11]

It is pointless to recontain Croce's piece within the logic of enlightened criticism, because it is precisely the demise of that logic that she bemoans and performs. However, Bhabha's own article tends to reconstitute certain commonplaces of precisely the critical positions from which Croce claims to write. It could be claimed that he too misses the radical polemic of her work, for, in the terms he will provide to describe the phenomenon of "survival" — and the communitarian values it entails — it might be possible to read Croce's piece as itself caught within the logic of survival, a criticism that survives the demise of the traditional critical paradigms. Bhabha uses terms such as *experience* and *analysis* somewhat loosely or even interchangeably. It will be necessary to render them more precisely to understand the polemical performance of Croce's article. Ignoring Croce's otherwise incongruous interest in a work's "express intentions" — no, in the producer's intentions, for she has not seen the work — we need to examine what new critical, aesthetic, and ethical reconfiguration her article seeks to bring about.

Ostensibly, Croce charges Jones with a facile politicization of art, one that serves to render the work more easily consumable. Jones's intimidations are those of a self-performing identity (or victimhood) that at the same time makes the political demands accruing to that identity in the economies of cultural diversity and multiculturalism. But perhaps we could invoke the notion of an "acting out" to question some of the article's assumptions about "activist" and utilitarian art. In "Acting Out," Jean Laplanche and Jean-Bertrand Pontalis stress the distinction between the verbs of action in Freud — *tun, wirken* — and the verb of Latin root, *agieren*, which is not active.[12] This inactivity of "acting out," its exemption from a performative rationality in the technical sense, might be thought as precisely the modality of aesthetic performance. At the same time as they talk of the nonactive verb, however, Laplanche and Pontalis also stress that the verb is often used *transitively*. This curious combination of a transitive verb that is nevertheless denied the efficacy of action implicit in the transitive perhaps captures the very performativity of the aesthetic: it is an action that exhausts itself in itself, producing no "action."

This sense of "acting out" returns us back to the first two questions posed by or with regard to Jones's piece: the question of victimhood and the power of representation, and the related question of death, survival, and the sublime. The dissociation of *Agieren* from action in the instrumental sense clearly problematizes any attempt to use the charge of "acting out" to accuse Jones of presenting political activism as art. The problem with the piece would seem to be a political *inactivity*. In fact, this performance problematizes the notion of acting out in very interesting ways. Laplanche and Pontalis — quoting Freud — insist that the patient "acts it before us, as it were, instead of reporting it to us" (4). In this case, however, Croce's aesthetic concern is quite the reverse: this is not performance; it is "unintelligible" as theater. Instead, it features people "who are terminally ill and talk about it" (54). What Croce resents, in fact, is what the analyst seeks: the report. Jones brings reportage into the dance and thereby threatens performance; for, if death cannot be contained at the level of *récit*, it at least regains its aura of (negative) presence through the pure immanence of narration or performance. The problem with Jones's piece—with its play of performance and reportage—seems to be that it accepts neither form of mimetology: neither immanence nor mimetic denotation in the *récit*. Performative narration is transected by the *récit* and the containment that the *récit* enacts is threatened by the moment of its *narration* or *performance*.

At the same time, then, acting out is not self-exhausting, because it is a repetition: "the subject, in the grip of his unconscious wishes and phantasies, relives these in the present with a sensation of immediacy which is heightened by his refusal to recognize their source and their repetitive character" (Laplanche and Pontalis 4). In other words, we cannot, by another logic of mimesis, reconcile performance with the presence of self-performance, the self-revelation of the subject or action in its immanent unfolding. As Derrida writes in "Living On—Borderlines":

> What we have here is not that conclusion, readily drawn these days, using a logic of truth as presentation substituted for a logic of truth as representative equivalence, according to which new logic the narrative is the very event that it recounts, the thing presenting itself and the text presenting itself—presenting *itself*—by producing what it says. If there is performance here, it must be dissociated from the notion of presence that people always attach to the performative. What is here recited will have been that nonpresentation of the event, its presence*less* presence. (145–46)

We must also resist overstating the difference that the performativity of dance introduces into the text itself. In Jones's case, the alignment of "people who are terminally ill *and* talk about it" (Croce 54; emphasis added) retains a conjunction that separates. In other words, if we are to read the performance through the lens of acting out, we must necessarily question the notion of actualization as well as of action.[13]

Laplanche and Pontalis's linkage of "acting out" to the question of communication is particularly apposite in the context of a debate triggered by anxieties over the status of the critic and the possibility of communication within a critical paradigm. We have already pointed out how Croce's article is caught between a critique of the exclusionary practices deriving from Jones's performative identity politics and an uneasy feeling of "cozy complicity." What the critic does not reflect on, however, is the impact of the specific communication—the performance of death, rather than its mere "acting out"—on the traditional critical paradigm. Where Croce feels disarmed by death, she presents her reticence as a form of etiquette rather than as a necessary response to (the idea of) the work. Might it be that Jones's politics and performance of "intimidation" are something more than an opportunistic or "utilitarian" political ploy—and that they find expression precisely in a piece that problematizes the notion of an "acting out" of death?

If acting out needs to be thought in terms of the repetition compulsion, as Laplanche and Pontalis argue, the iterative will need to be an anterior—not a repetition, but a *répétition*. Not mimesis, but rehearsal. This, perhaps, is where Croce transgresses the function of the critic: in thinking that her task is to review a *rehearsal* rather than a performance. But how does this recognition of a cultural rehearsal of death impact the ideals of critical distance, objectivity, and disinterest? As Michel de Certeau observes:

> There is nothing so "other" as my death, the index of all alterity. But there is also nothing that makes clearer the place from which I can say my desire for the other; nothing that makes clearer my gratitude for being received—without having any guarantee or goods to offer—into the powerless language of my expectation of the other; nothing therefore defines more exactly than my death what speaking is.[14]

("Jones presents people (as he has in the past) who are terminally ill and talk about it" [Croce 54]). Speech, writing, criticism, and performance—how might they relate? What does it mean to see death performed? What room does it leave for critique? Whose death is the performer performing—his own or mine? All of these questions derive from the work's status as *répétition*, which can be thought of either as a collective and ritual function or as a personal attempt to come to terms with death. Does the intimidation Croce experiences lie in the performer's usurpation of *my* death, or in his failure to usurp it—that is, in the forced recognition that only *I* can perform my death? What is more frightening, a confrontation with death forced on us by another, or the refusal of that other to appropriate that death for us? This perhaps is what Croce inadvertently touches on when she observes that "this kind of dance had a built-in resistance to criticism—not to writing but to criticism" (56). Death threatens criticism because it threatens the fiction of alterity and distance on which Enlightenment critique was grounded. Or is it threatening instead because it cannot establish the fictional reciprocity on which a communicative community would be founded?[15] When Jones seeks to intimidate and exclude, he intimidates because he raises not only the fear of death, but also the fear of death's expropriation. What is most to be feared—my death, or the death of my death? If I am to die, I am to be silent. But if I am not to die, then I have no position of integrity from which to speak.

We must beware of becoming embroiled in a philosophical discourse on writing, however, for it is crucial that we respect the specificity of Jones's piece as a *performance*. By invoking, perhaps inadvertently or thoughtlessly, the clinical terminology of "acting out," Croce's article in fact foregrounds the function of the performance; for an "acting out" would be a performance in the mode of a prescriptive and prescripted mimesis: what such a performance performs is the *fiction* of performance. Consequently, what Jones's piece would perform would be not the truth of death but the fiction of performance. It is not a question of eschewing performative representation by "really" dying, but rather of refusing to "really" pretend, and thereby of performing the reality of a social and aesthetic fiction. Croce would be right when she does not "deny that *Still/Here* may be of value in some wholly other sphere of action, but it is as theatre, dance theatre, that I would approach it. And my approach has been cut off" (54). This is not theater in the sense of a ritualistic acting out—an impossible, reiterated exorcism— nor in the sense of a self-immanent actuality. The self-sufficiency of presence ("here") is disrupted by the acknowledgment of a temporality ("still") that renders it silent, renders it "still."

The critical question then would be what "work" is the piece doing on death? Or rather, how does it put death to work? This critical question—this possibility of critique—is precisely what Jones seems to foreclose. The idea that a performer might be "terminally ill" raises the question not only of the termination of his existence, but also of the termination of his illness. The point would not be to ontologize the performers—*Are* they "sick people" or *are* they "professional, international-class dancers"?—but rather to show how the very idea of their "termination" is itself intrinsic to, and disruptive of, such ontologies. They are not, then, speaking a truth about death but performing the fallacy of silence. In Derrida's terms, we have not the truth about death in a denotative mimesis, nor the mimetic, apocalyptic performance of the death of truth. Or, in Freud's terms, the piece indeed "crosses a line" that would separate "acting out" and working through. We could no longer say with Freud that the patient "acts it before us, as it were, instead of reporting it to us" (Laplanche and Pontalis 4)—for instead we see how the *récit* (including that of the disinterested critic?) always functions as an acting out.

It is not without relevance that the debate around *Still/Here* should concern the *status* of the performers: Croce refers to them as "sick people" while Jones's publicist, Ellen Jacobs, insists in the next issue of the *New Yorker* that the piece's subjects "are not 'victims' but, rather, witty, smart, and feisty heroes" (11). The question seems to be precisely one about the nature of being and the performance of being. In short, can one "be" a "victim"? Could it be that sickness is not the condition of a subject, but rather the sickness *of* the subject, as a subject? In which case—and the impossible chronology of "acting out death" would imply this—the problem concerns the impossibility of the subject recounting his own death. "Acting out death" would, in fact, be the fantasy of recounting from the position of an other-than-life the totality of one's existence. This would be the point at which death rather than life would be the origin of being, for there would be—to reiterate de Certeau—"nothing that makes clearer the place from which I can say my desire from the other" (194). In other words, the possibility—which Jones's piece apparently refuses—of "acting out death" would serve both to posit the possibility of a transcendence (I witness death and do not die) and the very possibility of subjectivity ("I" am completed only through death, or, rather, through my imagination of it). Thus, the question of "victimhood" goes to the very heart of the subject. Is victimization the denial of subjectivity? And, if not, how would such a subjectivity perform itself? What does it mean—in other words—to talk of "victim art"? What is a victim and how does he or she produce an art?

Although the debate around Jones's work can be read within the specific context of a polemic surrounding "utilitarian" art and the role of the state in funding such work, there is more than politicization at stake here. The outrage that Croce experiences when confronted—or not confronted—with Jones's work derives not from a simple, transgressive introduction of politics into the realm of the aesthetic, but from the sense of a paradoxical fusion of a subject-centered politics and an ethics of the victim; for the condition of the victim is the condition that prohibits the enactment or enunciation of subjectivity. "It is in the nature of a victim," Lyotard writes in *The Differend*,

> not to be able to prove that one has been done a wrong. A plaintiff is someone who has incurred damages and who disposes of the means to prove it. One becomes a victim if one loses these means.... In general, the plaintiff becomes a victim when no presentation is possible of the wrong he or she says he or she has suffered.[16]

Thus, to create as aesthetic subject a work that attests to the damage done to one's subjectivity is in itself to undo the work of victimization. If you can bespeak the wrong, the wrong is merely a damage. Not only *can* it be made good, it implicitly *is* made good in the performance or enunciation. In the terms of Croce's critique, what we have here are "people ... who are terminally ill and talk about it"—indeed, who not only talk but dance as well. Accepting for a moment the nomenclature "victim" (itself problematic and politically fraught) as outlined by Lyotard, what would be the impact of these dancers dancing and speaking their illness? If the fact of death and terminal illness is somehow unspeakable, what does it mean to speak of it? Does the development of a body of work around the thematic—but also the enactment—of death mark a definitive break in the possibilities of the aesthetic? And would that break be the paradoxical conjunction that allows a subject to speak of his or her loss of subjectivity?

From a perspective opposing—yet somehow rejoining—Croce's, one might argue that the *presentation* of a wrong that cannot be represented risks reducing the wrong done the victim to the status of a damage, something that can be made right. This would be the danger of trivialization—aestheticization, one might say. But this does not seem to be Croce's concern; what worries her is the role left the critic in such an art. "By working dying people into his act," she complains, "Jones is putting himself beyond the reach of criticism. I think of him as literally undiscussable" (54). What is being threatened is the critic's ability to *judge*—in other words, the very status of the (aesthetic) tribunal. The question of the critical faculty is necessarily the question of the possibility of litigation. The "voyeurism" that Jones's piece induces is the condition of the critic in the face of a wrong—in the face, that is, of a damage that refuses all judgment, aesthetic or otherwise. Croce's question would be whether the aesthetic realm is the correct realm for the articulation of such a wrong, because the notion of transcendence she invokes seems to act as a form of "talking cure."

Aesthetic representation is implicitly to be understood not as the description of or the longing *for*, but rather as the enactment *of*, transcendence. If death has been demystified by the systematic killings of the wars, life has thereby been robbed of its transcendent meaning, which lay in death. The annulment of individual life functioned also, Croce seems to imply, as the conclusion of a life that thereby sealed off its individuality. It is only in death that the individual—through annihilation—becomes an individual. The function of "the group" is not only to deny the individual his life (through "politics"), but to deny him his death. In fact, Croce is inverting the traditional ethical structure, because she rejects entry into a collective that transcends the individual life. Her critique of a performance bases itself on a recognition of the performative function of all speech acts: to speak of being a victim is to be a victim no longer. What this transcendent aesthetic enacts, of course, is a secondary repression of the victim. One can prove that one is a victim only by refraining from proof—which implies access to the practice of law, or to the judgments of a critic—in silence. What we need to examine with regard to Croce's critical endeavor is the relationship of aesthetic judgments of taste to a discourse of justice. Croce, in fact, conflates critical and ethical judgment to the extent that the disarming of aesthetic criticism is read also as an ethical problem.

Jones's work does not trivialize death by making a wrong into a litigation and thereby forcing the audience to judge. He is unacceptable not because he forces us to judge—thereby reducing himself to the level of a plaintiff before a court that is scarcely able to adjudicate—but because he refuses judgment, while yet refusing to be silenced. To this extent, such "victim art" presents victims—which is precisely what a victim cannot do—without proposing a metadiscourse that might resolve the wrong. In essence, what Jones threatens is the assumed unrepresentability of the "wrong." He traduces a certain modernist understanding of the sublime. The aesthetic problem—as opposed to the critical—seems to be that Jones's piece suggests a "crossing of the line" between death and representation. By refusing to "act out" death—refusing in other words, the ritual function of art—the performer does not "perform" it, does not bring it into the realm of immanence, but rather demonstrates the *function* of death within a mimetological aesthetic.[17]

In her review of *Still/Here* for the *Village Voice*, Deborah Jowitt discusses the two textual levels of the work—the dancers and the projections of survivor workshop interviewees—and concludes of the former: "Jones, I think, intends their dancing as a metaphor for life, for unquenchable spirit. I can see it. But I also shudder at the irony: those bodies and spirits looking out from the screens, speaking out on tape, are under siege. And these incredibly fit and glowing people are their messengers, witnesses, and surrogates?"[18] This comment is crucial for an understanding of the ways in which death might be thought of as a possibility of representation rather than as its impossibility. Respecting for a moment the line that Jones's piece so disturbingly seems to cross, we might schematically organize life and death in *Still/Here* around the split of dancers and film "victims." The dancers, we are told, represent the "unquenchable spirit," the "life" of those seen confronting their suffering on-screen. This the reviewer sees as an "irony." But the irony consists in the fact that the *actual* life of the dancers—"these incredibly fit and glowing people"—becomes a mere *metaphor* for life. The act of performative representation mortifies the bodies of the dancers into metaphoric existence. "Real" life is thus distanced and merely implied (the "spirit" of the interviewees from the workshops?), whereas the living bodies before us become rhetorical. In other words, representation mortifies, not because it is secondary to the immanence of "life," but because the very conception of life as an integral whole depends on and springs from a death.

To this extent, Jowitt's supposition is also reversible. The terminal illness of the interviewees serves as a metaphor for the vitality of the dancers. I am not proposing any "vitalistic" reading that would stress the "heroism" of the survivors and the ineradicability of life. Instead, I wish to show how the attempt to bring death to life necessarily reveals the death to which such a task condemns life. If an unquenchable life of the dying renders metaphoric the "fit and glowing" bodies of the vitally alive, then the people on video are likewise metaphors for the subjugation to representation that those dancing bodies undergo. The deathliness of those represented on video itself symbolizes those whose own living bodies have been mortified as mere signifiers of the dying. One dies not by signifying death, but by signifying at all. The video might be said to "represent" the death at the heart of performance. Homi

Bhabha, then, would be wrong to recur to the aesthetic presuppositions of modernism to defend Jones's work. His assertion that for the modernist it is precisely a work such as Jones's that "demands that we acknowledge the difference between the HIV-positive dancer as person and the HIV-positive persona as role, *especially when they inhabit the same body*" (20) surely misses the point of Croce's argument. The two no longer can be dissociated by a simple act of modernist faith. Just as the reviewer for the *Village Voice* had to "shudder at the irony" of fit, healthy, glowing bodies speaking out—acting out—for the terminally ill people on video, so the aesthetic quarantining of dancer and patient fails to stem the spread of an epidemic. There is a death in the reduction of the healthy bodies to the secondariness of a representation. Representation itself kills—this is the work it performs upon the bodies of those who represent.

The question raised by Jones's piece is nothing less than the possibility of a *beautiful* death. Traditionally, the "beautiful death" raised essentially ethical questions. What is particularly troubling about this work, perhaps, is the operation of the term *beautiful* within more strictly defined aesthetic parameters. Of course, an aesthetically beautiful death has never been particularly troubling in and of itself: Where would opera and ballet be without this genre? But such deaths always take place at the level of the *referent* of the work of art; in Jones's case, death enters into the very signifying system, questioning precisely what this referent would be. Lyotard argues in *The Differend* that beautiful death is a redemption from individual physical death through a passage into the collective, understood as an ideal ego; a sacrificial death—even where that death is a punishment of law—in which we will our death by accepting the law and thereby pass over into the eternity of the collective. What Lyotard does not address, however, is that alterity of death—"there is nothing so 'other' as my death, the index of alterity"— of which de Certeau speaks. The sense of "voyeurism" the spectator might experience confronted with Jones's piece can be understood at two levels: first, there is a limit to all empathy, your death is your own; but second, the very alterity of the death itself indexes my relationship *to* death. In de Certeau's terms, my death is not just "other," it is the *index* of all alterity. Is there any name that might be accorded these performers within a traditional critical scenario that might serve the function of an identification? It would seem that the only such function would be the "acting out" of death—a ritualistic *fort/da* game with mortality that performance might play. By refusing to merely "act out," the performers radicalize alterity—"yes, it really is my death"—and therefore threaten alterity in that second sense, the sense that allows me to think of my life making a sense I cannot yet know. Mortality is ob-scene.

The ritualistic elements of performance—of the performance of death specifically—must be tied to this sublime unrepresentability of death. As Freud noted in his "Some Thoughts for the Times on War and Death," "It is indeed impossible to imagine our own death; and whenever we attempt to do so we can perceive that we are in fact still present as spectators."[19] The very imagination of death is the survival of death: or, in other terms, the *performance* of the imagination takes precedence over the *representation* of death itself. That Freud should cast this as a *specular* relationship is particularly interesting in the light of Croce's complaint that Jones's piece is "intolerably voyeuristic" (54); for why would this voyeurism be intolerable, when in fact the specular relation—central to the function of imagination—is precisely that which renders *tolerable* the representation of death? What exactly is intolerable in Jones's performance? In fact, Freud argues that the specular—imaginary—relation to one's own death finds a specifically theatrical expression in the modern age: "at bottom," he argues, "no one believes in his own death" (289), and while this might provide us with a comforting fiction of immortality, as a result "life is impoverished, it loses in interest, when the highest stake in the game of living, life itself, may not be risked" (306). In other words, life itself is trivialized and impoverished by our inability to believe in our own death. One might almost say that the possibility of *imagining* death—the sublime possibility, that is, of surviving death through imagination—renders death itself mundane.

Freud proposes a cultural antidote: "It is an inevitable result of all this that we should seek in the world of fiction, in literature and in the theatre compensation for what has been lost in life. There we still find people who know how to die" (291). The theater serves the function of making death real again—but we must remember that making death real means making it *un-imaginable*. In other words, the ritual function of death in the theater would not be its imaging and performance of death, but rather the presentation of its unimaginability—its refusal to reassure us that imagination transcends death. In Freud's model, then, the ritual function of death in the theater would not be sacrificial. The point is not to transcend death by representing to oneself *through the death of another* an image of death. On the contrary, the point is to observe someone who still "knows how to die"—whose death cannot be subsumed under the self-sublating work of my imagination. The work of voyeurism that so troubles Croce would be precisely the work of an imaging that thwarts imagination.

Now, one might argue that the representation of death for me by another—or, indeed, in Jones's piece, the representation of the "sick" by the "healthy"—enacts precisely the movement of imagination that Freud talks about: I have the representation of death that does not threaten me. This would be a sublime experience, inclusive of the transcendence that the sublime implies. So what is intolerable? What we find here are people who "know how to die": the locution itself is ambiguous. Are these people who can imagine their own death and can therefore transcend it (through knowledge)? Or is "knowing how to die" knowing how to die *properly*—knowing, in other words, what one cannot imagine? Knowing *that* one cannot imagine? Knowing how to die is not a prescience: it is unprecedented. Does one who knows how to die know what death *is*? Is knowledge a *form* of, or a *lack* of, imagination? Is it a cognition or a *technē*, a know-how?

Freud certainly seems to imply the latter: I cannot live because I cannot properly die—my death has been rehearsed in the imagination. The imagination would, at bottom, be the name for that *répétition* implicit in the impossible "acting out" of death. Meanwhile, the people who know how to die, die unimaginable or unimagined deaths. Their knowledge is a form of ignorance that retains for death the immanence of the unique. But, as Croce argues, the problem with this piece by Jones is that the figures do not "act out" death: it is not of the nature of a *répétition*. To insist, as Homi Bhabha does, on the ways in which the traditional dichotomy of signifier and signified can be reasserted within the body of the performers in this piece is to reduce their death to a ritual of the imagination.

In certain ways, Freud's analysis—written in a time of war— uncannily reflects Croce. "After two world wars and the other unspeakable terrors of our century, death is no longer the nameless one; we have unmasked death," Croce argued, "but we have also created an art with no power of transcendence" (59). Freud, meanwhile, argues that the war changes our concept of death because it brings death into the real: he writes of "the altered attitude towards death which this—like every other war—forces upon us" (14:273). What we need to understand, however, is precisely what Croce could mean by "unmasking." For Croce, although we can name and imagine death, we seem unable to transcend it through art. But, as Freud points out, quite the opposite is true. War reminds us that our imagination of death is, indeed, only that—and that the transcendence that imagination enacts must remain purely imaginary. Croce—even where she argues for death's entry into our lives—can conceive of that entry only in the imaginary. This is why Bhabha's analysis is wrong: the distinction (within one and the same body) between that which is death and that which is its representation is no longer tenable. The performer does not transcend death—death itself transcends our imagination, making us real, giving us life. What the terminally ill remind us is that they can die only for themselves. The ritualistic function that distinguishes death from the performer—and, through the performer, from the audience—no longer works. The purgative effect of the death of the other is lost precisely because the other asserts its alterity rather than its identity with us through that death.

Of course, Jones's attempt to offer an aesthetic framework for death may in itself be problematic, but not for the reasons adumbrated by Croce.[20] What we have here is not a surrender of "the aesthetic" to the contingencies of political correctness, but a rather radical pushing of the limits of the aesthetic into the realm of the ethical. In his response to the piece, Homi Bhabha comments quite rightly that Croce's piece itself demonstrates an interest that is purely ideological, and he, in turn, seeks to defend the supposedly communitarian elements of Jones's work. But, in a sense, Croce's argument is also a search for community, a community based on critical interaction: to this extent it is paradigmatically "enlightened." "If survival has no place in the esthetics of transcendence," Bhabha writes, "perhaps this is because it is a form of being that is somewhat undecided, ambivalent about the dialectic of art and indeed the direction of life. To survive, technically, is to continue after the *cessation* of a thing, event or process: to carry on in the light and shadow of a break, a trauma, a trial, a challenge" (20). This foregrounding of the question of "survival" is particularly apposite for a debate in which various levels of survival can be isolated. Jones himself "survives" the death of his partner, Arnie Zane. The performers "survive" their illness. Croce's criticism "survives" the performance that supposedly renders it impossible. Can we read these survivals as in any way parallel, homogeneous—or even as repetitions of each other?

I have referred en passant to some of the troubling aspects of

Croce's racial and sexual vocabulary, and I think we need to ask what it means for Jones to "survive" the death of his partner, Arnie Zane. Croce writes that "Bill T. Jones seems to have been designated by his time to become the John the Baptist of victim art. (His Christ was Arnie Zane, who died of AIDS in 1988.)" Perhaps the most striking thing about Jones's "survival" is the effect it has on Zane—the Jew becomes Christ (again). The temporal logic is skewed too: Jones will be the prophet—John the Baptist—of the coming of that which has already gone (Zane). Jones's survival is itself an "event" in the development of modernism, according to Croce:

> The concerts that Bill T. Jones gave with his partner Arnie Zane, were different from the ones he gave after Zane's death, though both were fairly typical of the post-sixties atmosphere of "conceptual" dance. Talking and singing were mixed with dancing; dancing was mixed with non-dancing. It was Jones who split the mixed media from the message, with his bating of the audience. (58)

In essence, the passage from Judaism to Christianity in a process of what Tony Kushner calls (paraphrasing Croce) "morbid fetishization," is a passage out of the modernist discourse of the sublime; for what does it mean to make a fetish of the dead man whose cultural significance as a Jew (the binaries of black and Jew fascinate Croce) resists the fetish? What does it mean, in other words, to fetishize the dead body that signifies (through the Judaic interdiction on fetishes) the impossibility and sublimity of signification? By supposedly fetishizing that which paradoxically resists and represents fetishization—the corpus of his dead Jewish partner—Jones moves outside the parameters of modernism as Croce would define them.

This would be the significance of the chronology, of Jones playing John the Baptist to someone who has gone, rather than to one who is yet to come; for the ultimate question of survival—at least for Croce— is that of modernism itself. Can it too live on after a rupture, a trauma, a trial? As Lyotard has famously decreed—in a temporal inversion reminiscent both of Jones's prophecy and of the temporality of a pathological *répétition*—"A work can become modern only if it is first postmodern. Postmodernism thus understood is not modernism at its end but in the nascent state, and this state is constant."[21] The prophet of what has passed, Jones would be the postmodern prophet of the modern, even as Croce seeks to invoke the criteria of modernism to reject him. This, of course, raises questions of the racial, religious, and ethnic codings of Croce's model: the iconophobic Jewish modernism prophesied by the black dancer who is "uninterested in conforming to the stereotype of the respectable black choreographer" (56). Kushner's paraphrasing of Croce might in fact phrase the paradox of the postmodern: it draws its strength from the fetishization of that which resists and condemns the fetish.

But, how do we think the thematic of death in regard to the specific sexual politics of the Jones–Zane relationship? In fact, Freud's characterization of the distinction between the mundane death of imagination and the fiery, enlivened death of wartime proves uncannily prescient. Imagined and transcended through imagination, death, he argues, "becomes as shallow and empty as, let us say, an American flirtation, in which it is from the first understood that nothing is to happen," whereas this unimaginable death functions like "a Continental love-affair in which both partners must constantly bear its serious consequences in mind" (291). But what would be the consequence of such a love affair, of this *Liebestod*? A loss of self in the passion of love? An unwanted pregnancy? Or, in an age of AIDS, the very possibility of death. In fact, Freud's metaphor is more than a metaphor for us. If, in a time of war, the possibility of love is reawakened by an acquaintance with death, we might say that the reverse is now the case; it is love that has "redeemed" for us the possibility of death—of a consequence of no consequence to the act of love itself.

But, of course, Freud's own comparison—the flirtation as opposed to the affair—is enclosed within a tropology of heterosexual romance. And, as Croce pointed out, it is against the romantic imagination of death that Jones's piece seems to work. Would it be possible to push the argument a little further? To play—as Derrida plays—on that "triumph of life" that we understand in such positivistic and vitalistic ways? Or, beyond Derrida, to reverse not only the process of the genitive—but also of the *generative*? The answer, surely, is not to engage in a counter-discourse of the homosexual subject. Even if the tone of her response is juvenile in its clerical nostalgia for "decadent blasphemies," one can at least sympathize with Camille Paglia's citation of Wilde—"that anti-philanthropic warrior for art"—when she excoriates "the current cant and sanctimony about homosexuality" (10) that has helped polarize debate; for it is this polarization, perhaps, that leads Croce to simplify in turn. Although the tenor of the publicist's defense — "Rather than a work about AIDS or about dying, *Still/Here* is a work about living, and its subjects are not 'victims' but, rather, witty, smart and feisty heroes" (8) — is emotionally appealing, it begs the question of the relationship of death to subjectivity. How might we know death without imagining it? How might we render it neither generative and procreative in a "romantic" (or, indeed, Romantic) sense, nor self-enclosed as a truth in the metaphysical sense? Perhaps we cannot: but I suggest that we begin by recognizing the materiality of those bodily signifiers of death whose own signifying function is itself under threat of death, by insisting not — as Bhabha tends to — on "the difference between the HIV-positive dancer as person and the HIV-positive persona as role" (20), but rather on the *différance* that would undermine such binaries.

What is at stake for Croce and her supporters is, indeed, a discourse of re-generation and redemption, as Robert Brustein makes clear in a letter claiming that "reality without transcendence turns us all into voyeurs. . . . the visionary gleam rather than any narcissistic glitter is what redeems American art" (10). If the central concern of the debate seems to be the question of aesthetic transcendence and the illegitimate politicization of aesthetics, Brustein's analysis deals not with the self-transcendence and self-alienation of the subject, but rather with the redemption of "American art." The project is collective in a political rather than a humanitarian sense.[22]

In his letter of response to the *New Yorker*, Tony Kushner touches on a level of rhetoric that betrays both Croce's aesthetic and her ideological assumptions in this regard. He questions her comparison of Jones to a contemporary, David Gordon, whose very different career trajectory is reflected in a new piece being staged at the same time as *Still/Here*:

> Might I suggest, indulging in some victim paranoia, that David
> Gordon's play (which I hear is wonderful) is invoked in her attack
> because it sets up an opposition lurking beneath Ms. Croce's
> politics of anti-political art? Ms. Croce tells us that Mr. Gordon's
> piece is called "The Family Business" and that it's by Mr. Gordon
> and Ain, his son. Mr. Jones, with no son and no family business
> but only a dead and, according to Ms. Croce, morbidly fetishized
> male partner, is trapped by "charisma" and "narcissism," of
> which gay men are invariably accused. (11)

Kushner's point is well taken: the triumph *of* life and the triumph *over* life are enacted through the act of procreation. Implicit throughout

Croce's article is the assumption of the conciliatory power of procreative sexualities once translated into art; for, as Brustein makes explicit, Croce's desire to create and sustain a public sphere through the practice of criticism itself constitutes a form of "family business"—the creation and procreation of a sphere of discursive intimacy. Taking seriously Jones's challenges to modernist aesthetic and critical assumptions, I think we need to insist not on the transgression of the border in *Still/Here*, but rather on its maintenance as a separation and conjunction of presence and iteration. It is a hymen that is not ruptured.

Notes

1. Arlene Croce, "Discussing the Undiscussable," *New Yorker* (December 26, 1994–January 2, 1995): 54–60.
2. All letters cited from the *New Yorker* (by bell hooks, Robert Brustein, Tony Kushner, Ellen Jacobs, and Camille Paglia) appeared in "In the Mail," *New Yorker* (January 30, 1995): 10–13.
3. Patricia Clark, *New York Times*, March 5, 1995, sec. 2, 5.
4. At this point, I shall not conjecture upon the seropositivity or negativity of Mr. Jones's dancers, though the thrust of my argument would not necessarily hold this to be irrelevant to an analysis of the work.
5. Jean-François Lyotard, "The Sublime and the Avant-Garde," in Andrew Benjamin, ed., *The Lyotard Reader* (Oxford: Basil Blackwell, 1989), 196.
6. Sigmund Freud, "The Theme of the Three Caskets," in *The Standard Edition of the Complete Psychological Works of Sigmund Freud*, trans. and ed. James Strachey in collaboration with Anna Freud (London: Hogarth Press, 1953–75): 12:295.
7. Jacques Derrida, "Living On—Borderlines," in Harold Bloom, Paul de Man, Jacques Derrida, Geoffrey Hartman, and J. Hillis Miller, *Deconstruction and Criticism* (New York: Continuum, 1979), 78–177.
8. Susan Sontag, *New York Times*, March 5, 1995, sec. 2, 5.
9. Jürgen Habermas, *The Structural Transformation of the Public Sphere: An Inquiry into a Category of Bourgeois Society*, trans. Thomas Burger with the assistance of Frederick Lawrence (Cambridge: MIT Press, 1991).
10. See Joyce Carol Oates, "Confronting Head-on the Face of the Afflicted," *New York Times*, February 19, 1995, sec. 2, 1.
11. Homi K. Bhabha, "Dance This Diss Around," *Artforum International* 33:8 (April 1995): 19.
12. Jean Laplanche and Jean-Bertrand Pontalis, "Acting Out," in *The Language of Psychoanalysis*, intro. Daniel Lagache, trans. Donald Nicholson Smith (London: Hogarth Press, 1973), 4–6.
13. Indeed, Laplanche and Pontalis are unhappy with definitions of "acting out" and argue that the work to be done "presupposes a reformulation of the concepts of *action* and *actualization* and a fresh definition of the different modalities of *communication*" (6).
14. Michel de Certeau, *Heterologies: Discourse on the Other*, trans. Brian Massumi, foreword by Wlad Godzich (Minneapolis: University of Minnesota Press, 1986), 194.

15. De Certeau notes how "The melancholic says 'I can't die'; the obsessive says, 'I cannot not die' ('Above all,' says Freud, 'the obsessed need the possibility of dying in order to resolve their conflicts')" (192). As bell hooks writes of Croce, "she is obsessed with his story."

16. Jean-François Lyotard, *The Differend: Phrases in Dispute*, trans. Georges Van Den Abbeele (Minneapolis: University of Minnesota Press, 1989), 9.

17. Lyotard in fact differentiates the forms of silence that the differend necessitates: "The survivors remain silent, and it can be understood (1) that the situation in question (the case) is not the addressee's business (he or she lacks the competence, or he or she is not worthy to be spoken to about it, etc.); or (2) that it never took place...; or (3) that there is nothing to say about it (the situation is senseless, inexpressible); or (4) that it is not the survivors' business to be talking about it (they are not worthy, etc.). Or, several of these negations together" (26).

18. Deborah Jowitt, "Fight for Life," *Village Voice*, December 20, 1994, 87.

19. Sigmund Freud, "Some Thoughts for the Times on War and Death," in *The Standard Edition* 14:273–302; 289.

20. Interestingly, an article on Jones's life in the November 28, 1994 *New Yorker* describes Jones's attempt to frame the death of his lover and partner Arnie Zane as a bedside performance and Jones's second thoughts about the appropriateness of this gesture. This article is also of interest—in the light of the issue of procreativity and the arts—for its revelation that Jones is, in fact, a father.

21. Jean-François Lyotard, *The Postmodern Condition: A Report on Knowledge*, trans. Geoff Bennington and Brian Massumi (Minneapolis: University of Minnesota Press, 1984), 79.

22. Brustein nevertheless takes Croce to task for not sufficiently conflating the concerns of the nation and the concerns of mankind, hoping that "in future Arlene Croce will find nothing human alien to her critical sensibilities" (10).

a(Bridge(d

ACTING OUT WITH THE CECIL TAYLOR UNIT

ACTING OUT WITH THE CECIL TAYLOR UNIT

Fred Moten

For me it's more interesting, in a way, to look at the construction of bridges than it is to look at musical scores. Here we are. [Opens a book on bridges.] Here are the cable-stayed bridges. The first ones, of course, were done in Germany. The Germans also came up with the heliacal bridges. The first one was done in 1953. And these were all over this river. I think it's the Rhine, too. It's extraordinary. They come in two different kinds. There's the fan shape and the harp shape, you see. When you go into Cologne by train you'll see the most extraordinary bridge. It looks like a huge piece of sculpture.

But then, oh boy, I wish I had that book—I don't know—I lost it—the Calatravas bridges. Now, Calatravas's bridges—and his teacher Christian Mann—he's got another conception of bridge building now—and roadways—that we just—we just don't understand that shit here. Give us time, however.

Anyway, some of those pictures, they're incredible . . .

—Cecil Taylor, from Chris Funkhouser,
"Being Matter Ignited: An Interview with Cecil Taylor,"
Hambone 12 (1997): 27.

0

Suspension. There is performance in the absence of the recording.

Expansion, incision, excursion; fold in, act out, like what Nathaniel Mackey calls "the sexual cut."

> You got me all wrong on what I meant by a "sexual 'cut'" in my last letter. I'm not, as you insinuate, advancing severance as a value, much less pushing, as you put it, "a thinly veiled romance of distantiation." I put the word "cut," remember, in quotes.

What I was trying to get at was simply the feeling I've gotten from
the characteristic, almost clucking beat one hears in reggae,
where the syncopation comes down like a blade, a "broken"
claim to connection. The image I get is one of a rickety bridge
(sometimes a rickety boat) arching finer than a hair to touch
down on the sands at, say, Abidjan. Listening to Burning Spear
the other night, for example, I drifted off to where it seemed I was
being towed into an abandoned harbor. I wasn't exactly a boat
but I felt my anchorlessness as a lack, as an inured, eventually
visible pit up from which I floated, looking down on what debris
looking into it left. By that time, though, I turned out to be a
snake hissing, "You did it, you did it," rattling and weeping
waterless tears. Some such flight (an insistent *previousness*
evading each and every natal occasion) comes close to what I
mean by "cut." I don't know about you, but my sense is that
waterless tears don't have a thing to do with romance, that in fact
if anything actually breaks it's the blade. "Sexual" comes into it
only because the word "he" and the word "she" rummage about
in the crypt each defines for the other, reconvening as whispers at
the chromosome level as though the crypt had been a crib, a
lulling mask, all along. In short, it's apocalypse I'm talking, not
courtship.[1]

Open, break, enclose like what Jacques Derrida calls "the law of the
law of genre" and its whole im/possibilities.

> . . . the law of the law of genre. It is precisely a principle of
> contamination, a law of impurity, a parasitical economy. In the
> code of set theories, if I may use it at least figuratively, I would
> speak of a sort of participation without belonging—a taking part
> in without being part of, without having membership in a set.
> With the inevitable dividing of the trait that marks membership,
> the boundary of the set comes to form by invagination an internal
> pocket larger than the whole; and the outcome of this division
> and of this abounding remains as singular as it is limitless.[2]

The metaphorics through which the cut of the law seemingly must be
described, explained—no, generated—would mark its existence as a
function of a real sexual difference, one comprehended rather than
apprehended, perceived rather than conceived, visible and determined,
subject to light. Such an idea of sexual difference stands in opposition
to that which engenders and is engendered by Peggy Phelan's notion of
performance (of the real, *of the whole*) as "the genre of art in which
disappearance (the failure of the given to be seen to remain fixed in an

arrested position) is part of the aim of the work[,]"[3] a genre in suspense and span:

> Performance art usually occurs in the suspension between the
> "real" physical matter of "the performing body" and the psychic
> experience of what it is to be em-bodied. Like a rackety bridge
> swaying under too much weight, performance keeps one anchor
> on the side of the corporeal (the body Real) and on the side of the
> psychic Real. Performance boldly and precariously declares that
> Being is performed (and made temporarily visible) in that
> suspended in-between.[4]

But Phelan knows that something remains in performance. It is perhaps an unmarked, invisible, and undetermined something, but it paradoxically projects light in unrecordable passion and exigent flash as submerged natality and encrypted revelation. This trace of the temporary seen is perhaps the something that remains in Derrida's formulation of the law of genre and one wonders what that essential remainder—*the law* of the law of genre—has to do with performance. One wonders whether that law is the imminent and locatable singularity whose withdrawal is that out of which or from which performance is generated. That remainder, whose disappearance is held precisely as that which is said always to be to come, generates performance; for Derrida, it is a constative mark arrested as invagination. So that again it might be said—and is, indeed, implied by Phelan—that the law of the law of the genre "genre of performance" is the paradoxical and complex singularity of sexual difference. It is, more generally, the interminable and arresting oscillation between purity and impurity, natality and disappearance, determination and indetermination that ensures that any valorization or conclusion of impurity or disappearance has, at its heart, purity and natality in a law no less immutable than its mirror image. In that image the presence of the impure and the disapparent is located at the heart of the pure and nascent present. And the interplay of original and image is the in/determinate structure of the law and of the law of the law. Sex works this way. Does race work this way? Does sexuality? Are either manifest by and/or as "an internal pocket larger than the whole" where "the outcome of this division and of this abounding remains as singular as it is limitless"? Here Derrida would deploy ineffable and inevitable, happy and tragic singularity to instantiate a written disruption of totality: by way of an augmentation, scrawny cry, or piercing scream, metastory or metavoice, growling recitation or hummmming sigh (sound's written disruption of voice); by way of what emerges either as the embodiment of the difference sex makes or as the emergent subjectivity of a sutured, unstable, reciprocal gaze, a dual—aural-visual—un/doing of arrestment. We'll try to get to performance as an undoing of arrestment and see what this veiled brilliance sounds like. I think it might sound like something on the other side of a rickety, rackety bridge.

So let's say that being is not but nothing other than what is acted out in groups; this is to say, in an abounding echo of Derrida's divided echo of Heidegger, that what is acted out in groups "speaks always and everywhere throughout language."[5] Let's say that what is performed in performance, what is organized or arranged, is the improvisation of ontology, of that which interrrupts or erupts from or out of ontology to the extent that ontology will have never arrived at what is acted out in groups even/especially when the question of what is acted out in groups phases into the question of being. Let's say that what interrupts and erupts from, divides and abounds, ontology is (the) ensemble—its sound, spacing, taste, visuality, meaning, smell, touch: content.[6] The way (the) ensemble operates, the way it acts—out from outside, out from the opposition and interinanimation of out/in epistemological and ontological formulations, out from outside the house of being, out of the restrictive harmonics the one inside has formed with what has been called thinking and its codes in an improvisation of the opposition between harmony and rhythm and in the reverberate halloo that is between and improvisatory of elements and their collection—opens up for us an improvisation of the ontology, and the ontological idea, of performance (its space, its sphere, the primacy of the privacy of what has been called its experience), one that drives through the opposition of the appearance and disappearance of encrypted, differentiated genres/ identities that are themselves oscillating between purity and impurity. In/visibility, dis/appearance, product/process are the axes around which the phantomic "ontology of performance" would revolve. I want to improvise through them and through their arrangement of the constellation (event/action, rituality/mundanity, structure/agency) at which occurs the annular-interruptive renewal of things, of the way things are ...

By way of the trace[7] of The Music's[8] performance, by way of the step away of genre/s, we're off! on some out improvisations: of out where ensemble links the improvisation of the divided and abounding— invaginated—whole with the improvisation of the improvising musical group's performance; of the sound—and the extra-sonic particularities

of the production of sound—of the Cecil Taylor Unit, divided, Cecil
Taylor, abundant, Cecil   will sing
                    linger and   collapse
music   falls
before   down

        descension

Cecil descends, sounds, moves down, is out in many respects: of the
outside/s that The Music constitutes—of narrow and superficial understandings of (the) tradition, of certain harmonic constraints, of certain
assumptions regarding tonality, of prior notions of totality and its
relation or opposition to singularity, of the solo and the dominant theorization of its emergence from and disappearance within the group,[9]
of, therefore, a theorization of disappearance-in-performance that in
some ways anticipates that of Phelan; of outside/s only in the context of
the group, or so it would appear, like that fold or invagination made
visible by and in the law of genre, the one that extends and deepens
the totality it ensures by way of violation, an extending and deepening
violation that is never an erasure or disappearance or is only a disappearance in the partial way that erasure performs, a "foreshadowing
description"[10] of the outside Set—the interinanimation of one and many
that is our fate, "this is not prophecy but [foreshadowing] description,"[11] that divine Egyptian trace of fixity to which Amiri Baraka[12]
sometimes negatively and warily refers[13]—takes in;[14] of the unit/s of
performance, the song form, the song and its collection, the tune and
the normal lineup of tunes, the "Standards" (of performance); of the
set, which is to say the party, the jam, the get-together gathering logos,
outside of the imaginary disappearance of the logos in another kind of
writing, another composition, another movement through composition
and its other, another improvisation of improvisation.
    But here nothing follows for me but questions, ones that ought to
make you go back and question the sharpness of a chain or run of asser-
tions about the out of the music. Like: (A) What is the Cecil Taylor
Unit?

the unit is present in Cecil's "solo" performances as surely as he "leads"
(structures or feeds) the performance of the unit; the subject of ensemble is embodied in the piano, rhythmic orchestra of unit, playing as

Ellington played, orchestra held in the instrument, instrument become orchestra, each extensions of a single, divided, and abounding body

Is it him alone, a set continually invaded or complicated, divided or abounded, by a dominant singularity around which it is structured and which is violent to or excessive of that structure? Is the unit that which erases singularity in the name of a unity in which the singular reappears undifferentiated? Does Cecil participate without belonging and is that participation encoded in the name the Cecil Taylor Unit, a unit of which Cecil is (not) a member, a unit dis/allowed by his non/membership? Is Cecil the living principle of invagination or the improvisation of that principle, an anarchization of that principle that would place the whole within the field that emerges between deconstruction and reconstruction? Embedded in these questions is the possibility of an invagination of invagination, the sense of what is out from the outside, the outside that is not brought back in. (B) What is it to be out in The Music? What is the sound of this "out" and where is the sexuality of Cecil's music-poetry-dance-performance? Wherein lies the cut that exists within and for a single sex, a sex that is one or, at least, perhaps, the same? How's that sound and how's that sound performed or acted? How does out, the outness of the sexual cut within the same sex, sound? This is to ask: What's it sound like? But it is also to ask: How would it sound if it sounded? *Does* it sound? Is the out of The Music, The New Black Music, The New Thing, Cecil's music, the music of the Cecil Taylor Unit, the out of a sexuality that, while out, is not always as overtly referenced as the other elements of his identity or identities? What would an out performance—an acting out—be and what would the (homo)sexuality of Cecil's music, if there is a (homo)sexuality of this music, sound like? What would it look like? (C) What is the relationship between a music of an outside sexuality, a music in which that sexuality is out, overt, visible as identity, and the music of blackness as another (an other) outside identity? What is the sound of a certain misogynistically and hyperheterosexually politicized black manhood and how is it related to, diluted, changed, silenced, disappeared by Cecil's sexuality? Here we can think Cecil as the site of an ambivalence not only regarding the complexities of individual sexuality or the sexuality or procreativity of an aesthetics, but regarding the revolutionary (im)potency of a highly gendered and heterosexualized black politics and the multiple status and conflicted terrain of the outside, as well.

For LeRoi Jones, The Music is the site of an "American Sexual Reference: Black Male,"[15] an out and visible sexual mark, an out, black heterosexuality indexed immediately to shadowed act, haunted and deferred action, motivated and concealed acting of a black revolutionary politics of which Cecil is outside because of an out sexuality and what Jones saw/heard/read as the pale cast of a concomitant aesthetics sicklied o'er with a debilitating—which is to say feminizing, homosexualizing, whitening—boho-intellectualism that dilutes the native black/straight/male hue of resolution, subjecting the act to the displacements of nomination.[16]

Yet, Cecil is a fundamental figure in and prophet of the black musical outside. As such he is the member who disrupts and allows the black political unit/y and displaces the "home" Jones would hear in The Music. Out-from-the-outside Cecil is located at the center of Jones's ambivalence. It is apparent in his writing on Cecil, writing filled with so many veiled and submerged distancings, critiques, outings.[17] These writings are the site of a dis/appearance or other appearance or complication of appearance of the outside, an oscillation of im/purity tied to an equally ambivalent rejection of and immersion in the (myth of the) European that also, ironically, characterizes Cecil's work, whose conceptualization is even today still bound to the notion of a critique of a Euro-aesthetic absence of emotion and the correspondent hegemony of an inauthentic intellectualism disconnected from its home or origin, which is to say from the *feeling* that would predict—prophesy, determine, foreshadowingly describe—it.[18]

Is jazz a kind of closet, a withdrawal of (homo)sexuality negatively echoed in real and mythical carnal origins in explicit and illicit (hetero)sexuality? But what of the inevitable, always already out and out from the outside (primarily male homo)erotics of ensemble or of the feminized romanticism of a pianism of the body that is never not racialized, never not coded as the non-European, as the non-European within the European, even as it is coded as effeminate, overemotional, lustful, uncontrolled, animalistic, or at least infused with too much anima, possessed, transportive, out, ecstatic, gay? What about Taylor's approach to the piano, stabbing at sounds in the form of a seduction, the piano's *embodiance*, the body from outside occupying the instrument by way of incremental penetrations, gestures emitting light light sound in the course of out out movements? What about the structures of a certain interplay, in the performance of the solo and in the "solo performance," where ghosts or living spirits return like Jimmy Lyons, saxophonist and longtime member—improviser in and out—of the unit, the love never not sexual that they outwardly express and that is always put in (their) play and in their position in the improvising ritual of the cut as if acting out in groups were another name for the unit, another name for (the) ensemble?

Is Cecil out? Is there something on the order of an affirmation of his identity/identities (an out blackness [or, negatively but more precisely, an out non-Europeanness] or an out queerness) or is there an acting out or performance of it that becomes a kind of disappearance, a free and out negation of identity—lingering emergences in/from the fissure between and outside as well as in groups: the unit, blacks, queer—and identities operative at this point, here, in the silence of an unmade declaration or of unasked questions? Would this redoubled or undoubled outness be the locus not of universals of performance but the performance, or improvisation, of universality and the space or sphere, never not public—for the space of performance, the site of the creation of new models of reality, the rearrangement of the relations and the particularities of representation/ resistance/idenitity is that proletarianizing reconstitution of the public sphere of which Oscar Negt and Alexander Kluge speak, the site or precondition of politics, of a politics that improvises resistance—where performance or improvisation or (the) ensemble, the Cecil Taylor Unit, occur as one another's other selves?[19]

I

Appearances of *The Motion of Light in Water*[20]

> *When walking somewhere along Eighth Street, on the side of an army-green mail collection box I'd noticed a black-and-white mimeographed poster, stuck up with masking tape, announcing: "Eighteen Happenings in Six Parts, by Allan Kaprow."*
> —MLW, 110

> *There was general silence, general attention: there was much concentration on what was occurring in our own sequestered "part"; and there was much palpable and uneasy curiosity about what was happening in the other spaces, walled off by translucent sheets with only a bit of sound, a bit of light or shadow, coming through to speak of the work's unseen totality.* —MLW, 113

After a while, a leotarded young woman with a big smile came in and said, "That's it." For a moment, we were unsure if that were part of the work or the signal that it was over. But then Kaprow walked by the door and said, "Okay, it's over now." — MLW, 113

And of course, there still remained the question for me over the next few days: how, in our heightened state of attention, could we distinguish what a single happening was? What constituted the singularity that allowed the eighteen to be enumerable?
— MLW, 115

It was lit only in blue, the distant bulbs appearing to have red centers.

In the gym-sized room were sixteen rows of beds, four to a rank, or sixty-four altogether, I couldn't see any of the beds themselves, though, because there were three times that many people (maybe a hundred twenty-five) in the room. Perhaps a dozen of them were standing. The rest were an undulating mass of naked, male bodies, spread wall to wall.

My first response was a kind of heart-thudding astonishment, very close to fear.

I have written of a space at certain libidinal saturation before. That was not what frightened me. It was rather that the saturation was not only kinesthetic but visible. — MLW, 173

But what this experience said was that there was a population — not of individual homosexuals ... not of hundreds, not of thousands, but rather of millions of gay men, and that history had actively and already created for us whole galleries of institutions, good and bad, to accommodate our sex.

Institutions such as subway johns or the trucks, while they accommodated sex, cut it, visibly, up into tiny portions. It was like Eighteen Happenings in Six Parts. *No one ever got to see its whole. These institutions cut it up and made it invisible — certainly much less visible to the bourgeois world that claimed the phenomenon deviant and dangerous. But, by the same token, they cut it up and thus made any apprehension of its totality all but impossible to us who pursued it. And any suggestion of that totality, even in such a form as Saturday night at the baths, was frightening to those of us who'd had no suggestion of it before.*
— MLW, 174

The Music looks (doesn't look *sound?*) like that. That: which is to say these: both of these performances and both of the theoretical for-mulations they imply regarding totality and singularity, visibility and invisibility, event and trajectory, structure and agency, process and product, rituality and mundanity. So that what you get to is an improvisation through, rather than an unretheorized or unreconstructed or unresuspended bridging of, the gap between the unseen totality of Kaprow's fragmented, singularized, modularized performance and the visible undulation of bodies cognized as a mass, the iconic dynamism of a seen totality. Number and mass—and the onto-epistemo-ethics they carry—are slain here; singularity and totality are both improvised, yet the arresting, fascinating, abjectively affective experience of the sublime (that which is experienced as a kind of *temporal distancing* and the out interinanimation of disconnection as it manifests itself in the Saint Mark's bathhouse and in an apartment/performance space on Second Avenue) marks the infusion of a deep sexual energy, brings the experience to a felt and theorized stop or, more precisely, reveals the internal complication of seen/seeing aspects, the narrative of the experience, the imagined objectification of that which philosophy demands be described as subjective experience, that which Wittgenstein—unrhythmic philosophy's most self-conscious a/rhythmicist—must recite, the climax that is never not to be seen in its formal similarity with ... *jazz* and as ... *ensemble*. Cecil's music is an acting out disconnected neither from Kaprow's performance (out/sharp weird as in unexpected or outside the house, though still bound up within a certain set of inside exclusionary protocols that continue/d to animate the Western avant-garde and mark its determinate relationship with that tradition from which it would break) nor from the performance at Saint Mark's (an acting out as the performance of out—as openness and [homo]erotic publicity and the concomitant undermining of the complex that revolves around the juncture of perversion and solitude—though this *performance* of out is a proscribed revelation, an unconcealment with concealment at its heart and as its frame, hidden and held, a publicity both real and virtual), though both remain, finally, inside, which is to say never fully emergent in or as that public sphere that would call *differentiated* experience into question by being the rationalization of a certain desire for the experience of ensemble. Nevertheless, these performances and their transmission give us a transcendental clue that is both manifest as (with all its critical and sexual energy in tact) and a refinement of (which is to say out from the outside of the inside/outside distinction around which these performances are constructed and improvisatory of their corollary numerical distinctions—count and mass, minimum and plenitude) Delany's framing of them.

   Variation of not on
not
but
of
a theme. The Music is an improvisation of the clue. This is held as a
possibility of the encounter, of descent and the ascension of dissent, of
an active destruction of the bridge out from the outside of any nostalgia, gratitude, and hope—even Cecil's—that won't hear what a fall—
through the cut/castration/invagination—makes possible

blue light, light's motion (in water), mediation
   the question of the elision of either blackness or homosexuality
in the paradox of the making visible-in-writing of experience (another
"homographesis"—its occularity and invisibility):[21] the abyss between
columns waiting to be bridged[22]
   the bridge (rickety, rackety [unsounded—which is neither to say
written nor unspoken—] language) collapsed: plummet. descent
   like before as the "to come," a future/metaphysics, the "to come"
of and as the withdrawal (even as that withdrawal is figured in the
shadows of space and experience: the double column is the site of a
withdrawal, the space of a potential suspension, a bridge between what
appears and what withdraws: and what withdraws is the future, the "to
come" that is forged in practices that are set against a background, all
of which must be written: autobiography of and like a cut, slice of life,
connection); the "to come" is unknown, comes in the space of a suspension, and the suspension has a double meaning: improv is not just
movement in suspension, the temporization of the frame

                              See, it's not the fact but the
vision (and its attendant *sound*; its *content*, which I wanna bring out
now) of male homoeroticism, of the homoeroticized body as totality or
the totality of the sexual—the writhing mass that seems to operate
beyond any notion of singularity—that is liberatory for Delany. And
this is connected to a certain understanding of speculative fiction (the
refined, expanded denotation of science fiction that Delany employs)
as a mark of the totality of the discursive, the total range of possible
sentence/incident, the implicit deconstruction of any singularist and
set-theoretic conceptions of the total: a wider range of sentence and
incident, not a suspension of the sententious (à la Homi Bhabha) or of

the experiential (à la Joan Scott). The future metaphysics of the out, of the "to come," of the speculative, is, instead, what's already given in the descriptive and prescriptive totality present in Delany's work as anarchic institution: the collapsed bridge marks the space-time, the externalizing gap and caesura, of a new institution: ensemble.

Scott deftly argues against any simple experience of totality, any simple visualization or perception, any unthought rendering of a/the real or whole; but the moment of Delany's affirmation of totality is also the moment of his critique of a no less problematic valorization of modularity, the imposed experience of fragmentation that he sees as a framework and opening of the postmodern. Scott doesn't think Delany's vision as the critical and comparative (or, more precisely, dialectical) one it is—he experiences the orgy retrospectively in relation/opposition to an earlier, no less visualized or experienced sexual tableau that is formally aligned with Kaprow's happening. It is not a simple critique of modularity, no simple or naive desire for a hypersexual plenitude and openness—indeed, elsewhere in his work Delany engages modularity in an encounter governed by something other than the spirit of an absolute, if impossible, negation (think, for instance, of the extended attempt, initiated in *Triton* and extended throughout the *Return to Nevèrÿon* series and beyond, in the form of various prefaces and appendices, to offer the framework for "a modular calculus," something that is nothing other than the calculation of event, world, subjectivity, objectivity that the happening shows in all of its impossibility). What Delany is attempting to do is make a double distinction or cut— Dedekind-like, if you will (one that would allow the historian/poet to improvise a field unbounded by the illusion of one and many in a way similar to the way Dedekind's cut provides an essential tool for the building of a mode of operation for mathematicians within a field bounded by one and many)—between the impossibility of a calculus of the world, the event, art, the happening, subjectivity, objectivity and their reality and between experience and calculation. This cut, which is the field within which the opposition/relation between one and many is improvised, is also the site, or can be the site, of a certain holo-aesthetic nonexclusionarity if we let Cecil reemerge in his submergence; it doesn't take much to imagine that he might have been playing too that night, not far from Kaprow's happening, his music the heretofore unheard (of) sound animating the scene in and for which it is absent.[23] As we shall see, the (sound of the) said exists. As we have heard, the seen remains.

"The rhythm is anacrustic or, as I should call it, *encountering*." Thus writes Gerard Manley Hopkins to Robert Bridges (May 30, 1878) in an epistolary description of one of his poems addressed to his most faithful reader. The sentence is quoted as an example of the use of the word *anacrustic* in the *Oxford English Dictionary*. *Anacrustic* is the adjectival form of *anacrusis*, "a syllable at the beginning of a verse before the just rhythm; a thesis with which a rhythm begins, an upward beat." The (a)rhythm of anacrusis engenders counting and countering, appositional and contrapuntal sound-from-outside: engenders but does not determine. There is no bridge between parallel narratives.

Cut it visibly into tiny portions. The visible cut makes the whole invisible. Visibility, which is not necessarily transparency or even app(e)arance, is important for Delany. The echo of Ellison is important for Delany for two reasons: because the trope of a certain self-understanding of blackness—knowledge of invisibility—is here operative for Delany with regard to homosexuality as well as blackness; because the echo is sound, is sounded, and that sound's exigence always belies and improvises any too-simple valorization of vision. The echo is sound. The echo is music. Organization. There is no bridge, but an encountering, between parallel narratives; an apposition, an apprehension, an invention, nondetermining rhythm come upon, generative and disseminative discovery, acting out in groups. Writes Cecil: "From *Anacrusis* to *Plain* patterns and possibility converge, mountain sides to dry rock beds, a fountain spread before prairie, form is possibility; content, quality and change growth in addition to direction found."[24] Invention, descent into a gap blue-lit in the deconstruction of the blue(s), the reconstruction the blue(s) holds, the blue ghost's geometry, a reading of light's motion, do not so mistrust the desire for fixity that that mistrust vanishes what remains. Light remains in blue refraction; motion shifts and doesn't capture what dis/appears in play or what dis/appears as "play" "between" light and water. There is no bridge, no play between. No vanishing, just look again. "'Look,' he said. Jimmy's eyes had already followed Beauford's [Delany] anyway, but he just saw water.

there is no bridge

"'Look again,' Beauford said. Then he noticed the oil on the surface of the water and the way it transformed the buildings it reflected."

"... it had to do with the fact that what one can and cannot see 'says something about you.'"[25] Organization. The oil is music. "Complex vision." Plain: plainsong, plainchant, "the medieval church music still surviving in some services of the Roman Catholic Church, properly sung in unison, without harmony and with no definitely measured rhythms

     before the just rhythm   descent

         premature, post-expectant   ante-ontological

                       . Its groupings of notes have, however, a strongly rhythmic character, but it resembles the free rhythm of prose, whereas that of 'measured music' is comparable to the rhythm of [non-free] verse."[26] Nothing "now spoken, now written—in both directions, over the gap." Nothing in "that suspended in-between." Plainsong, music in blue light, uncontained by the *inadequate meaning* of the word *motion*, music, organization, reflected in oil, activation of a descent, music at Saint Mark's.

2

a

José,
the essay calls upon its readers to meditate on the necessary relation between utopia and publicity in the most general, as well as in a quite specific, sense.[27] The condition of possibility of that publicity is a certain assumption of totality, that for which the picture of utopia gives or is a reason, according to Adorno. The subjectivity or agency of that publicity is ensemble (structure of feeling + *mode of organization*) or, perhaps, the (politicized) continuous body. This is the constellation, admittedly a bit convoluted, from which I start.

b

Crimp's essay was rousing and moving. A/rousing and moving, like your paper. You saw, but also *heard*, Crimp's essay, and the mention of that occasion raises the idea or possibility or, even, actuality of a certain encounter between—no, conflation of—the critical and the erotic, the theoretical and the e/a/rotic. So that, because of my particular interests,

I'm already thinking here in anticipation of further manifestations of the Seen-Said, Seen-Sounded.

c

"A vast and lost gay male lifeworld." This connection between the vast and lost is like Jameson's "impossible totality" and its relation to utopia. For Jameson—in *The Geopolitical Aesthetic*—this loss is of the possibility of description. What the relationship is between description and prescription (or actuality and ideality, the present and the [temporal/spatial/bodily] nonpresent, truth and falsity, negation and affirmation), on the one hand, and utopia/totality (a kind of absolute publicity?), on the other, will have to be thought, and, at least for me, it's necessary to do so in the context of an interrogation of *echoes* as well as specters, *phonography* (phonography of Giorno's text, how *sound*, if not voice and all its baggage, works and plays there: soundwriting) and photography: the nonexclusionary ensemble (feeling/organization) of the sensual and the sexual; the devotion to an abstraction not immediately indexed to (the loss of an) absolute singularity, to an absolute singularity of presence, manifest in voice, broken by itself as writing. Hearing Crimp's essay is not immediately indexed or reducible to hearing his voice. The "neutralization of the phonic substance" (of which Saussure speaks and which Derrida's writing echoes) implied in only *seeing* Crimp give a talk is too stringent. I hope to show that this ain't just me being picky, that that neutralization is fundamentally tied to heteronormativity and to an oppressive *privacy* that can make itself felt even in public as some regressive interiority of acting out.

d

Is there only one utopia? Again, what is the relationship between totality or world and utopia? What was Crimp's utopia? Why was it utopian? What was/is the transformative potential of queer and/or public sex? This is not to question the fact of that potential but to request/ion an outlining or description of that potential in some detail. This stems from a possible affirmation of certain practices that would be connected to the necessarily negative or negational aspects of utopian and transformational formulations. It seems crucial to entertain—contra Bersani—"utopian hopes and possibilities" while keeping

in mind how such hopes are lost in certain attempts to manifest or con-
cretize them. This is the bind that Adorno is so clear about, so clear in
his dialectical relation to; but what I'm wondering is whether a certain
movement can be made via particular attention to the actual performative practices of queer/public sex. I know this is what the attention to
Giorno's text is directed toward; I just want to reestablish this thread
so as to pick it up in a different way than you do later on. My thoughts
are working against the backdrop of Adorno's notorious aversion to
practice (or performance), an aversion manifest in his inadequate attention to the actual practice—modes of organization, production, performance—of jazz(-as-utopian-art). In short, is there a description of queer
sex that sees/hears in it not only a negation of heteronormativity (at the
level of structures of feeling), not only—paradoxically—a negation of
its status as negation (Bersani's redescriptions), but hears/sees/projects
an affirmation—of, let's say, a radical anormativity or a normativity of
nonexclusion—that exists at the level of practices and organization as
well as structures of feeling? A *social* hauntology. Then it's possible to
take Bersani's warnings as seriously as is needed—taking into account
the "race trouble" you rightly diagnose—while giving queer politics
the "dose of utopianism" it needs, and while giving utopianism the
affirmative queering it needs.

e

When you say "Utopia lets us imagine a space outside of heteronormativity," I pause. The sentence can imply that utopia is a space that
allows the thought of an outside or within which the outside can be
thought. Is the particular outside you discuss here—outside of heteronormativity—utopia or a condition of the possibility of utopia? Is utopia
the totality within which the outside is thought or is it that which exists
outside of a necessarily restrictive totality? In short, your sentence
echoes the famous sentence of Wilde that you and Bloch echo and raises
some of the same questions concerning the relation between utopia and
world, particularity and universality. I'm trying to think about this stuff
and so I dwell on it here.

f

So how to combat that which Bersani sees as a danger, something we
saw manifest, in a certain way, in Earl Jackson Jr.'s talk, which we heard

(and saw). I bring that talk up because it remains resonant for me. I hear the echoes of it, not in your paper, but off to its side somewhere in my own head. This gets me back to the a/rousing and the moving, the theoretical and the earotic, though not just as he tried to play them. This has to do with the way I was a/roused and moved by your paper—in particular, by the first quotation from Giorno or by how your paper carries and transfers Giorno. That's the echo, 'cause I was a/roused and moved by Jackson's paper, too, his recountings of his encounter in the bathhouse in Oakland. The echo is also of my reaction to some of Delany's stuff ("Street Talk, Straight Talk" and *The Motion of Light in Water*), of a certain interinanimation of the theoretical and the earotic that I've been trying to work out in relation to him and Cecil Taylor, Baraka (I'm thinking of Baraka's description of music as well as of his play *The Toilet*—a phobic enactment of a kind of double negative way before Bersani), and Baldwin (there's a real cool moment in Leeming's biography about Beauford Delany showing Baldwin how to look at the motion of light in oily, standing, gutter water), which has to do with a certain interconnection of communal mourning, communal sex, communal musicianship—never not homoearotic—in jazz and in the (literary) phonography of jazz. I think my own arousal—no doubt too easily, no doubt at the level of panic and phobia, but, you know, with a certain theoretical slickness—in part as a function of a certain male heterosexual longing for sexual publicity, for a certain omnipresence of sex. My arousal is working, then, on two negational fronts: against my own sense of my own heterosexuality (internalized heteronormativity) and against a general, external heteronormativity that has to do with—that is marked most essentially by—the enforced privatization and paradoxically inter-subjective solipsism of sex. But my being a/roused and moved—by Jackson's paper, by Giorno's words in/and your paper—is also shadowed by some disappointment, and I want to explain why that disappointment is a function of the reemergence of heteronormativity (in the specific, broader sense I allude to above and to which Bersani's critique bears some complicated relation) in these texts and, no doubt, in my reading of them.

g

Anyway, what I've been trying to say is this: I'm still thinking about sentences like "The idealization that his prose produces is, within the scope of my analysis, an example of the way in which a rich remembrance of sexual utopia feeds a transformative queer politics," from the perspective of one who persists in some of the kinds of criticisms your paper anticipates. But, on the other hand, I'm convinced about the need for utopian thinking and think it necessary and possible to think this combination of remembrance and longing, again, in relation to an affirmation. Again, the transformationality of queer/public sex is bound up as much in its affirmative moment (practices that offer a transcendental clue or model for the nonexclusionary and improvisational organization of sex/uality and of the social, more generally) as in its negative moments (challenging heteronormativity) or in the negation of those negative-utopian moments that Bersani sees as the trace of anti-utopian, hetero-normative, hierarchical, etc. structures in queer/public sex. What a sexual utopia would be—public, ensemblic, but not reducible to *any* publicity, *any* communality—is discernible in Giorno's text. But I'd argue that our already existing sexual dystopia is there as well, and not just in/on the train. Am I wrong to imply that in your text and in Giorno's text and in a way that is tied to the complex of writing/memory/spectrality, utopian longing bears the trace of a certain nostalgia? Are you satisfied that you have eliminated such a trace or do you think it impossible that such an elimination could take place? In your view, is the presence of such nostalgia either nonproblematic for or, deeper still, necessary to the utopian? That the critique of the past that is as necessary a part of utopian thinking as the critique or negation of the present is not as strong as it might be? Obviously, I'm very wary of nostalgia, think it to be fundamentally anti-utopian. And my "charging you with nostalgia" is totally enabled by your paper, which is also constantly giving evidence of a nonnostalgic but memorial utopian longing. So that when I write "How?" in the margins of your paper, in response to your claim that "The space of the Prince Street toilets and the practices of public sex that are rendered in the writer's narrative engender a certain transformative possibility," I'm not, again, questioning *that* it's true but wondering *how* it's true, as in, "how to build a free society?" So that I'm soliciting from you some kind of Montell Jordan response: "This is how we do it . . ." (Sorry.) You might respond: "Well, Giorno tells us how. He writes it." But here, I would say, those issues regarding writing, performance, recording, presence or the present, spectrality, memory, to which I have alluded arise. What arises, too, and please forgive the pun, though I'll have occasion to linger in it for a while, is (the question of) will. I wanna try and say something about the relations of will to utopia (Adorno's formulation) and political desire (longing) and impulse. Finally, I wanna try and say something about what might be thought about as a utopian *drive*, in its relation to performance, writing, reading, listening as forms of transferential-resistant memorial longing.

h

> We can still read a powerful political impulse in Giorno's text, an impulse that is detectable in the acts that are being transcribed, in the spaces that are being conceptually rendered, and in the performance of writing his public sex history. Of this list I am most interested in the latter. The listing of public sex culture that Crimp performs in "Mourning and Militancy" can be read alongside Giorno's text as an act of queer worldmaking. More specifically, I see worldmaking here as functioning and coming into play through the performance of queer utopian memory. Utopia, then, but an understanding of utopia that understands its time as reaching beyond some nostalgic past that perhaps never was, or some future whose arrival is continuously belated. A utopia in the present.

Things move in a certain direction: some questions: How can the memorial detach itself from the nostalgic? What is the performance of memory? Perhaps the second addresses the first; perhaps the memorial escapes nostalgia by virtue of the distancing—maybe even metacritical—force of performance. This would also tie up with the determining present-ness (live!) of performance as some theorize it. Thus, the utopia in the present would be this performance of queer utopian memory, a memory without nostalgia by virtue of the performed present-ness of this particular memorial field. But what, then, about the critique of presence, of its metaphysics, that is all bound up in writing, in the transcription of the act, or even in the transcription of the theoretical encounter? What does recording or transcription do to a notion of memory, of utopian memory, that is articulated through an ontology of performance that operates within a metaphysics of presence even if that presence is subject to or is itself articulated through disappearance? The point is that this notion of queer utopian memory has a political force rendered dormant by a real struggle going on between the demands of a disappearing presence and the imperatives of transcription. Of course, there is an immediate demand to extend and deepen anything we were thinking about as recording and transcription. The acts are not the acts transcribed. The transcription is a transference and the transference is a transformation. This puts even more pressure on memory because it is more complicated than disappearance. The transformation of transcription is neither simply present nor the simple disappearance of the present. All this is not in the interest of a dismissal, but a sharpening: to really get the present down.

And what about sound: of the recording, of the transcription? More generally, and this has to do with these questions concerning the present, what of the material substantiality of the act, particularly as this understanding of the performance of the present seems inevitably to slide toward a kind of spiritualism, if you will? Here again the shadow of the question of writing or transcription's relation to material/phonic substance haunts the question of transcription's relation to the sensuality and materiality of the sexual act. Rather, if we are to think through the way a utopian sensuality is present or performed, we gotta think about the mechanics of the transfer of the sensual in/through signification, both spoken and written, as memory and history. This is the question of content and its relation to the very idea of collective memory. I should say, too, that the question of aurality in particular is important to me: of Giorno's delivery, of Adorno's and Bloch's dialogue. A clue. Can utopia, and utopian sexuality in particular, survive the neutralization of the material (phonic) substance? Can the particular features of the performed present of queer utopian memory survive the transfer of material substance (sensual/sexual content)? It seems as if the utopian demands a substance or content that the disappearing present of performance—this safeguard against nostalgia-in-memory—must precisely disavow. So you introduce Bloch and Adorno in order to set this problem up: the conflict between a notion of utopia in the present that safeguards against both nostalgia and empty wish and a notion of utopia whose essential function is a critique of the present. Again, this is where performance comes in: it requires both the present and the disappearance of the present. Neither prophecy, nor nostalgia, but description is what you advocate by way of Giorno. Fate. (Foreshadowing) description, transcription by way of the performance of memory. Narration as a kind of acting out. Insubstantial pageant.

This is a real deep problem: How to guard against the problematics of the metaphysics of presence while maintaining that necessary allegiance to content/substance and its transferentiality. This conflict—

between the materiality of content and the disappearance of presence—
is tied very much to that that exists between the cognition of totality
and the apprehension of particularity. Here, some attunement to the
very real question of transferentiality is absolutely crucial. For it is
transferentiality—as improvisation, as recording or transcription, as
production and reproduction—that is everything here, though what is
demanded is the deepest attention not only to the motion and drives of
transfer but to the material elements, sites, and agents of that transfer.
Before. What the recording does to the politics of time; the transference
of content (memory and aspiration). Prologue and Epilogue.

i

Adorno says, "And insofar as we are not allowed to cast the picture of
utopia, insofar as we do not know what the correct thing will be, we
know exactly, to be sure, what the false thing is." You add:

> Dialectical thinking, especially what Adorno refers to as "the
> determined negation," enables us to read Giorno's text as
> something other than a nostalgic foreclosure on future political
> possibility. Instead, via the lens provided by the above materialist
> philosophers, we can understand Giorno's text as pointing
> beyond the barriers of our current conditions of possibility,
> beyond the painful barriers of the AIDS pandemic, it lets us see,
> via a certain conjuring of "the past," and for many of us we see
> this past for the very first time. These pictures of utopia, a phrase
> that is derived from further comments that Adorno makes in the
> dialogue, do the work of letting us critique the present, to see
> beyond its "what is" to worlds of political possibility, of "what
> might be."

The present is false, the utopian future is correct, in Adorno's formulation. But it's unclear what this does for you. The utopian doesn't always
jibe with determinations of the present as true or false. What would the
music of the future be? Cast a (true) picture. Have a vision. Prophecy:
anti- or ante-utopian? Do we cast a picture of the future that allows us
to see more clearly the present? Or is it that our not being allowed to
cast a picture opens this more clear seeing? Adorno says that we are not
allowed to cast a picture. One assumes he means that we are not
allowed to cast a true picture. Is this a good assumption? You operate
under another frame: that we do, or at least Giorno does cast a picture,
but that picture is not of utopia-as-future, but is rather the picture that

is called or is a function of "queer utopian memory." Am I too picky? Is the distinction between not being allowed to cast a picture of utopia and casting false pictures of utopia unimportant, so unimportant that Adorno slips between them without a problem? You know this shit, this intersection of the problems of temporality and the problems of representation (in Jameson's sense), is massive. The temporal frame of your encounter with Adorno is real complicated. Implicit in your thing seems a certain equivalence between critiquing the present and seeing beyond it that is precisely what Adorno would never allow. For Adorno, it is the false or unallowable picture of what is beyond the present that allows us to see the present. For Adorno, the impossible picture of utopia that we cast functions only to allow us to see the truth of the present's falsity. For you, the critique of the present allows us to see beyond the present by way of a "conjuring" of the past. And the performance of memory makes possible a critical view of the present that, in turn, makes possible a vision of the future. If my recounting of queer utopian memory is close, good, because it seems cool and interesting. At first glance, it also seems not to have a helluva lot to do with Adorno's understanding of utopia. The determined negation of the present by a necessarily illegitimate view of the future turns into the determined negation of the present by a performed memory of the past, which, in turn, helps to produce a vision of the future. Not prophecy but description, which is to say description given the force of legitimate prophecy, a force given in and by a narrational relation to the past. But how is this not mere nostalgia? I guess, again, it would be saved by performance, by yet another temporal shift, this time to a present that disappears.

j

> From the depth of the inebriating darkness of that underground
> cave, stretching my cock to the sky, I shot a big load of cum,
> straight and glorious. Perfectly arisen and accomplished, and
> perfectly dissolved back into primordially pure empty space.

The performance—narration, description, transcription, recording, casting, conjuring—of the memory is crucial. Your utopian thing is a really complicated temporal convolution, a temporal *ekstasis* that, paradoxically, keeps turning back in on itself—no, pointing outward because the vision of the future is both legitimated and undermined by its determined relation to the past. I guess the real *ekstasis* would be given by and as performance, by whatever material and sensual content is transferred in the transcription/reception of the act portrayed. *That the utopian exists in the reader's arousal is my fucking point.* It is not in the virtually ecstatic climax of the picture Giorno casts, precisely because, in that picture, the very publicity of the sex seems to me to fade—along with the material/substance of the act itself—into "primordially pure empty space." This is what I was trying to get at in suggesting a relation between the deictic and the ecstatic. Here I wanna critique that relationship. It's the "egocentric particularity," as Russell would say, of Giorno's dick that I'm at odds with, for, as everything moves in the story toward its free expression, so to speak, we see an ecstasy that only prefaces a fade. That's maybe the trace of some of that Zen stuff that Ginsberg and them were always covering, comfort with a kind of nothingness that I can't fathom and that parallels a set of determinations of male orgasm as loss (rather than transfer) of substance, as release into *nothing*ness (the misogyny of *much to do about*), which is, it seems to me, the reprise of a whack kind of spiritualism (a spiritualism that excludes the material) and is also sex-negative to the extent that the publicity and ensemblicity of sex is negated and to the extent that the old view of sex as a miniature kind of, or preface to, death unless alloyed with a hetero-reproductive intent is replicated. So that this ain't some veiled valorization of an enforced reproductivity in the old sense of the term, though, ultimately, it is in the interest of a certain reproductivity of performance that has to do with the transfer of substance and content rather than the making of babies and, therefore, some imposed heteronormativity. And the absolute necessity or force of the transfer of substance in gay male public sex, for instance, is a big and crucial thing anyway, especially given the AIDS pandemic. It's all about the political force of the transfer/reproduction of fluids, sensations (or sounds, another part of the reason that the dominant visuality of Giorno's account and your reading are problematic for me). Acting out. In groups. But the group disappears (in a way that is countered, for instance, by Delany's descriptions of public sex in *The Motion of Light in Water*). All this is not to say that Giorno's stuff is in some ultimate and final way anti-utopian. Rather, one wants to imagine some transfer of the utopian substance of Giorno's writing and that transfer does occur, and not in some purely metaphoric way, in your reading and writing. You could say that this is about the uses of the erotic in critical/theoretical discourse or in the encounter between artist and critic. After Giorno's climax, you write:

> This, I want to suggest, is certainly a picture of sex, a casting of a picture of sex, but, in the same instance, it is also a picture of utopian transport and a reconfiguration of the social, a reimaging of our actual conditions of possibility, all of this in the face of a global pandemic. The picture rendered through Giorno's performative writing is one of a good life that was and never was, that has been lost and is still to come. It performs a desire for a perfect dissolution into a "primordially pure empty space." After this scene in the Prince Street toilet Giorno runs out and grabs a train in the nick of time. Once on the train the author feels himself once again overwhelmed by the crushing presence and always expanding force field that is heteronormativity: "I said goodbye and I was out the door in a flash, onto the train going uptown. It always was a shock entering the straight world of a car full of grim people sitting numbly with suffering on their faces and in their bodies, and their minds in their prisons." This experience of being "shocked" by the prison which is heteronormativity, the straight world, is one that a reader, especially a queer reader, encounters after putting down a queer utopian memory text like Giorno's. I think of my own experience of putting down his text, at some predominantly straight coffee shop, near where I live, and looking up after the experience of reading *You've Got to Burn to Shine* and feeling a similar shock effect.

But it's a transport away from the social (here one takes Giorno at his word—the impersonal or depersonal, apolitical, nonideological or postideological is what's encoded in that arc's trajectory; this is contradicted by the actually sensuous materiality of the sexual-social practice, the active collaboration and engagement of the Prince Street Toilet Ensemble, of its organization). Rather, there is a recrudescence of privacy, isolation, darkness, almost a reification of the closet, almost a denial of the possible erotics of publicity as we move toward this valorization of empty space. How is that utopian? For me, the utopian is not primordially pure empty space and primordially pure empty space is not or must not be allowed to become our understanding of a space outside of the prison of normativity (the necessity of this disallowal is held in the fact that Giorno's arc moves from a highly privatized sexual climax to the admittedly whack but admittedly real publicity of the subway car; it's as if public sex reduces to intensely privatized experience and then publicity itself is reduced to the space of heteronormativity, whose alternative is the empty space of that intense privatization, thereby establishing an equivalence between public space and heteronormativity that operates as a kind of conceptual surrender to the already existing world). That move from an extreme ego-phallo-centric field to empty space is not the site of a reconfiguration of the social; it is the site of the disappearance of (the condition of possibility of) the social, the inversion (a word I've been trying real hard to avoid: I don't intend this pun but precisely its opposite, though maybe my intentions don't amount to much) of *ekstasis*. Part of what must be insisted upon here is the necessity of a kind of temporal ecstasy or *ekstasis* of temporality to utopian thinking. But we also gotta see how easily some version of that *ekstasis* can turn into a black hole, so to speak, from which no vision/light escapes. Thus, the incompatibility of deixis and *ekstasis* and the absolutely necessary copresence of utopia and invagination. A true pointing out abounds out from the outside.

And you're right to think about the correspondence of Giorno's shock and the reader's shock, especially the queer reader's shock, upon putting down such a text as Giorno's. But there is a difference. It seems to me that the reader's shock might also be at the fading or disappearance of the erotic substance/content of the text; Giorno's shock is at the emergence into heteronormative space, a space that is profoundly de-eroticized but is also public. Thus, Giorno's text is complicit in the de-eroticization of the very publicity it had served to eroticize and the reader is shocked by this even before putting the text down. How to think and counter this de-eroticizing of publicity? And how to think that de-eroticizing in relation to the inversion of ecstasy? One wants simply to point out a relationship between the ego-phallo-helio-logo-centrism of Giorno's text and the de-eroticization of publicity that accompanies the fading/disappearance/neutralization of the erotic content/material/substance into empty space. The valorization of privacy, of empty space, seems to me to be a constitutive element of the heteronormative field, one all bound up with a certain understanding of property in/and its relation to agency.

You're working this temporality strangely; this notion of the copresence of the never was and the still to come seems to undermine precisely that valorization of the present of performance that I took you to be trying to deploy in the interest of a critique of these old notions of utopia. This combination of loss and *l'avenir*, of was and never was, bears the trace of both nostalgia and infinite deferral and even a kind of sex-negative echo, the shadow of a kind of avoidance of fluid exchange or transfer, as I said earlier, something like what Edelman might call a nonreceptivity. Still, is this negative, this negation, all bad? Or unnecessary? Or anti-utopian? I don't know. Can the orgasm be nonsolipsistic? What about the solo in sex? Not simply masturbation, but rather, a kind of detachment? This has to do, of course, with jazz, the absenting of jazz in Adorno/Giorno, its dissolution. Is any orgasm ever nonpremature? One wants to think of that specific prematurity of birth (Lacan) as well as of a certain prematurity of orgasm (Adorno) in order to do maybe another turn on Freud, toward some of the stuff that Brown and Marcuse are on, that utopian drive, that erotic drive, the move toward ensemble, toward ever greater and greater unities. All in the interest, then, of a kind of jam session, polymorphically/polyphonically perverse, a relation to the utopian that Adorno/Giorno couldn't see or hear or taste or touch or smell. Adorno couldn't see it in jazz or anywhere else. Giorno sees it in jazz, which is to say jizz, but it's an already contained solo flight, as Ellison would have it, into disappearance. But we'll keep going.

k

Adorno:

> The commandment against a concrete example of Utopia tends to defame the Utopian consciousness and to engulf it. What is really important here is the will that it is different.

The importance—if not the triumph—of the will. Forgive. Scandal. Here, given all the sexual connotations of will, is Adorno's valorization of privacy, of genius, coming back as a kind of solipsism and as a surrender: resign(eg)ation. The will is different. Can the will be different? Can there be an emergence of the will from solipsism? And is it enough simply for the will to be different? This is to say, can we be satisfied with a notion of utopia that is only given to us as negation? You say that the will is different in Giorno. OK. But this is not simply unproblematic. Yet, if the will, problematic in that it implies a certain solitude, a certain absenting of publicity, is sidestepped in the name of an ensemble that is different, a different agency or organization or subjectivity, even; if the subjectivity of the ensemble is different, if the mode of production of the ensemble is different, present and critical of the present, to come in the present and of and for and in the future (to be transferred, reproduced, figured out: later), then this would be significant. And it is there in Giorno, but endangered by him and by any simple critical valorization of a different will. You say:

> Adorno . . . was speaking out against a trend in socialism (and in humanism in general) where utopianism became the bad object. Utopianism could only exist via a critique of the dominant order. It had no space to exist outside of the most theoretically safe-guarded abstractions. In a roughly analogous way, the pictures drawn by Giorno are also bad objects insofar as they expose gay men to acts, poses, and structures of desire that may be potentially disastrous. But, as Adorno teaches us, the importance of casting pictures is of central relevance. The casting of a picture helps us arrive at a critique of hegemony. Adorno explains that: "If this is not said, if this picture cannot—I almost would like to say—appear within one's grasp, then one basically does not know at all what the actual reason for the totality is, why the entire apparatus has been set in motion."

Yeah, it's just the particularities of the picture and those particularities' relation to totality that must be rigorously thought. Bloch quotes Wilde on the necessity of utopia to any worthwhile map of the world. And here one thinks of what might be the place of utopia in an aesthetics of cognitive mapping. A map of the world as utopia: that's a description of the future. Utopia must be total. Not just one spot on the map. You say, "Queer worldmaking then hinges on the possibility of mapping a world where one is allowed to cast pictures of utopia and include such pictures in any map of the social." And all one can say now is that missing in this formulation is what's also missing from Giorno's text: a picture of utopia as the totality of the map rather than as simply a spot on the map and an attentiveness to the ensemblic and public nature of the subjectivity that would inhabit that world.

|

> In 1994 [Tony] Just completed a project that attempted to catch exactly what I'm calling the ghosts of public sex. The project began with Just choosing a rundown public men's room in New York City, the kind that was most certainly a tearoom before it,

like the Prince Street toilets that Giorno describes, was shut down
during the AIDS/HIV public health crisis. Just then proceeded to
do the labor of scrubbing and sanitizing the public men's room.
The preparation of the space is as central to the series as the
photos I choose to focus on here; the only evidence of this aspect
of the larger project is the clean spaces themselves—Just's labor
only exists in the ghostly trace of a sparkling men's room. His
documentation of this project was committed in the form of color
slides and photographs . . . that focused on the bathroom's
immaculate cleanliness and the details of such a space.

Ghosts and specters now, in the photograph. "The urinals, tiles, toilets
and fixtures that are the objects of these photo images take on what can
only be described as a ghostly aura, an otherworldly glow. This aura,
this circuit of luminous halos that surround the work, is one aspect of
the ghosts of public sex that this paper is interested in describing." The
return to aura and therefore to a distance that is, paradoxically, all
bound up with presence (I'm implying a connection between writing's
breakdown of the metaphysics of presence and mechanical reproduction's breakdown of aesthetic aura—photo*graphy*!) is a bit troubling,
like Peggy's spiritualism, like Giorno's willed trajectory back to primordially pure empty space. Is that the space these photographs represent?
If it is, one would want to be sure to think some real or possible materi-
alization of the ghosts. Let the bodies of the spirits the photos would
capture be there. Makes me wanna think, again, about the sound of
the photograph. Elegy. To render these ghosts visible, to think their
sign as aura, is to get caught up in a figural economy that does have
consequences.

Meanwhile,

The ghosts slide into visibility when we consider the substance of
such ghosts. In part, I see the ghosted materiality of the work as
having a primary relation to emotions, queer memories, and
structures of feeling that haunt gay men on both sides of a
generational divide that is formed by and through the catastrophe
of AIDS.

We gotta think about the substance, if you will, of ghosted materiality:
how these elements are to be thought together. José, you do it by way of
Williams and within the ocularcentric field. We gotta check on this.
One wants to be attuned not only to structures of feeling but to modes

of organization. The structure of feeling, as Williams describes it, operates kinda like the transferential agency of ensemble, like what one
would think of as content in contradistinction to meaning. This is, for
Williams, "the true source of the specializing category of 'the aesthetic
...'" It is, for him, an "unmistakable presence." And here we could say
that the aesthetic is bound up with a notion of presence as/in a kind of
transferential force and not that form of presence which produces as its
counterpart a kind of metaphysical distance that has been called aura.
Here, again, a bit of a contradiction, I think, between you and the folks
whom you invoke. On a kind of technical level, aura and structure of
feeling don't go together, though definitely you don't mean aura like
Benjamin did. Nevertheless, the trace of Benjamin (and by extension
Adorno) remains, especially since you're talking about photography. At
any rate, in Williams the aesthetic isn't all bound up with aura, though
it is, at the same time, connected to a certain reconfiguration of autonomy (after which Said works). That autonomy is precisely bound up in
or with what is not covered by formal systems, though it is, as Williams
points out, not an autonomy that implies some abstraction from the
social, an abstraction that Giorno certainly flirts with. For you, the
structure of feeling that bears the trace of a vast social network is rendered visible by Just's work. An intense specificity and a broader map
are given there: something like an aesthetics of cognitive mapping.
"Due to the obstacles imposed by certain preconceptions of materiality,
preconceptions that are often manifest as visual myopias, one cannot
see the ghost of public sex in Just's project. But, if an eye is sensitized in
a certain way, if it can catch other visual frequencies [Now note here a
certain echo, of Ellison on the lower frequencies but also of sound as
such, the echo of an otherwise excluded sensual register, suggesting that
one of the visual myopias that hinder true conceptions of materiality is
that that is caused by an exclusionary allegiance to the visual itself. As
if only looking makes you not see as well.] that render specific distilla-
tions of lived experience and ground level history available, it can potentially see the ghostly presence of a certain structure of feeling." Now, all
I can say is this: I got a certain wariness about this equivalence of
ghostly presence (ghosted materiality) and structure of feeling. It seems
like what Williams is after is a kind of transfer of material, of content.
And we might think this transference as a kind of haunting, but we also
might not. I don't know if all the ghost stuff is necessary. These determinations of spirit still trouble me. But, after all, just as what I'm after

might not be properly called spirit or specter or ghost (though it has something to do, finally, with breath), it might also not be properly called transference, but rather something more precisely thought of in terms of a certain encounter between resistance and drive. Finally, I'm not all that comfortable with structure of feeling either. When one is all bound up with these notions of spirit, feeling, and so forth, one is in danger not only of a certain absenting or reduction of materiality (actually, an almost silly formulation to make with regard to Williams, I guess), but also in the even graver danger of a loss of action or of its name. It's as if too much attention is given to the ontological field so that, for instance, the critic who can discern these ghosts, these structures of feeling, even a certain ghosted materiality or a social and political map, might very well remain unattuned to what is operative in the artwork as another mode of organization.

m

> The emphasis on tile, in conjunction with the foreground of
> emptiness in the rooms, makes one think of an echo chamber.
> Through an associative chain, the connotation is one of rever-
> beration and echoing. The pictures, through the negative charge
> of absented bodies, instill in the spectator a sense of emptiness.
> Such an emptiness is not the project's teleological objective;
> rather, that space of emptiness is meant to make other worlds of
> sexual possibility available.

The sound of the photograph! This negative charge is what you're getting from Adorno. But is the determined negation an emptying? I can't get with empty space as a space of possibility (it's an almost puritanical echo that bothers me, the prefigurative shadow of what Susan Howe might call—even as she reenacts it—another enclosure), though I see here a much more clear deployment of Adorno: there are lots of negative-photograph puns for one to make, but the point is this: how to deal with the limitations of negative utopianism that Adorno knows and outlines so well. Utopia is only given to us as/in negation; nevertheless, we are (for)given to cast a picture of utopia, to put forward a positive image, so to speak; but, ultimately, we are commanded to refrain from any such image, from any such concretization. Just like Donne says: we are called upon to call God's name, but no name is adequate, and therefore caught within the double bind of a command to suppress that drive to which we are given. For me, the only possible solution demands a close examination of the nature of the drive and of the commandment. Why are we given/driven to representations of utopia (or totality, or God)? Why are we commanded to suppress that drive? What will come about as a function of the surrender to that commandment? What will come about as a function of disobedience? Is annihilation really the condition of possibility of utopia? Is AIDS, the "agency" behind the absenting of those bodies, a necessary condition of possibility for utropian (did I mean this or is it a typo? I better leave it in) sexual possibility? This ain't a nasty trick question. It's not just one of those do-bad-things-have-to-happen-in-order-for-good-things-to-happen questions. Really, it's about the difference between annihilation and improvisation, nothingness and publicity. Methodological point: one can assert either that the picture of utopia negates the already existing world or that the negation of the already existing world makes possible a picture of utopia. You seem to split the difference here: *a picture of* the negation of the already existing world makes possible a picture of utopia (the Just case); a transcription of a self-negating or unsustainable utopia creates a temporary negation of the already existing world (the Giorno case). But there is, in "the echoic specter of a sexual cut," an affirmation. Meanwhile, you're caught up in a kind of chicken/egg thing between (pictures of) utopia and negation. They go together, but which comes first? Always implied, as Adorno knows, in the idea of utopia is an affirmation or (potential) concretization: how to improvise that against the commandment.

> One reading of the absence of people and acts in these photos
> that riff on public sex would consider these representations of
> a hollowed-out, mournful, and fetishistic space as that of
> determined negations, the casting of pictures that represent
> utopia through the negative.

Past and, at the same time, never, this utopia. And how to think it in relation to the absenting of people and act that concludes Giorno's positive rendering of utopia? But you, by way of Derrida, would go past Adorno's persistent dialectic.

> Within dialectical terms, Just weighs in on the side of determined
> negation, since, when one tries to unpack a dialectical opposition
> between "the act and the potential in the space of the event, in the
> event-ness of the event," we see, with great clarity, what Derrida

has called the "eventness" of the space. Just's work represents the ideality of utopia while also representing the importance of effectivity and actuality. The negation of physical players and its choice to represent absence permits a viewer, strangely enough, to occupy a space both inside and outside of the predictability of such an established dialectical pattern.

Now, I can actually get with this in a certain way, as long as we can make a distinction between the empty space that Giorno achieves and the empty space that Just moves into and shows. But I don't think such a move works, because it becomes clear that Just records a negation that Giorno initiates. One needs to affirm the utopian in Giorno rather than affirm the negation of that utopia that he initiates and Just mechanically reproduces. But to tighten or further compress the distinction between ideality and actuality that new technology renders unsupportable or impossible, while necessitating a "hauntology" that is beyond or outside ontology and dialectics (of course, it would be my contention, that the resistant force of ensemble had always already been operating in or at that outside) according to Derrida: the mode of organization of public sex gives a clue, bears the trace of what it is not. And the ideal is manifest not in/as absence but in/as an actuality that is not. To affirm that utopia is an actuality that is not yet, an actuality that is to come, a material subjunctivity. The real as a speculative fiction in Delany's sense, or foreshadowing description, description of fate: that which has not happened yet. Not inside/outside but out from the outside, pointing out of itself, out from itself, nondeictic *ekstasis*. Affirmation of the ideal actuality.

n

The double ontology of ghosts and ghostliness, the manner in which ghosts exist inside and out and traverse categorical distinctions, seems especially useful for queer criticism that attempts to understand communal mourning, group psychology, and the need for politics that "carry" our dead with us in battles for the present and future.

But the use of the ghost and its complex hauntology carries a kind of danger, too. Not just the possible eclipse of materiality, but the identification of ghostliness and negation that forecloses the possibility of an affirmation. Or, rather, one should ask about the possibility of a ghostly affirmation. Sex-negative, HIV-negative, photographic-negative, dialectical-negative, negation of the present.

To really think the eventness of the event is hard: it requires some real meditation on the event's singularity, its relation to presence and to the present as well as to iterability. These things are connected to the "to come" of the event, the orgasmic element of the to come. If it's always to bear the trace of a determined singularity, then that would be problematic. Which is all to say that the eventness—the ghostliness—of the event is the site of some major questions. And all of those questions are framed within a mode of thinking that, even in its outest, extra-dialectical guise, is conditioned by and in negation. Even Derrida's postdialectical hauntology is essentially negative. I just don't see how worldmaking, as opposed to world picturing, can be negative. So that one wants to beware of certain determined and valorized ephemerali-ties, and this is precisely what you do in your critique of Odets's yang about a psychological epidemic. Yet, in the appeal to structures of feel-ing, ghosts, auras, and all that, you make something of a similar move. And, for me, the necessity of affirmation ought to, on the one hand, guard against that very valorization of the (HIV) negative that you're wary of, while disallowing some silly reversal wherein HIV-positive sta-tus marks some kind of affirmation of an earlier, utopian, free, public sexuality. No simple equivalence between HIV-positive and sex-positive; no simple equivalence between HIV-negative and sex-negative; never-theless, some attunement to the dangers inherent in the fading/reduc-tion of materiality and publicity and in negation's exclusionary dismissal of affirmation. A tale of two negatives and two positives. Two forms of, specters of, affirmation and what these affirmations—as well as these negatives—have to do with utopia. On the one hand, the problematics of a too-stiff adherence to the dialectic; on the other hand, the prob-lematics of any affirmation of the negative or any negation of the affir-mative that do not see an interinanimation. Negation and the limit. Affirmation and abundance. Invagination and utopia.

out

Utopia is (Ellington's orchestra, his instrument; the Cecil Taylor Unit) acting out in groups. Thelonious Sphere Monk. Meanwhile, they're selling this really bad pizza where the Five Spot used to be. One thinks, then, of the possible relations between politics and the public sphere, on the one hand, and models of reality and utopian thinking, on the other. What's performance/improvisation got to do with these? Perhaps this: new models have got to be seen not in the interest of a canonization, authentication, or simple representation and against the exigencies of commodification or fetishization, but rather in the way that improvisation is, or, more precisely, utters and hears, seeing, *improvisare*, seeing outside, seeing ahead, foreshadowing description outside itself. It's not about the imperviousness of what exceeds, say, the documentarian or the recorder; it's the ineradicable tie of that which exceeds to the improvisatory practices of ensemble. This is no simple safety, but the way the whole ruptures exclusionary totalizations.

What has acting/out/in/groups to do with that indifferent identity that corresponds to both an affirmation and a knowledge of freedom-justice-truth-beauty that would seem to spring from an insistently previous endowment, one free, paradoxically, from the in/determinations of an im/possible natal occasion? Perhaps performance is neither the disappearance of the event nor the disappearance of any possible product or trace (the record is neither definitive not disapparent): perhaps it is, rather, that which disappears the conceptual apparatus/scheme of in/differentiation (the oscillation between singularity and totality).

Improvisation sees/sounds

> deeper, plummeting attunement or enrapture

> > Sometimes a thousand twangling instruments
> > Will hum about mine ears, and sometimes voices
> > That, if I then had waked after long sleep,
> > Will make me sleep again; and then, in dreaming,
> > The clouds methought would open and show riches
> > Ready to drop upon me, that when I waked
> > I cried to dream again

> > > > phrases from an "exemplary"
moment in the canonical imaginary's imaging of that encounter which founds and disrupts it, before us

> > > premature postexpectancy, insistent/evasive previous-
ness, a speaking without foresight that is, in its extrarepresentational-
ity, always a foreshadowing description; the theoretical resources

embedded in the cultural practice of improvisation reverse the definition its etymology implies and the theoretical assumptions that etymology grounds. That which is without foresight is nothing other than foresight.

Cecil, between where we are and the present, between where we are and no place, takes it to the rickety, rackety bridge and sounds.

The bridge is over. The bridge is out.

Notes

1. Nathaniel Mackey, *Bedouin Hornbook* (Los Angeles: Sun and Moon Press, 1997), 42–43.
2. Jacques Derrida, "The Law of Genre," in W. J. T. Mitchell, ed., *On Narrative* (Chicago: University of Chicago Press, 1981), 55.
3. Peggy Phelan, *Unmarked: The Politics of Performance* (New York: Routledge, 1992), 91.
4. Ibid., 167.
5. Jacques Derrida, "Différance," in *Margins of Philosophy*, trans. Alan Bass (Chicago: University of Chicago Press, 1982), 27. Allow me to insert a rather lengthy passage here in the hope of some audible overtones:

   "What we know, or what we would know if it were simply a question here of something to know, is that there has never been, never will be, a unique word, a master-name. This is why the thought of the letter *a* in *différance* is not the primary prescription or the prophetic annunciation of an imminent and as yet unheard-of nomination. There is nothing kerygmatic about this 'word,' provided that one perceives its decapita(liza)tion. And that one puts into question the name of the name.

   "There will be no unique name, even if it were the name of Being. And we must think this with-out *nostalgia*, that is, outside of the myth of a purely maternal or paternal language, a lost native country of thought. On the contrary, we must *affirm* this, in the sense in which Nietzsche puts affirmation into play, in a certain laughter and a certain step of the dance.

   "From the vantage of this laughter and this dance, from the vantage of this affirmation foreign to all dialectics, the other side of nostalgia, what I will call the Heideggerian *hope*, comes into question. I am not unaware how shocking this word might seem here. Nevertheless I am venturing it, without excluding any of its implications, and I relate it to what still seems to me to be the metaphysical part of 'The Anaximander Fragment': the quest for the proper word and the unique name. Speaking of the first word of Being (*das frühe Wort des Seins: to kreon:* [*der Brauch:* usage, enjoyment, to brook, to let something present come into presence: unconcealment, nearness]), Heidegger writes: 'The relation to what is present that rules in the essence of presencing itself is a unique one (*ist ein einziges*), altogether incomparable to any other relation. It belongs to the uniqueness of Being itself (*Sie gehört zur Einzigkeit des Seins selbst*). Therefore, in order to name the essential nature of Being (*das wesende Sein* [which is nothing other than this uniqueness, this one-ness, the state of being one, the singleton]), language would have to find a single word, the unique word (*ein, einziges, das einzige Wort*). From this we can gather how daring every thoughtful word (*denkendes Wort*) addressed to Being is (*das dem Sein zuge-sprochen wird*). Nevertheless such daring is not impossible, since Being speaks always and everywhere throughout language.'" [The difficulty lies not so much in finding in thought the word for Being as in retaining purely in genuine thinking the word found.]

"Such is the question: the alliance of speech and Being in the unique word, in the finally proper [*propre*, ownmost, authentic, *eigentlich*] name. And such is the question inscribed in the simulated affirmation of *différance*. It bears (on) each member of this sentence: 'Being/speaks/always and everywhere/through/language.'" (27)

6. I should now say that I'm writing a book called *Event Music* (of which the stuff you're reading now is a part), the first part of a project whose general title is *Ensemble and Improvisation*. This book tries to work around and before and through being totally enabled and prompted by LeRoi Jones and his essay "The Burton Greene Affair" (see LeRoi Jones, *Black Music* [New York: William Morrow, 1968], 136–39), an essay that describes the performance of an ensemble consisting of Burton Greene, a white pianist whose "'style' . . . is pointed in the direction of Cecil Taylor, and one would also suppose, with Taylor the Euro-American Tudor-Cage, Stockhausen-Wolf-Cowell-Feldman interpretations," and Pharoah Sanders and Marion Brown, two black saxophonists who, if we extrapolate to Brown from Jones's description of Sanders, want "to feel the East, as . . . oriental m[e]n." It's an improvisation of some texts of which "TBGA" is the lead voice, the voice always marked by what seems to be its immediate supersession.

There's what Mackey would call a stammer in "TBGA," a divided (and abounding) articulacy that undermines and exceeds the rhythmic marking of racial difference that Jones would discern and deploy. The ensemble is heard by way of the improvisatory interplay of Jones's representation of Greene's sound as a stuttering search for materiality (the percussive) and Pharoah/Marion's flowing extensions into and of spirit (*anima*/breath): the ensemble is heard through the incompatibilities Jones projects in the cut between syntagmic order and eventual break.

Way outside, yet in the tradition of the outside, toward that tradition's end, in and out of Jones's spirit, the book consists of notes toward a phenomenology of totality by way of a more precise understanding of the phenomenon of singularity, by way of a critique of their interinanimation and idea. But the thing is that the note toward goes way beyond, like words don't go there, they go past there, through the image of a phenomenology to improvisation. Yes, we have experiences of singularity *and* totality and it's not at all my business to deny them: rather, I would think their ground. That ground—paradoxically anarchic, before us and without origin but for that which is not but nothing other than the cut that it allows—is ensemble (in other words, the generative cut is where ensemble is and ensemble is the condition of possibility of the cut; note that such circularity is what is meant by what remains to be seen in "an insistent previousness evading each and every natal occasion" or what we'll have seen later as "premature post-expectancy"): no vague mass/oceanic feeling; no aggregate count/analytic stance; no whole given only in falseness. Ensemble is in the cut like another kind of *epochē*, generative and profoundly historical: indeed the epochē that is the very essence of history. The cut is the condition of possibility of the improvisation of difference.

The reason for this long digression is this: Cecil Taylor is a central figure in "TBGA" and thus in my book "about" "TBGA." His name comes up as that which Greene either hopes to or actually does arrive at: if he hopes to, thus can only hope to, then Cecil is black; if he doesn't, then Cecil is whack, because Euro, because arty, because gay: indeed, the ambivalence toward Cecil and toward his own identity is so much of what "TBGA" is about and that ambivalence is not just about whether Cecil, and, for that matter, any European-influenced black artist like, say, Jones is black enough, a black-enough man, a manly enough black man, it's a political ambivalence, one in which ensemble and its experience continaully emerge, in which the sense of the whole comes out precisely in the representation or transmission of a certain transportation and a certain refusal of assimilation or acceptance of the condition by which one happily is driven by that which cannot be assimilated by anyone, which never is to be seen as essential to or the proper of anyone, that is, spirit, a certain outwardness that disrupts the exclusionary totalizations, the murders, which Jones's poeticity intends. So, if I say my book is not really about "TBGA" or Jones, it's not to say it is about Cecil: it's just to say it's about the ensemble experienced and represented all throughout all of their stuff: about, which is to say ab/out, out out, way out out from the out: so maybe it is about all of these things, about in the way ensemble is (I know this is a kind of fake etymology or illegitimate split, unsanctioned caesura between syllables, but if I sang it like that no one would say shit, so let me have it): so that it's all about "TBGA" and all about what "TBGA" is all about: a turnabout or a turn on the meaning of out in and for the Cecil Taylor Unit).

7. Inasmuch as memory, vision, echo imply a certain enabling disability to access this music in language, I make no attempt to speak of it directly, thereby hopefully enacting an improvisation through its dis/appearance that will have been, itself, this music. I've been trying to linger in this music; I've been preparing myself to play with Cecil Taylor . . .

8. "The Music" is a term that was often used to describe what is, perhaps improperly, known as free jazz. Free jazz was also known as "The New Black Music" or "The New Thing"; these names indicate that this music is marked by a certain interconnection of novelty and racial identity, by the hope or drive for a revolutionary blackness. The term, as I hope to show, is also sexually marked in complicated ways. As I echo the term, I would like Cecil Taylor's music and his re/definition of music to resonate: he argues that anything is music if it is organized according to certain principles. I would add that perhaps The Music is the organization that improvises principles.

9. Ralph Ellison puts this formulation most clearly: "There is a cruel contradiction implicit in the art form itself. For true jazz is an art of individual assertion within and against the group. Each true jazz moment (as distinct from the uninspired commercial performance) springs from a contest in which each artist challenges all the rest, each solo flight, or improvisation, represents (like the successive canvases of a painter) a definition of his identity: as individual, as member of the collectivity and as link in the chain of tradition. Thus, because jazz finds its very life in an endless improvisation upon traditional materials, the jazzman must lose his identity even as he finds it" (Ralph Ellison, *Shadow and Act* [New York: Vintage Books, 1972], 234).

10. Derrida, "The Law of Genre," 52.

11. Ralph Ellison, *Invisible Man* (New York: Vintage Books, 1972), 564.

12. This is not a simple question, nor is it a simple whom. When, as earlier (see note 6), I speak of Baraka, I will be speaking of LeRoi Jones. You should be aware of this name change or name reversion even if I don't have the time or space to delve into that reversion's significance. For more on that significance, see my book without a title if it ever emerges as a book and keep in mind that the complicated outness of

Cecil's music, of The Music, has much to do with the transformations that Baraka's/ Jones's names would invoke, reflect, engender, create.

13. "Set. The Egyptians called it Set. If you try to fix anything—you can't fix anything— that's death. You can't fix anything—the thing's in motion. So you *Set* it—that's a death grip. So they're trying to Set this thing, this status quo" (Amiri Baraka, "Cultural Revolution and the Literary Canon," in Anne Waldman and Andrew Schelling, eds., *Disembodied Poetics: Annals of the Jack Kerouac School* [Albuquerque: University of New Mexico Press, 1994], 17).

14. Bill Corbett's phrasing on late Phillip Guston's ("As they grip me I grip them and mind is harmonized with matter and I take the outside in"), in *"From Phillip Guston's Late Work: A Memoir,"* 10, (spring 1994): 193. There's something outside harmony—a cluster—I'm after as it gets to go past.

15. See LeRoi Jones, "American Sexual Reference: Black Male," in *Home: Social Essays* (New York: William Morrow, 1966).

16. See, it was never about (the loss of) action's name, for Jones; it was always about or against interpretations, interpretation as such ("the Euro-American Tudor-Cage, Stockhausen-Wolf-Cowell-Feldman interpretations" as examples of a dominant epistemological mode or metaphor for Euro-classical musical performance, interpretation as a Europeanist desire for fixity, determination, artifactuality [Jones, "The Burton Greene Affair," 138]).

17. The trajectory of Jones's attitude toward Cecil Taylor in the 1960s is complex. What I'm arguing here is that "TBGA" approaches a nadir in that trajectory. This extremity is marked by a certain harshness born of the determinate exclusions forged within a certain black cultural nationalist moment in Jones's work and thought. My work on Jones seeks the liberatory as form and impulse in that moment, even in the midst of that moment's violently reactionary framing.

But "TBGA" is just a moment of extremity vis-à-vis Cecil and what he came to symbolize for Jones, a moment articulated through the objectifying and ontologized differentiation of the music of the ensemble that Jones *reviews*; it is therefore necessary to trace the trajectory of Jones's understanding of Cecil in the brief and inadequate approximation of its fullness that we can derive from Jones's writing on Cecil elsewhere in *Black Music*. In "Present Perfect (Cecil Taylor)," a 1962 review of Cecil's contributions to a Gil Evans production titled *Into the Hot* (Impulse A-9), Jones champions Cecil's position on and as the creator of the cutting edge of a black but still Westernized avant-garde:

"Cecil's tunes on this album create, by their sincere attempts at perfection of a form that is still not completely understood, a musical environment that will make the fingerpoppers shudder. It is an orchestral language that Cecil is pointing towards; a language that still conceives of verb force, i.e., the solo exclamation made fierce by improvisation.

"Taylor and the others are making music that is exactly where we are. It is as exact in its emotional registrations and as severely contemporary in its aesthetic as any other Western art."

Cecil's music marks the present for Jones, the contemporary emotional space of a "we" whose differentiation is only implied and for whom Cecil's hybridized, incomplete, unperfected, perfect orchestral voice can still speak as vicious modernism, fierce blackness.

Also, however, in 1962, we see the ambivalence I have spoken of in Jones's understanding of Cecil. In "Cecil Taylor," a review of *The World of Cecil Taylor* (Candid 8006), Jones calls into question the spatial constitution of the present that elsewhere Cecil had been seen shaping and articulating. At the very beginning of the essay, Jones asks, "Is there really a 'world' of Cecil Taylor?" and in that question lies implications that, I would argue, play themselves out most fully in the problematic mention of Cecil's name in the context of Greene and certain members of the Euro-American avant-garde. In "Cecil Taylor" there is still the valorization of what has emerged for Jones as Cecil's relation to a necessarily hybridized jazz tradition, one to which the revision of "the most terrifyingly maudlin pop tunes" remains essential; but, in raising that question of the topography of the new that originates in an ambivalence toward enabling/disabling mixture, Jones moves, by way of the particularities of Cecil's music, toward those extremities of differentiation that play themselves out in "TBGA" and, more forcefully, in "American Sexual Reference: Black Male."

18. "Feeling predicts intelligence": see Jones's liner notes to *The New Thing in Jazz*, in *Black Music*, 172.

19. See Oskar Negt and Alexander Kluger, *Public Sphere and Experience: Toward an Analysis of Bourgeois and Proletarian Public Sphere*, trans. Peter Labanyi, Jamie Owen Daniel, and Assenka Oksiloff (Minneapolis: University of Minnesota Press, 1993).

20. Samuel R. Delany, *The Motion of Light in Water: Sex and Science Fiction Writing in the East Village, 1957–1965* (New York: Plume/New American Library, 1989), 110. All subsequent references will be marked *MLW* in the text.

21. Lee Edelman, *Homographesis* (New York: Routledge, 1994).

22. The double columns: the mundane particularity of an autobiographical text and the general constitution of the subject in desire. For Delany, those columns are marked by the space they leave: between writing and its deferral, between legitimacy and illegitimacy, between straight and street, between the realistic and the phantasmerotic, lies "[t]hat locus, that margin, that split itself [which] first allows, then demands the appropriation of language—now spoken, now written—in both directions, over the gap"(see *MLW*, 17, 25–26, 30, 212). See also Samuel R. Delany, "Straight Talk, Street Talk," *differences*, 3:2 (1991): 21–38. Joan W. Scott says that "[i]t is finally by tracking 'the appropriation of language . . . in both directions, over the gap, and by situating and contextualizing that language that one historicizes the terms by which experience is represented, and so historicizes experience itself" (Joan W. Scott, "The Evidence of Experience," in Judith Butler and Joan W. Scott, eds., *Feminists Theorize the Political* [New York: Routledge, 1992], 36). Can performance be so historicized or thought? Phelan finds hope in such bridging, hope that Delany offers and counts on in taking us to the bridge, Williamsburg, Brooklyn, language. I don't know.

23. Unheard not coincidentally, in the way that for much of the scholarship of the Lower Manhattan avant-garde of the late fifties and early sixties, the music of Cecil and many others—musicians/poets/black—remains unheard, held in a kind of irrecoverable background. This is a whole other issue, and I'm not accusing Scott of this, though I am accusing her of something that is connected to this: a certain occularcentrism, even in the midst of her critique of the hegemony of vision. I just wanna exercise some caution, to ask if there is something to be heard in Delany, to argue that, yes, that which is to be heard is Cecil, that the performance of (the) ensemble, the acting out in groups that Cecil performs, is the resonance to which Scott's critique is unattuned. Searle says that the background is "that set of non-representational capacities which allows all representation to take place" (Searle, John R. *Intentionality* [Cambridge: Cambridge University Press, 1983], 143); I don't wanna ascribe that kind of exclusive generative force to the music, but I do wanna say it was a real and complex part of what was going on.

24. Liner notes to *Unit Structures* (Blue Note Records, 1967).

25. David Leeming, *James Baldwin* (New York: Henry Holt, 1994), 34.

26. Phonocentrism is not just the differentiation of speech and writing and speech's concomitant hierarchization. It is, too, a certain split within speech that separates sound
from the (meaning of the) spoken word and immediately and imperceptibly thinks
the spoken word as visual mark with visible transformationality demanding, say, a
Warminskian *reading*. Transformationalities of sound are lost and then found in the
metaphysical overvalorization of the spoken and the kind of subject implied by a
certain understanding of disembodied voice—whether by Plato or by hooks.
    The phonologocentrism that Derrida critiques is compensated for by a valoriza-
tion or revelation of writing that he diagnoses rather than invents—or invents in the
old high way of invention: discovers, discloses, comes upon; for the phonocentric
spoken word is, as he suggests, never not written, is not but nothing other than written, not but nothing other than the visual mark in that it is reducible either to a fixed
or enportraitured visualizing interpretability or an undecidable but no less visualiz-
able readability. This is a reduction that excludes sound in the interest of an impoverished and inaudible understanding of meaning, an understanding of meaning that
is indexed to the similarly impoverished reduction of history (and temporality) to
the past or to that which is dominated by the past: the exclusion of sound produces
a past and visualized mark, the always already written, which is to say already *dif-
ferantiated*, word.
    Toward future history, dissemination, or improvisation rather than interpreta-
tion because history is the future, too; but all prior analysis has been posterior, has
been has been, of the has been. So that interinanimation of sound and meaning as
ideational representation of a past conceptual field or a past reality (or present reality inevitably represented—*because* represented—as past) has eclipsed the possibility of sound/meaning as projective mode of organization.
    No need, though, to always start and end with sound: rather, mark and work
through its exclusion in the instant/interest of a holoesthetic field that is available to
us in the cut, the unbridgeable (at least within an unimprovised, unfunkdafied
understanding of the bridge—lingering, suspension, variation of) distance, between
genres and sensualities. History is the future too, improvising the cut of prophecy
and description, played that tomorrow, gon' play that yesterday, all the way back,
way back, as we do a little something like this, hit it:
    Linger in the unbridgeable distance so that improvisation is not necessarily
indexed to sound. The cut is where ensemble is. For instance, in the untranslatabil-
ity that emptily centers the interinanimation of sound and graph.
    A change is lost—kinda like Wittgenstein's problem (there is no phenomenology
but there are phenomenological problems; no adequate language for phenomenology)—in the cut between phenomenology and physics, their inadequate languages.
There is no language of music, no langauge of the phenomenality of music, no language of the way music improvises through the opposition of phenomenality
(ephemerality, changingness) and physicality, that would not falsifyingly "translate" it into a virtual visuality or spatiality, a seeing aspect itself immediately denied
as subjective and not objective, a hierarchization of the senses.
    Let the abstract show us the future as another model of reality, another mode of
organization—not decontextualized, not without descriptive force, but with
utopian, yeah, okay, thrust as well.
    Form is only an extension of content: (content is always principal, says Baraka)—
yeah, it takes content out, farther out, out from outside, manifests the most radical
improvisatory organization that the content bears.

27. José Muñoz, "Ghosts of Public Sex: Utopian Longings, Queer Memories," *Policing
Public Sex*, Dangerous Bedfellows, ed., (Boston: South End Press, 1996): 355–72.

Body Bildung

LAURENCE RICKELS TALKS WITH KATHY ACKER

Laurence A. Rickels

What I've always found so strong and futural about Kathy Acker's work is its close encounter with adolescence, not as the phase or phrase everyone has to be beyond rather than stuck on, but as a level of intervention and reception that is always there, for example, whenever you're in groups. The force field she works is what Freud called group psychology. Acker's work shows how the problems of adolescence or group psychology are always there, even or especially in one-on-one relationships. I'm thinking of Acker's great dialogues (examples from *Blood and Guts in High School* come to mind), which are completely organized around the adolescent metabolism or perpetual ambivalence machine, in which making up alternates with breaking up. It reminds me how over and over again we try to form couples, we try to be in individual therapy, we try to stay with the transference, and all the while we're always still being pulled back into the group with all the problems we face being in groups. Adolescence is a blender: the teen rebounds between extremes and short attention spans (for example, between asceticism and sexual or self-destructive excess), because the two sides of parental guidance or identification—the mother, the father—need to be mixed into the assimilated identity of ego or group member. The building blocks of development—early identification, sublimation, superegoic sadism—get libidinally mixed up between couplification and group processes. It's the group that permits teens to get around their parents, who are too out of it or off-limits to give them their sexual license, which they receive instead from the group. But even as their sex comes groupie-fied, teens receive another set of orders from the group—to form couples and reproduce (or reduce) themselves. Yet, the group reserves mega-ambivalence for the couples, which are the genitals of the group but which the group is ever dissolving back into itself. Group psychology isn't just a symptom; it's not a problem of masses that are already a measure or mass of psychopathology. We are in groups. In Acker's work, language stays tuned to the ambivalence that comes between groups and couples. It is a language that asserts identity, communication, then automatically group-formats the one-on-one.

Art that makes contact with the adolescent turbulence inside us and then takes a walk on this borderline risks having outer work experiences with midlife criticism types who really hate that they love teenagers. That's why the critical rep or rap given works of ambivalence is that it's adolescent, which is then further name-called perpetual, pathological, you name it. Journalistic critics (I mean the middlebrow types, like Camille Paglia, at the top of the best-sellout list) forget the adolescent origin of their otherwise happy medium (which lies in the keeping of journals or diaries), while at the same time acting it out in the decontextualized, empty run of a short attention span. The deferred adolescents among us (who are at the one remove from perpetual adolescence that's only a heartbeat away from crisis coming soon) interpret the Teen Age only one-way. But the always foreclosed other way is what adds the stereo context (that of ambivalence, transference, or reading) to our understanding of cultural—that is, cathected—phenomena. The mono turn-on that shuts down the stereo describes from the inside out the one readily identifiable form of adolescent acting out that is around, along for the writing, in open hiding inside midlife criticism.

> LAURENCE RICKELS: Did *My Mother: Demonology* start out with a particular identification, projection, or demonization?
>
> KATHY ACKER: It started out as my fascination with Laure's work and with Bataille and with wondering what that generation, two generations ago, was thinking. I was amazed reading her work that the same preoccupations that I have are there too. I mean, just to read in that little essay Bataille wrote about her (it's at the end of her collected works) that when she was in her twenties she lived with a guy in Berlin and he had her on a dog leash. What? That's really uncanny. The work Bataille and Laure were doing in the thirties was model building from the ground up. Neither the democratic nor the post-Leninist model was usable, so they turned to anthropological work and started looking into myth and sacrifice to come up with a new ground for a new social model. Whereas Breton settled for Stalinism after psychoanalysis, Bataille and Laure were looking for something else, where irrationality would

not be just a matter of mental functions, and sexuality would be something more than just the repressed. We're in a similar situation today with regard to Russian communism and democracy.

In her search, Laure also looked consciously as a woman, which greatly interested me. That's how I began to get interested in relations of women to demonology. It really has nothing to do with Laure's work. But that never bothered me. So the two came together. And sometimes chance meetings are rather wonderful, because they're never chance, of course. So it was by chance (in other words, by some determination that doesn't have a name yet) that, in the course of working through Laure's texts, I became interested in witchcraft. And this started my novel. The witchcraft material presented another history of women, or another history—one not written by and about dominant men. And it told of a time when there wasn't so much gender and orientation splitting. But that's still content. It's the process that always takes over in my work.

When I began writing *My Mother: Demonology*, I was worrying that I was internalizing certain censorships. Any member of a society does, as Ulrike Meinhof once mentioned. I used to go to sexual writing for my writing freedom. That place was no longer available to me, due to the changes in our society, and due to my own writing history—I didn't want to repeat myself. All writers are scared of internalizing restrictions; we're looking for places of freedom that take you by surprise.

I read the witchcraft material, and dreaming did surprise me. Dreaming became a technique for deciding the next move in the writing. I don't know how, I started dreaming about what I had just written that day. I started dreaming what I was writing. Once I realized what was going on, I started using it as a writing technique. What would happen (it's especially clear in the *Wuthering Heights* section), I would rewrite, appropriate, whatever: plagiarize, copy (slash-and-gash method) *Wuthering Heights*, and that night I would have a dream, and the dream would be about *Wuthering Heights*. So *Wuthering Heights* changed as I dreamed it. I didn't interpret the dream—like I dreamed about two basketballs lost in a pit and I told myself, in the dream, "Well, you don't have to interpret that!" I would leave the dream alone and use it to interpret the text.

The work with dream comes out of work with the body: you can't separate language and the body from the realm of the imagination. At the end of my version of *Don Quixote*, I started turning to the body as a resource for new models of writing. That was the first time in my life that I started looking at narrative—that *Blood and Guts in High School* came together as a narrative really amused me. I've never been interested in creating characters or stories. I've never been interested in creating anything. I turned to narrative when there was nothing else to turn to. There had to be some kind of narrative, but one that wasn't only a means of control. It was at this time too that I became interested in tattooing, as an art that isn't just on the body but goes into the body. I started to wonder if sitting in the body there was a narrative that was something else. What do you hear when you're listening to the body, as in bodybuilding, or in sex? What are the language movements? I'm always looking for narratives that I don't make up but that I'm already hearing. *Empire of the Senseless* was where I first worked on the relation of body to language, but there it was more writing about something than really doing it. It took me until this book to know what I was doing with that body/language relation. Now I'm exploring connections between masturbation and language.

LR: Can you describe some of your techniques?

KA: Like I said, I'm interested in languages we don't have access to. I was asked to write a piece for *Parquette* about bodybuilding, and I found out that I couldn't do it. So the piece became about why I was blocking. And I realized when people were doing things like bodybuilding or whatever (I'm sure dancers are the same way) there's a very complicated language going on, but it's not verbalized, it's almost *unable* to be verbalized. So people like bodybuilders and dancers sound stupid. I wondered how could I describe language that won't allow itself to be described and why won't it allow itself to be described. Why, when I do it, does it seem very complicated, and the minute I stop doing it (because I thought I would just go to the gym, work out, do a diary) it's gone? I wondered if it was the same language-barrier problem as in sex. I've often noticed that when I'm having sex, especially during the movement toward orgasm, I'm having a largely mental affair, images look as if they can be verbalized, but after it's all over I couldn't tell you what was going on. So I wanted to be able to access that language too.

LR: How can you do that, though?

KA: Well, with the masturbation project, I literally stick a vibrator up my ass and start (up my ass! I mean up my cunt) and start writing, and it's working really well.

LR: Do you think masturbation may already be a different kind of access or approach to sex? More like writing or reading? I mean, it would be hard to imagine having sex with someone and being able to write at the same time.

KA: You'd have to have a really willing partner.

LR: But that kind of stop-and-go would already be masturbation. Like when you interrupt yourself to turn to your favorite page.

KA: Maybe you could use a recorder.

LR: Ever since Freud went on the record, people have been wondering how to get their dreams down before resistance sets in.

Freud and Abraham and company had these really willing and ambitious patients who would keep notepads right next to their beds so they could write it down right away, or they would even start using recording devices. But what always happened was that resistance still had the last say. The handwriting was illegibile, the recording was staticky, or only the statement of purpose or the reminder to write down or record the dream would be repeated: "Write down the dream."

KA: There's a lot of resistance. But with dreaming, if you work hard at breaking through the resistance, it gets easier every time. By the time I finished *My Mother: Demonology*, because the book is really my "Interpretation of Dreams," I was waking up five times a night so I could write down my dreams. I trained myself. I had a hard time *not* dreaming, because the dreaming became so important. I tried to give my body rules, like Wake up now, Sleep, You're allowed to sleep. But something told me that I'd rather dream than be awake. I was having a real problem not sleeping twelve hours a night and not waking up five times to write down the dreams. I had to stop myself dreaming. At the end, I really felt that I was just raping "myself." But something had broken open.

LR: Sounds like you completely technologized yourself. But you also fed the machine; is there that element in the masturbation project too? Where you write something and then it's replayed in fantasy?

KA: Dreaming and masturbation are different techniques of writing. The writings I get from masturbation aren't fantasy narratives but are descriptions of architectures, of space shifts, shifting architectures, opening spaces, closing spaces. I don't know yet what to do with this writing in regard to narrative; right now I suspect that the language accessed during sex has some relationship to Kant's categories. My narratives at the moment are based on dreams. Dreaming is something you don't think you can control. And it's something everyone does; one doesn't have to desire to dream. With the masturbation, all I really do is put the vibrator up and start writing. I mean, there's some resistance, but not the major kind. I want to experiment with techniques where you don't climax and see what language is there while you hold off orgasm. Bodybuilding involved a great deal of resistance and I had to turn to other texts, I had to turn to Canetti, for example, on that, and I realized that the language I was trying to access was a meditative language, about breathing.

LR: Nietzsche said that all style is breathing.

KA: I think he was right.

LR: So the techniques you're working out, they started with bodybuilding and tattooing?

KA: Yes, the tattooing in a way, bodybuilding definitely. I thought about five years ago: I'm either going to have to stop bodybuilding or I'm going to have to incorporate it in my work in some way. It was becoming too important to me and there was a real time problem. But how do I incorporate it in my work? I don't want to write about bodybuilding. (I'm not Harry Cruise!)

LR: I guess, when you forget about the individual characters involved, bodybuilding is about metabolism in a big way.

KA: It's also about breathing.

LR: Right, and writing. It's totally technomediation: you're externalizing big-time or you're internalizing at the same time. What gets internalized is something like tattooing, I mean the scarification and internal bleeding that go down when you build up muscle. But if not bodybuilding, which you were into before you came to the Coast, what changes has California introduced into your work?

KA: The change would be all the girls, these crazy wild girls who are part of the San Francisco scene. They're the main characters in the new book. I think it's the first time in my life that I'm living in a girls' society—it's like girl's school. I've got to get out of here! I want to graduate! But there's real safety here too. Here's a tremendous freedom in daily living that I've never had anywhere else. My strongest desire (it's beyond desire, it's a need) is to make it possible for people like me to be in society. Perhaps it'll have to be a different society. This society tells me that a woman after thirty doesn't have a body unless she has children. You can't even be a whore after thirty. What I'm seeing in San Francisco is the emergence of a community of younger women that seems revolutionary, and also a relation to the body that I've never seen before with women. There's a play with gender, too: I say "women" but I'm not even sure. This could be the emergence of a place for me, where a woman of color like me (Jews have only been passing as white for centuries) and a queer (I'm so queer I'm not even gay) is no longer marginalized out of existence.

LR: Could you say something about your drawing? Is there a separate story to that?

KA: I always worked very closely with artists, but now that I've moved to a big press I had to drop the collaborations. The house felt it took away from the literary value of my work. I said my work doesn't have any literary value, so leave the pictures in. They were going to *give* my work literary value, they said. So that's why I started drawing, because if I draw the pictures they're part of the work, and they've got to stay in. That's why I do it. But I can't draw.

LR: This kind of property dispute is a real feature of your reputation. I'm thinking of your reinventions of the notion of plagiarism. Was that all along part of your work?

KA: Yes, but it wasn't there because I was *thinking* about plagiarism. I grew up basically in the conceptual part of the art world, and I was trained to think about writing a certain way. You have an intention, then you set up the experiment, you go ahead and do the experiment as you set it up, and anything that's outside that experiment detracts from what you're doing. The experiment was never about, say, good writing. I had other rules, like "Don't rewrite, don't do anything unless it's part of the experiment." It was only artists who understood what I was doing in my early work; to the literary world it was absolutely revolting.

In my first work, I wanted to figure out what identity was. It was a really simplistic experiment. I just jotted down every day what I did, it was that stupid: I did this, I thought about so-and-so. Then I tried to figure out who I was the easy way, through the process of elimination. So the person I could say I most wasn't was a murderess, because I didn't think I'd ever murdered anybody. I started looking into biographies of murderesses and I picked pre-Freudian ones because I didn't want to get involved in that specialized language. So I went to Victorian biographies of murderesses and basically got every one you could get and started copying them. But when I copied them I put them into first person so there was this real autobiography and this false autobiography. And then I went on from there. And I didn't know what was true and what was false by the end of it; I couldn't tell anymore. But I didn't have any theoretical language to talk about it. I can always talk about the theory afterwards. It's hard to talk about this business with language and the body because we don't really have much theory to go on. By now it's easy to talk about identity and construction because all the theory's been done. But in those days I was just wanting to do this, I didn't really understand it. All I had was R. D. Laing. I didn't have much.

By the time I got to *Blood and Guts in High School*, though, I realized that I wasn't interested in this business about identity at all. Identity was obviously constructed; it wasn't a big problem. What I was interested in was the texts I was using. It wasn't interesting writing diary work, I was boring myself to death; but it's very interesting to use other texts. I didn't understand why—I knew I didn't want any narrative, I didn't want characters, but I had this fascination with copying. I started reading Foucault, Deleuze, Guattari. So, suddenly the theory had started to form in me, so I could start understanding what I was doing, which meant I could do it more. I find I can't write without having another text in front of me. I mean, accessing language is like having another text in front of me. Or writing a story someone told me. There's no such thing as nothing.

LR: Something has to be metabolized.

KA: Writing is either hearing, listening, reading—or it's destroying.

LR: Did you find the constructed identity of the murderess, the constructed identification with these murderess narratives, suddenly having some kind of effect upon you? You chose something you felt was completely other, and then you incorporated it into the body of your work.

KA: I did six months, six chapters; I'd take six months off, do six more months. At the end of each six months, I'd have a sort of nervous breakdown. It made me quite crazy, crazier than the writing has since then. People ask me, Doesn't it make you wacky writing what you write? No, actually, writing balances me.

LR: But then you reach a certain limit, whether it's a breakdown, an exorcism?

KA: It's totally like a possession. But only with *In Memoriam to Identity* did I begin to realize that.

LR: There's a kind of melancholia here, all the way to *My Mother: Demonology*. Plagiarism or whatever you want to call it is like an improper burial or it's like taking something in, keeping it a secret and alive, metabolizing it, yes, but more within the limits of recycling. The contours of the foreign body are still recognizable, like the vampire asleep in the crypt.

KA: What I was thinking of while you were saying that was the ritual they have in Haiti for incorporating the dead, which is kind of the basis for the entire society. Is that how you would see the relation to the mother in *Demonology*?

LR: Your relationship to your own body is always at the same time the relationship to your mother's body. And that's always the problem because the mother's body is also off-limits, which is why it becomes a kind of limit to one's pleasure. That's the static or resistance, the melancholic legacy jamming the connection to one's own body.

KA: I've often noticed that the men in my books are stick figures. In the new book, there are basically only women, girls, except for Bush, another stick figure, but how does he fit into this body politics? Is the father's body just that foreign? Does he have a body?

LR: The father is all about the kind of death that doesn't lead to melancholia; his mournable death is the antibody we inject into our systems to get rid of mother or demonology, but also maybe to get rid of the body altogether.

KA: There's one little paragraph that is very personal, which goes something like this: "O says, 'My mother wants me to suicide because she suicided. I try to find a father to get rid of my mother but there are no fathers around anymore.' All of the whores agreed with O: It was the end of the white male world."

LR: It's the struggle between the antibody and the drive to incorporate the only body that's around, the body that's missing, the mother's body.

KA: It's one feminist line that men are different from women; for instance, men are aggressive, women are kind and gentle. If that's true, for women there is no fear or trembling involved in the incorporation of the mother's body; there is no demon aspect. Which isn't true at all.

LR: But there is one difference: the only chance the father gets to come alive is the one the daughter has to libidinize or animate him so that she can be pulled out of the mother bond.

KA: And libidinization of the father is the biggest no-no. At one point there was a movement among the wild girls in San Francisco to write the hottest stories they could and it was all father-fetishizing. You know: I want to fuck Daddy.

LR: Right at the time the family was being invented, in the eighteenth century, those bourgeois dramas were already picking up on it.

KA: It's totally hot. Now everyone's favorite sin is the glorification of child abuse. We all know that fathers want to sleep with their daughters.

LR: It's amazing how in California (or maybe it's worldwide by now) one thinks that one can externalize something like that and get rid of it, I mean without taking it in. As with the sexual harassment charging down university corridors. Pedagogy is, certainly transferentially speaking, one of our biggest libidinal charges. Now teaching, seduction itself, must disappear.

KA: What scares them is the demon part of it. So instead we go for dehumanized bodies, robot bodies—seduction is removed from sex and teaching disappears.

LR: It's transmission without transference, or writing without reading.

Act Out/Turn On

THE MORE COMPLETE AVERSION

Laurence A. Rickels

I

It was like this. In the course of my work on "Nazi Psychoanalysis" I had uncovered, among many other closeted skeletons, certain determining conditions and contexts attending the invention of "acting out" as the cover-all designation it still is today, a label that advertises all the grief that an adolescent or the masses can give in terms of once and future psychopathology. These conditions were in fact in the beginning war-time conditionings. During World War II, analysis or analytic therapy was being mobilized on all sides of the total conflict to serve the psychological war and the psychic war economy. Group therapy was developed as the new and improved format for "analytic" treatment of war neurotics. After the war, this group model was recommended for treatment of sexual offenders. Thus, I had stumbled upon a collapse—or co-lapsus—of categories in the discourse of a certain institutionalization. The institution is that of "greater psychoanalysis." In addition to original analysis, all the schools of therapy, even as they claim to move far away from the most basic principles of psychoanalysis, ultimately are stuck on their destination as forever part of Freud's science. Included in this part that keeps remaining greater than the whole of its diversifications and improvements were all the corridors of military psychology.

I had just finished my *Artforum* interview with Kathy Acker, "Body Bildung," in which certain value-free theorizations of acting out and group psychology were already along for the exchange for a change. *Artforum* at that time was hard-pressed to perform a balancing act around a rather (shall we say) conservative article by contributing editor Donald Kuspit that just could not be kept out of the magazine.

My first version of a response addressed Kuspit's first version, which *Artforum* faxed to me before it had undergone any in-house copyediting. It was an eye-opener. I opened my response with a grammatological reflection on one of Kuspit's striking stylistic idiosyncrasies, which, technically agrammatical, represented and repressed a profound affinity with acting out. I was advised to drop that, if only because Kuspit's prose was always published in the magazine with the split infinitives edited out. But, in the meantime, Kuspit had seen my first version. Apparently unaware that his prose undergoes correction before it meets the press, Kuspit had composed yet another response (or so I was informed) that, contrary to his wish, would not be added on as a chain reaction. I was reassured that I would not be needing to read Kuspit's latest effort hot off the repression. But then, one day *Artforum* faxed an unsigned, untitled text to me, perhaps by accident.

All this by way of identifying what follows as the original version of my *response*. But first I will begin with the outer-corpus experience, with the piece of stray hostility that reached me by fax-ident. I give you the fax-you message intact and undisclosed.

II

Should I take Rickels' "reflections" on my text seriously? It's hard to do so: his text is long on rhetoric and innuendo, short on accuracy and understanding. He ought to be embarrassed by his grotesquely distorted account of the development of psychoanalysis and object relations. He hopes to drag me down—smear me—along with them. His play with "not see" and "Nazi" suggests as much. Perhaps the full measure of his mentality is his obsession with the typographical error that occurred in his text on Kathy Acker. Who's to blame? Me, the unconscious of the editors of *Artforum*, a virus lurking in the computer? Rickels has projective problems.

The article on Acker is an apologetics for adolescent acting out: it's okay, as long as it's literary. It's in defense of this privileging of the literary that Rickels attacks my unliterary text.

There's a peculiar contradiction here. If, as Rickels says, "acting out refers to dynamics internal to the analytic situation," what's it doing in literature and why does he tolerate it there? Because he's one of the literati, and the literati feel threatened by the psychoanalysts, who know know [typo in the original fax—L.R.] more about the psyche than they do. Indeed, literature has always pretended to know more than it does, and Rickels wants to maintain the pretense.

Acting out is not just a phenomenon of the clinical situation (where it can be contained), but socially prevalent, and not just as an "idiomatic phase or phrase of pop psychology or adolescence." It involves, at the least, the expulsion of primitive thoughts, and the inability to tolerate frustration, and splitting. As Bion suggests, it signals relational collapse—a general collapse of psychic linkage. In a sense, acting out is an ironical solution to splitting—to the dissociation of ideal and persecutory objects—for it provides a pseudo-link between them.

As for my splitting of infinitives, I reunite them, strengthening their link, by inserting a qualifying term between them. But why should I defend myself against a dupe of language like Rickels? Who is a shyster Derridean like Rickels—masking thoughtlessness by rhetorical manipulation—to lay down the laws of language? He just acts it out, as his rhetoric suggests.

III

In the last issue of *Artforum*, in the intro to my interview with Kathy Acker, the "encounter" with the midlife criticism of acting out I was already trying to have was at the same time a no-show: the very word "encounter," in other words, had been elided, typo-style, from its prescribed place between "close" and "with adolescence."[1] But in the evacuation of "encounter" from its sci-fi phrasing and teen phasing a connection with today's assignment was nevertheless acted out, displaced with regard to the absence, loss, or deprivation to which it owes its admission (I mean, omission). Acting out always catches on. Even its criticism, as in Kuspit's owner's manual to avant-garde acting out, is already stuck on it: right back down to the typographical level of the missing "encounter," which is where, Golem-style, the on/off switch operates.

Kuspit's tendency to totally split infinitives, for example, already has the look of acting out, which doesn't stay put when Kuspit has it where he wants it and leaves it there. The split along the linguistic lifeline is a literal, anti-metaphorical way another split has of getting in your type-face: the one that's out there in the delinquent and deviant behaviors Kuspit identifies at the lineup with certain art practices.

Kuspit's inside view of acting out turns on "splitting," the psychic mechanism Freud first addressed in his essay on fetishism (or gadget love by any other name). Through splitting we get the division and distribution of shares of one fantasy across gaps of omission or departure which are nevertheless "connections," missing but acting out, that skip the downbeat of loss and trauma. Acting out gets around repression by keeping the split that is there open (open in the case of split infinitives to the feel of live speech). Splitting goes to great wavelengths of an "oscillation" (according to Freud) "between neurosis and psychosis." In other words, the loss or absence the fetishist tunes in can, on this channel, be at once identified and not seen. This split-level view of how, then, the trauma of loss "goes" is what's along for the acting-out overdrive.

Acting out, the overriding post–World War II label that gets stuck on this mobilization of or access to the shifting border zone between neurosis and psychosis splits the trauma scene, divides and conquers for the time being the immediate evacuation effects of the first strike of loss, and thus skips the downbeat of psychotic shutdown. By keeping the split open, acting out gets around the fixed-front war of repression and its consequence in psychotic cases: the evacuation of all libido from the outside world, which is thus destroyed, back into the ego which overloads, short-circuits, disconnects.

Acting out's bypass operation around repression puts it up there with sublimation on a direct line to that different way some still call art. The access or excess of acting out, however, goes where no sublimation has gone before, into the borderline zone at once inside psychosis and between neurosis and psychosis.

In the face and about-facing of serial acting out, a word from our superegoical sponsor (the corporation or incorporation that issues the strict rule about never splitting the infinitive in the first place) seems in order, or keeps it there, an order taken this time around by an analytic concept's history or psychohistory. The concept of acting out that has been going without saying throughout these reflections acts out or splits its connections to a past it's making up or breaking up as it goes along.

The analytic interest in acting out doesn't begin with Freud, except after the fact. It was first through the study of "object relations" that acting out came to be linked to splitting and then reassigned the terms of a transferential cure: the acting-out patient, who has a low threshold for ambivalence, sets his relations in the concrete by splitting and bouncing apart his "objects" into "good" and "bad." In the everyday life of the child we can observe little one, once the tantrum subsides, announce that the bad child is gone now and the good one is back. Acting out rides out this split in every moment of reception, including that of the concept's own itinerary or history (acting out always catches on). Only around World War II did the study of object relations employ the term "acting out" in a sense compatible with, for example, Kuspit's art appreciation of delinquency and deviance. But this World War II application was never in sync with Freud's use of the term "acting out" (*Agieren*), which he referred exclusively to the analytic setting where repetition and remembering must face off in the transference. That's why, in 1967, Anna Freud convened the international psychoanalytic conference around the topic of acting out, calling for clarification of a concept that by then "covered" its distance from her father's use of the term. From the all-out attempt at the 1967 conference to address or redress the "diffuse expansionism" of the term, as the disconnection between Freud's sense of acting out as local to the transference and those applied psychosocial meanings that are still with us, to the match that is on right now between Kuspit and me, the preoccupation with acting out's meanings just never left the transference contest between remembering and acting out, a contest that pervades the concept's history.

Only by skipping a beat and getting stuck in a groove on the war record of psychoanalysis could the actors out of delinquency and, interchangeably, deviance be advanced as the true veterans of the twentieth century's psychological war efforts. This latest resort of the psy-fi colonization of the outer space of "psychosis" for treatability or adjustment (for the survival of the species) was first brought to us by Freud's close encounter with the shell-shock epidemic during the First World War. Freud's "Introduction to *Psychoanalysis and the War Neuroses*" made possible the consolidation of all preliminary findings or holdings under the equal separation between narcissism or ego libido and object-directed libido. Thus, from World War I onward (soldiers!), the more severe narcissistic neuroses or psychoses shift from the allegorical to the functional, from limit concept to borderline case. It doesn't really matter whether psychoanalysis in fact presented a cure-all for the war neuroses: in theory a newfound no-man's-land or borderline had opened up between neurosis and psychosis for advances or occupations by analytic therapy.

When the German military-psychological complex decided in 1918 that psychoanalysis was to be treatment of choice for war neurosis, and even planned construction of analytic institutes and clinics near the front lines to that end, it was of course too late; but it wasn't too late for psychoanalysis to score PR-wise on all sides of the peace that everyone was out to win. The myth of the healed war neurotic was to be the greatest success story of the analytic model, which thus gained admission into every department or discipline of psychological interventionism. But only the German military, psychological, and military-psychological establishments stayed with the analysis-inspired research into war neurosis: its cure and inoculative prevention on one's own side, and its infliction across enemy lines through psychological warfare. When World War II started up, Allied military psychologists suddenly saw themselves as way behind their German colleagues, with whom they had to catch up. In Britain, advances were first made under the pressure of total air war. World War I had for the first time provided large-scale uniform or uniformed populations for study under the new laboratory conditions of total war. In World War's Second Coming it was the new research resources of children and adolescents evacuated out from under the shadow of total air war that filled a vaster lab space for analytic exploration of a wider developmental range of human subjects. These children and adolescents were granted analytic or therapeutic supervision right from the start because it was assumed that the shocks of the target areas of air war had struck them the same way the hard shell of frontline combat affected symptomatizing soldiers. But then it was discovered that trauma number one for the children was the separation from their mothers that evacuation had brought about. That's how the British object-relations school of psychoanalysis (Wilfred Bion, W. Ronald D. Fairbairn, and D. W. Winnicott), which was developing under this air pressure, came to realize what Freud had already stressed for World War I war neurotics: separation anxiety cuts down the dotted line along which even the outbreak of war neurosis tears into childhood trauma. The object-relations analysts switched at this time and for these cases from individual therapy to group therapy, which is where the modern concept of acting out was first coming up for air war. In the zones of evacuation where the fit of juvenile delinquency with group-therapeutic "management" was first recognized, Winnicott saw through acting out as the repeater attempt to get back at the present and get back to a past prior to the trauma of deprivation and loss, which is thus the delinquent's disowned but perpetual present tense and tension, forgotten but preserved between Before and After pictures. This double take called for the kind of intervention (based on Melanie Klein's one-on-one approach, but now shifted to the group

level) that works regression real close to the borderline inside psychosis. Stationed at this border, analysis made first contact with psychosis,
which began to open wide. It's the nonstop interpretation of the transference, right down to the meganarcissistic demand that the transferences all ultimately address the analyst alone, that keeps the no's of
transference to the grind of acting out. Acts reenter verbalization and
their force as acts hangs on the words or rewordings. The patient's
whole poisoned world, reduced for the sake of understanding or follow-
ability to the rebound of the bouncing bad object, gets vacuum-packed
into the analysis. But this is too nerdy by half for the actor out who
splits the object scene. While the analyst is thus relocating the split ends
of acting out to a new settlement within the therapeutic relationship,
the acting out patient is out there trying to pull the analyst into the
poisonous metabolism of his p-unitive relations. Who's acting out
now? The concept of projective identification filled a need to give acting out's share in this breaking of a contract, the one the analyst cosigns
with his countertransference, a one-way determination. This concept
lays the blame, say, for the analyst's loss of patience and patients on the
self-fulfilling prophecies brought to session by the analysand.

In 1946, Fairbairn (with Winnicott's silent partnership) initiated
the object-relations move to make this package deal of analytic inno-
vations available to perverts at the same group rate. His first postwar
application of the lab work with traumatized soldiers followed the
bouncing bond of comradeship from the breakdown of defenses to
sexual offense. Fairbairn is able to relieve the inconsistency he's having
with his opening analogy between the psychoneurotic soldier and the
sexual offender by confining his comparison shopping to their lapsed
group memberships. Fairbairn's proposition: "the establishment of special communities for offenders—settlements with a group life of their
own, in which offenders can participate, and which is psychologically
controlled with a view to its gradual approximation to the life of the
community at large."[2] Missing the war experience with neurotic soldiers, Fairbairn takes better aim with the civilian population of perverts: "the establishment of such settlements would have the advantage
of providing a unique field for the scientific study of social relationships
and the factors which determine the nature of a group."[3]

The object-relations-school selection of perverts for the first postwar support groups and, thus, for group-therapeutic assessments of
group psychology, coincides with the introduction of "acting out," that

idiomatic phase or phrase of pop psychology or adolescence that is still with us. It's a time-release caption to the advance originally held by psychotherapists (including psychoanalysts) in Nazi Germany, who were real eager to apply the success story of Freud's encounter with war neurotics to a total victory through analysis: the all-out eradication-through-healing of the homosexual position or disposition (which since World War I marked the spot of the coming out of war neurosis under fire and the acting out of primal submissions through betrayal, desertion, even espionage). Nazi therapy culture thus faced sexual perversion right on within defense contexts of inoculation. The promotion of homoeroticism, for example, right on the face of Nazi culture was part of this all-out effort to inoculate the race (a race that had to be won against all odd men out) and grant it immunity from the other fact of life. After World War II, the pop-psychological concepts and conditions of acting out, homosocial double bind, homosexual panic, and latent homosexuality were among the inoculative measures taken in against the breakdowns, ultimately, of war neurosis. War-neurotic soldiers and civilians provided the research resource for the progress to be made in readjustment of psychotics and perverts. These dropouts from the group effort had to be not so much cured (since there is something about psychosis and perversion that remains compatible, after all, with war preparedness, mass membership, and merger with the machine) as readjusted, rewired, made user-friendly.

"Acting out" follows the logic of inoculation that is the wartime legacy of keeping up near-miss relations with internal enemies. It is a logic that requires total victory because it has a half-life that cannot outlast the explosive uncontrollability coming soon. It's paranoid all right: it sees the other's unconscious with total clarity, can recognize, for example, the remote-controlled acting-out currents that spark the selection of artist-mascots for mutual mass identification, but cannot see its own unconscious participation in this natural selection. The half-life of this controlling interest taken in the other is simply the effect of being able for the time being to "not see" or "Nazi" the continuity that is there, for example, between the two it takes to act out. That's why Freud was right: acting out refers to dynamics internal to the analytic session. When it comes to acting out, then, the work on transference must lead to work of mourning, and the timer of all the patient's other mournings must be set to the termination of the session in the here and now. It's time.

Notes

1. In the *Artforum* publication (reprinted as "Body Bildung: Laurence Rickels Talks with Kathy Acker" in this book), "encounter" was accidentally left out of the opening sentence. The published version thus suggested that what drew me to Kathy Acker's work was "its close with adolescence."
2. W. R. D. Fairbairn, "The Treatment and Rehabilitation of Sexual Offenders," *Psychoanalytic Studies of the Personality* (London and Boston: Routledge and Kegan Paul, 1952), 295.
3. Ibid.

True Confessions of a Talk-Show Audience Member

Rhonda Lieberman

Hi. Low.

In terms of cultural leadership, Chicago may have decided that the only intact interior designed by Mies van der Rohe is not worth preserving as a historical landmark, but it is the generative source of three popular talk shows: *Jerry Springer*, *Jenny Jones*, and of course *Oprah*. Following the custody battle regarding the fate of the Mies-designed Arts Club with morbid fascination, this reader was impressed by the scorn hurled in the papers by wholesome city developers toward the "uppity" "East Coast carpetbaggers" (i.e., architects, curators, and design professionals) and suspect "elitist" Arts Club members who stubbornly rallied to preserve the design monument. As the eternal present of Mies modernism rolls over in its grave, subsequent generations will sit upon its former site in the avatar of a new multiplex theater. So much for modern masters.

One doesn't have to read *The Western Canon* by the embattled Harold Bloom to suspect that "high" culture, like all of us, has something to whine about. I must come out as a fan and admit I consumed Uncle Bloom's whopping jeremiad with discreet grunts of pleasure. "Art is not a social welfare agency," Bloom provocatively declares, but rather helps us, individually, to learn how to overhear ourselves, how to endure ourselves, how to confront our essential solitude before death. So what could be bad?

We are having a crisis when any cultural text that isn't always enjoyable to everyone all the time is labeled "elite" (shorthand for evil and on speaking terms with the devil). Bad faith toward anything requiring active reading is so rampant that a student (a foreigner) had to remind me: "You know, your Excellency [my preferred form of address], we refer to wine experts when we want to know about wine, gourmets with developed palates when we want to know about food; what's wrong with having 'experts' who know about art?" Like the trusting gaze of an unabused child, his innocence refreshed me. According to Lacan, the only ethic was to be well spoken, *bien dit*. Although cultural "experts" may have jeopardized their authority in the recent past with sheer bad writing—ruining people's taste for thinking with the simulacrum of thought in the form of tortured jargon—we are beginning to confuse any earned difficulty with pretentiousness and are coming to the point where any text that doesn't go down as easily as a cultural Happy Meal is looked upon as a suspect bad object to be eliminated.

> You ask what you should watch.
> I ask how I should live.
> It's the same thing.
> *The Red Desert* (directed by Michelangelo Antonioni, 1964)

Because I daylight as a pedagogue, I thought, what better place for the ephebes to see a truly democratic text, a text that does not "exclude" the uninitiated reader, than at a talk show. I looked forward to the taping of the *Jenny Jones Show* with serene enthusiasm unalloyed by the narcissistic crisis accompanying the live sighting of celebrities I truly admire. Although I have nothing against Jenny, and empathize with her personal challenges with a migrating breast implant (god forbid), she fails to evoke the hysteria by which I experience the live presence of a truly sublime celebrity in my presence as a nauseous assault and commentary on my own person. This is cool, I bragged to myself, I can handle this. Although I enjoy the occasional Leibniz text in the privacy of my own home (Who doesn't? Only kidding!), I am at one with the global village. Some of my students were puzzled why we were taking this field trip to *Jenny Jones*. One had the cheek to inquire of me, the authority figure: "What does this have to do with art?" "Cultural context, honey," I patiently responded. "It's about how people represent themselves"—making a mental note to flunk her. Any student who made an intervention on camera was guaranteed special extra credit. As their guide and leader, I wasn't going to be caught in that audience without a shot at the glory. Ever the prepared pedagogue, I was ready with my comment (good for any topic). At the appropriate moment, I interject: "You can't look to others for self-esteem, you have to find it within!"

(Audience applauds wildly. I smile in a caring way. I drink in the fleeting elixir, like champagne, enjoyed by that fleeting chimera—audience top dog. My students are impressed. Jenny nods approvingly and scans the losers du jour on the panel for visible signs of enlightenment.)

Feeling very glamorous on the bus on the way to NBC, I reflected how part of the qualification to be a talk-show host seems to be overcoming some kind of personal challenge: for Jenny it's the breast implants; for Jerry Springer, disgrace when, as mayor of Cincinnati, he paid for a call girl with a personal check, thus seriously impairing his political career. Perhaps most empowering of all is to overcome a major weight problem; Oprah and Ricki Lake, the biggest talk-show queens, are triumphant former fatties. Rolanda Watts, a slightly unctuous but well-styled up-and-coming Oprah knockoff, tries to glom onto that trend by remarking that she used to be really fat. Jayne Whitney often refers to her fat childhood and inexplicably wears no shoes; running around in panty hose (are her feet too fat?), adding a subliminal taste of danger, as the viewer suspensefully waits for her to step on something sharp. Gordon Elliot, a British talk-show guy, is portly. Joan Rivers is a recovering tacky person, and still makes fat jokes, although she is now soignée and petite. Montel Williams is bald. Sally Jessy Raphael is a flaming pity-addict. Phil Donohue is a soft white man. Regis and Kathie Lee used to be considered losers, now they rule (while Kathie walks a dangerous line with relentless references to her perfect family). It is clear that talk-show hosts, like their guests, are in recovery. It's OK, in fact, required, to be flawed, to adequately consume them.

The talk-show audience member, too, does not emerge full-grown from the head of Zeus, but rather, must be produced, worked over in the audience holding tank by professionally giddy audience prep experts. *Jenny Jones* tapes playing on monitors, getting us in the Jenny mood, one prepper confides, "Jenny thinks of you guys as her co-hosts! She'll tell you not to interrupt, but pleeeeeze, yell anything you want whenever!" Interpellating us as trainable seals, we were tempted with the coveted "audience VIP card" awarded by preppers to well-performing audience members. As we were encouraged to behave with the rectitude of judgmental ten-year-olds at a food fight, I recalled why I avoided pep rallies in high school. Hectoring and ad hominem attacks were encouraged as the second audience prep person tweaked an outspoken sister in the audience for having a coiffure "like an ice-cream cone." At this point, after only twenty minutes of inanely bland "prepping," our resistance was low enough for us to laugh at this "witticism." In sum, it took about half an hour for us to be processed into witless zombies capable of yelling at a strange gentleman for wanting to date (gasp!) someone who came out as a "mistress and proud of it." Sufficiently stupefied, we were ready to enter the studio and learn, at long last, what would be the topic of the day. The walls of the *Jenny* studio were back-lit gables suggesting Early Salad Bar, or the food court at a mall. The insipid sea-foam and peach color scheme contrasted with the blaring disco music: decor and sound track coalescing ingeniously into the proper *Jenny* ambiance of bland rowdiness.

Early this century, wowed by the crowds in newsreels, Walter Benjamin predicted that film would close the gap between actors and spectators, eventually enabling everyone to be an "actor" on film, thus making the media text into an effective mirror, and potentially "revolutionary" outlet for its audience. Today, the TV talk show seems to be fulfilling his prophecy. With the recent explosion in talk shows (eclipsing game shows as showcases on TV for "normal" people), we have unprecedented opportunities to see the full diapason of humanity getting a shot of airtime. The next logical step, enabled by cable, would be for everyone to have their own talk show, evolving from guest to host, worms blossoming into "personality" butterflies.

I tried to remember this as I waited, like a gassed dental patient, fully hebetated by audience prep, to meet the affable Jenny, who lost no time before she *dissed* us: "excuuuse me, everyone, the Art Institute is here today," she tattled. She was wearing a long white cardigan that belied her aggressiveness. It is remarkable how well all that makeup photographs. She actually seems a lot less smarmy in person than she does on TV. We knew, since it was Jenny Jones, that the topic was going to be lame. "People who want to date someone they saw on a previous *Jenny Jones Show*" was the topic offered by the fertile brain of a *Jenny Jones* producer. Only a sufferer of Tourette's syndrome could possibly vocalize an opinion on this. Perhaps this nontopic in fact provided the essence of the *Jenny Jones* experience, as one of my more astute students proposed, because everything's an articulation of the void and whatever. I was glad I assigned the Maurice Blanchot. Still unsated as an audience member, I want to go back.

The three-hour taping was emotionally draining. One strained in vain toward the blandness for any scrap of affect to latch onto, eager to react (even with disgust) as a docile organ of the audience body, eviscerated of interiority, like a trained seal bobbing up to catch the clichés as they were thrown toward us, like stinky fish. My cheek muscles were sore from registering artificial bemusement. Days later, I watched myself at home on TV, a smiling and clapping, docile audience member, a ladylike version of Jack Nicholson at the end of *One Flew Over the Cuckoo's Nest*. I contemplated my essential solitude before death.

Serious Fun

THE *JENNY JONES* TRIAL

Gary Indiana

The sublime grotesquerie of the Talk-Show Murder Trial, aka *Michigan v. Schmitz*, was largely wasted on its principal figures, with the possible exception of the defendant, Jonathan Schmitz. A few days after being "ambushed" on the *Jenny Jones Show* into hearing his "secret admirer," Scott Amedure, declare his sexual interest in Schmitz's "cute little hard body," Schmitz bought a shotgun and reciprocated the ambush at Amedure's trailer home, blowing Amedure into kingdom come and himself into a second-degree murder conviction. (Schmitz was also convicted on a lesser charge of using a firearm in the commission of a felony.) There was a time in American jurisprudence when Schmitz's trial would have ended in an easy walk for the defendant. (In some states, notably Texas, the judicial anus of the nation, it probably still would be.) The conviction reflects a quantum cultural change in attitudes about homosexuality. One of the broader ironies of the Schmitz case is that chat shows of the type that triggered the crime have played their little role in bringing this change about. As became clear during the trial, however, any enlightening side effects of such shows are entirely unintended. For their producers, the condition of difference (whether social construct or gross pathology) is a cheap human resource, the exploitation of which spells profitable fund.

Amedure and a gal pal, Donna Riley, thought it would be fun to expose Amedure's secret passion to a nationwide geek-show audience, without first discovering if Schmitz was gay or straight. It would, they thought, be fun to find out that way. The producers of *Jenny Jones* thought it would make a fun segment, without first determining whether Schmitz had a history of mental illness. Schmitz, a manic-depressive, became elated at the prospect of appearing on TV, the fantasy solution to everyone's problems in a culture where "self-esteem" is the obsessive quest of those who don't have any but insist on looking for it in acts of compulsive self-exposure.

In the early days of misery TV, contestants on shows like *Queen for a Day* competed in abjection, hoping to win a washer-dryer or a new refrigerator. Several therapeutic generations later, such mingy material blandishments have shrunk beside the possibility of becoming famous for something, even something unappetizing, like weighing seven hundred pounds or having an affair with your stepfather. To paraphrase Nietzsche, people today would rather be monstrous than be *nothing*, and our culture tells them they are nothing unless they are well known. Jonathan Schmitz, a young man who had *loser* written all over him until *Jenny Jones* beckoned, clearly did not understand the devil's bargain that instant celebrity entails: everything in life comes with a price tag.

Schmitz claimed that he was never told his "secret admirer" might be another man. The *Jenny Jones* producers insisted that Schmitz had been cautioned that it "could be a man or a woman." Asked if this was true, one producer testified first that it wasn't, but quickly qualified by saying that, yes, it was. Jenny Jones herself, who had emoted a statement of deep regret on the air following the murder, testified that she had had nothing to do with writing the statement, and had been handed it moments before taping. She was not, in effect, responsible for anything that happened on her show, and neither was anyone else that she could readily name. Amedure's family is suing the show for millions. More saliently reflecting the times, Schmitz is suing too.

Schmitz's mental problems occasioned a familiar procession of paid psychiatric experts, a burgeoning medical subspecies that ruminates, funnily enough, between the nation's courtrooms and places like the *Jenny Jones Show*. Dr. Michael Abramsky described Schmitz's appearance at Amedure's trailer, shotgun in hand, as a "nonpredatory stance," to support the unoriginal idea (cf. the Jean Harris defense) that Schmitz's *intent* had been to tell Amedure to leave him alone, and then to commit suicide. Yet, it would appear to any reasoning mind that the latter intent would obviate the need for the former, even for the most bipolar of personalities.

Dr. Michael Garcia cited Schmitz's documented Graves' disease, a thyroid condition, as another, judgment-impairing affliction that helped push Schmitz over the edge, but had to admit on cross that

Graves' disease does not normally, or indeed ever, drive people to violence. Dr. Carole Lieberman, a "psychiatrist with expertise in media and communications," claimed that a humiliating incident at school and the *Jenny Jones* debacle "coalesced" in Schmitz's mind at the exact moment before he fired the shotgun, apparently causing an effulgence of brain goo that rendered Schmitz powerless to do anything other than shoot Amedure.

Specious as much of this was, one could credit the idea that Jonathan Schmitz was not a person who could prudently be exposed to unwanted sexual advances on national television. He had attempted suicide four times. His family had a long history of manic-depression. He went on a drinking binge after the *Jenny Jones* taping, and stayed up drinking all night before the murder. It isn't such a stretch to believe he committed it in a condition of "diminished capacity," a legitimate defense for first-, though not second-, degree murder in Michigan.

The conditions for diminished capacity, like everything else in American criminal law, vary absurdly from state to state. In some states, drugs and alcohol are excluded as influences on the ability to "form intent," because their ingestion is voluntary. Relatedly, Schmitz opted for diminished capacity over an insanity plea because Michigan, like many states, passed "guilty but insane" statutes following the John Hinckley not-guilty verdict, ensuring decades of incarceration for miscreants who really are too crazy to know what they are doing.

In fact, everyone involved in *Michigan v. Schmitz*, including the victim, seemed to suffer from some form of diminished capacity, an inability to make reasonable judgments, an unwillingness to separate the hallucinatory shimmer of publicity from the harsher textures of real life. There was plenty of blame to go around and nobody home to accept it. If Schmitz was a textbook case of homophobia run rampant, it should also be noted, just for the record, that Amedure, Riley, Jenny Jones et al. regarded him as just another cute little hard body to be played with, regardless of its psychological contents. On the *Jenny Jones Show*, Amedure said he first saw "the lower half" of Schmitz's body while the latter worked under Riley's car; Amedure fell in love with the lower half and never troubled to investigate the area above the neck. "You just want to pick it up," Amedure said, with the telling use of a neuter pronoun, "put it on a shelf, dust it off once in a while...." In Amedure's narrative, Schmitz was something like a bowling trophy.

That everyone can be played with in public without any risk to the players is a lethal assumption, but an easy one to make in a world that degrades and stupefies everybody equally. One part of it turns out to be true. Both Amedure and Schmitz thought going on TV would change their lives, and it did.

Burn, Signifier, Burn

Peter Canning

Aggression becomes a problem for human beings. And yet aggression is the very essence of drive, its urge, the thing that moves an animal— is the human not an animal?—to act. Under human law, the aggressive act is subject to challenge, being called into question by the very fact of language. Conversely, the act of aggression implicitly defies the law it transgresses and potentially forecloses all response from the Other of language and desire. By relating the manifestations of aggression to the symbolic matrix of the family (father, mother, child, Other), psychoanalysis is able to work out a logic and genealogy of institutions that supplement and clarify that of the Nietzschean tradition (Foucault). A dialectic of desire and *jouissance* emerges through the play of signifiers representing those familial positions and functions, even as they have been transformed or eclipsed by evolving institutions. Thus, the signifer of the father is proposed as a "law of desire" interrupting the *jouissance* of mother and child. And before that, the symbolic law prohibits the father himself from enjoying unconditional power over his family. However, the modern disciplinary institution presents the prospect of a system tending to eliminate the paternal function as unnecessary, thereby unwittingly exposing the child to the perverse and unchecked deployment of the *jouissance* of the Other, as incarnated in the set of institutions that take over and transform the maternal function.

It seems impossible to universalize a human essence of drive (beyond a set of biological universals) because each culture creates its own passage through the "discourse of the Other," expressing human passion in each instance by a unique assemblage of ritual performances. However, this discourse is a universal fact of language, realizing the human freedom to remodel and reinvent itself. From the moment that each culture begins to interpret its own humanity and nature, and to refashion this nature, aggressivity and drive become channeled into symbolic institutional functions whose meaning will give cause for thinking. This ritual and institutional discourse of the Other constitutes an unconscious in which humans move and act as living signs.

Discipline and Delinquency

The set of modern European institutions that Foucault identified as a "disciplinary matrix" was assembled and designed like a factory for producing human individuals. Its complex strategy has been to select and reconstruct the manifestations of human "nature" as they emerge, to fashion body and soul into a manageable individual, eventually subject to its own interiorized self-discipline. To this end, certain expressions of drive are elicited while others are suppressed and discouraged or forbidden and repressed. However, it is evident that institutions also cultivate, in spite of training and rules, certain "delinquent" behaviors that they officially discourage and pretend to eradicate—protocriminal impulses that take shape within families, schools, and other institutions purporting to suppress these energies or redirect them to "constructive" purposes. But the real lesson of Foucault is that this supposed subversion or perversion of discipline is, on the contrary, its very essence and truth. Everyone remembers a juvenile delinquent who became a policeman. But the true function of discipline is precisely to (re)produce a kind of variable perversion virtually indistinguishable from the agency of law and order.

If the aim of the perverse act is to demonstrate "the uselessness of the passage through the desire of the Other when the function of language is at stake," and the uselessness of the symbolic law that necessitates this passage (the law of the father),[1] then discipline is the institutionalization of perversion, a categorical imperative that precedes and bypasses the law. Institutions have little tolerance for desire and subjectivity, for they command their subjects like movable objects and modular functions. On the other hand, they have everything to do with the *jouissance* of power.

Power is the "differential element of forces," as Deleuze said, whose most elementary expression is command. Or rather, commanding is not expressing power, it is exercising it under human rules of engagement. Commanding is the *jouissance* of power, as is watching the command being executed or executing it oneself and performing a function of the Other. As institutions evolve, they sometimes forget their origins in the structure of command and control, or rather, forgetting this origin is in their very nature. The command becomes implicit in the statement of what is "understood" to be the story to be believed and circulated. What the institutional subject remembers is how to repeat, command, and obey, how to watch and evaluate and get the job done. Commanding is the "transcendental immanence" of human power, immanent in that it is interior to power, which cannot get anything done without it, but potentially so deeply internal that it becomes something transcendent to itself, something purely categorical. The category of power is universal yet cannot be positivized or materialized in itself. However, the category of command (or categorical imperative) presents itself abstractly as a structure of subjection that, when so internalized that the command to oneself seems to emanate from power itself, becomes indiscernible from the pure differential positivity of will.

The family presents itself as the genealogy and matrix of all institutions, not only as gens bearing the "name of the father," but as the source of institutional *jouissance* in commanding and obeying, and more fundamentally the source of the production of the human child whom it teaches to obey (and command) and to behave automatically and thus prepares for entrance into the disciplinary institutional matrix. This *jouissance* can be called "maternal" in the sense that motherhood has historically undertaken such preparation with some priority. Yet, the series of institutions through which childhood passes are something else, differing from maternity and family in that they invent their own training rituals and rites of passage involving various functions of society, while extending maternity and family into a mechanism for rearing and educating children. The delinquency that grows like a weed in the cracks of discipline thus has two distinct sources: a "paternal" source in that the imbecility of lawful authority tempts it to transgress and permits it to skirt detection; but also a more structural "maternal" source that uses the very form of discipline to bypass the law of the father altogether. More precisely, this perversion of discipline is already the essence of discipline, which is to concern itself not with the desire but with the *jouissance* of the Other (represented by institutional authority), a "power of abuse" (Apollon) that consists in practice driven by a categorical imperative, a superegoic use of language.

This power is invested in the development of will and command at the expense of desire and its questioning, its quest in search of its own truth.

A problem concerning the relation between discipline and delinquency is that the institutional subject experiencing the process, willing ignorance, "does not want to know anything about it." (A certain oblivion and senility form part of the paternal function.) The subject here is obviously not only the delinquent (who may, on the contrary, have a cogent account of what makes him angry, perhaps a story of abuse), it is also the representative of institutions, and of the law itself, who is not able to think about the *jouissance* of the Other that drives both criminality (transgression) and corrective repression and punishment in the name of the law. Perhaps all parties—between whom there is only a difference of degree, because everyone is both disciplined and disciplining, judged and judging—become intensely aware of the hypocrisy of the Other when the *cause of justice* (the distribution of *jouissance*) is in question. When a confrontation erupts, both sides may be aware only of an escalating demand for satisfaction and justice, which easily deteriorates into lust for revenge and exacts the maximum price from the Other. But who makes this demand?

The question takes us to the heart of the problem of the Other. The Other of *jouissance* is the source of a command, the source of power, authority and the voice and look of authority. At its core it contains a threat of violence, "ferocious and obscene" (Lacan), a "paternal superego" or *père jouisseur, Urvater*. This threat is the "content" of another expression of superego, maternal and corrective, punitive or encouraging, disciplinary. The threat of force is implicit, but violence breaks out when the agencies of power are perceived to have lost their authority to evaluate and distribute *jouissance* and their subjects lose self-control, erupting in rage. The *Urvater* is a retroactive projection of infantile narcissism into prehistory, a fantasy of omnipotence, provoked by the experience of impotence. It finds modern theoretical expression in figures such as Nietzsche's Nihilist or Sade's Dolmancé or Saint-Fond, prophet of the Supreme Being of Evil. Superegoic rage would find its determination in the absolute destruction of all paternal, maternal, and institutional authority, of its symbols, its knowledge and memory (all production and recording mechanisms), its signifiers, and its family matrix. This destruction ultimately reaches through "the womb of nature" to the annihilation of all being, a self-annihilation of the memory of life. All of this is enacted in the name of an Other, god or nature, who thereby self-destructs.[2]

The condition of the Other signifying *jouissance* is the emergence of language with its memory into the world. The Other is the source and agency of a power to command, to judge and evaluate life, to hold family or individual accountable for debt and wrongdoing. But once this system of responsibility—inherent in the structure of address—is in place, it becomes possible to imagine it removed and its signifying memory erased. The drive to erasure and oblivion (the death drive) is repressed by the signifying regime, but it remains urgent, motivated by the guilt and debt generated by the fact of language recording *jouissance* and demanding an account of our actions. This memory of the Other being contained virtually in the existence of language, and in life itself, it finally becomes necessary to destroy these and everything in order to erase the signifiers of *jouissance*.[3] Only the perversions (sadism and masochism) openly acknowledge this *jouissance* of power and its dialectic of destruction in their practice; others take measures to remain unaware of its existence or its structural necessity.

The Other is a kind of apotheosis or hypostasis of what makes social order. Its *jouissance* is the social inscription by which every body becomes marked for induction into a fictive and symbolic corporation. The challenge for perversion becomes to embody and represent this power of the Other, this superego, which it interprets and enforces as a will to *jouissance*. In the practice of discipline, it has invented a form of expression that can be purified into an ethical imperative, while retaining the essential elements of a determination of subjectivity that bypasses the question of desire (and meaning) altogether, in favor of a system of internalized rules and commands, a system of judgment.

If life were a certain and determinable value on Earth, its actions and passions would not raise controversy and the demand for judgment. The categories of judgment exude spontaneously from the structure of demand and address, and responsibility—but so also does desire, which addresses the Other as containing possible *jouissance* and giving possible satisfaction, and also addresses the *desire of the Other*, which, coimplicated in the subject's desire, cannot be reduced to any demand or command or category of power.

Even while being overrun by forces and institutions outside its control, the family continues to concentrate in itself the core of the Other, the matrix from which an individual emerges. Its libidinal dialectic and logic continue to possess the institutions that have rein-carnated and transformed it. At its nucleus, as abstracted by Lacan, the family puts into play a dialectic of desire and *jouissance*. This game has very serious stakes, for on its outcome depends the psychic welfare of a child, as well as the possible cure of its parents from the consequences of their own upbringing. As it has evolved into disciplinary institutions, the family function is life under judgment. Continual surveillance and evaluation, graduation and demotion, approval and denial, evolving together with behavioral programming and devices for remote control, tend to rule out any ethical engagement with another's desire. The question of paternity, at the moment its legal definition is being reduced to a function of genetic and financial accountability, deserves to be addressed in relation to the maternal function as they have evolved through their institutional avatars.

Father and mother no longer appear as themselves in institutions that extend the family into education, sick care, athletic and military training, correction, evaluation and judgment, all of which have evolved into separate functional routines or segments. The bureaucratic mind that serves as conscience of the institution and its awareness, inte-grating its perceptions, is maternal or paternal only in its unconscious function of incarnating the desire or *jouissance* of the Other. The mater-nity of this *jouissance* goes back to its origin in the fact of birth, in infant care, toilet training and early disciplining, the mother tongue, song, look, and body language. A series of institutional channels and tributaries recapitulates new disciplinary versions of these *objets a* rem-nants of maternal *jouissance*. In this process, fatherhood too becomes disciplinarized—as the failure of discipline to ground its own proce-dures in positive and universally recognizable values and criteria. Finally, this "ungrounding"[4] is itself the true universal, and that failure is thus constitutive of all institutional *jouissance* (the *jouissance* of the Other), which is founded only on its own power. The institution (espe-cially its university "brain") has no use for this insight or its signifier (the signifier of paternal blindness) and pretends to ground its power in knowledge and efficiency—which means, in practice, in fastidious oblivion and officious denial of its own brutality; whence the envy and suspicion among its subjects that imbeciles are in charge, and the rage for justice that is always threatening to burst into revolt and cancella-tion of the social contract. That rage is the residue of the *jouissance* of the infantile *Urvater* that is suppressed by discipline but symbolized by a paternal metaphor that it refuses to recognize in its own structural incapacity. It is exemplified by the Sadean rage for foundation that destroys every "false" ground until destruction becomes the only ground. Thus, institutional perversion tends to oscillate between cynicism (manipulation of imbecility) and nihilism. In this sad economy, desire would represent an opening of power to something outside its control, which would force it to recognize its own subjectivity in the desire of the Other that cannot be objectively evaluated.

In this context, delinquency runs a virtual "broken line" through the core of discpline. It can mean many things, from a game of cynical perversion to a menace to society from the return of the primal father; but it always potentiates a flicker of desire, a possible "phallus" poking into the institution from outside (or showing through from within). A social body is shaped by cultural techniques for modulating bodies and souls. There are no delinquency training courses in schools; the streets and playgrounds are the nurseries, prisons and reform schools still serve as finishing schools, for budding and evolving reprobates. The Nietzschean question remains unanswered: What type of human being is evolving and being cultivated by a certain mode of social organization?

The Delinquent Family

There are crucial moments of decision—on the part of parents and institutions as well as of the children they rear—determining the course of entire lives, when a certain path is chosen, when a "calling" is registered, or when something goes wrong and the developing individual either goes into systematic failure mode (self-sabotage) or chooses delinquency and criminality (or gets interpellated and identified as a criminal, and internalizes this identity). This channeling occurs not by a mere gradual drifting, but in critical bifurcation events during the process of individuation. Some are "scenes" that recur at critical junctures—where it is determined, for example, that a child is "no good"—singularities recurring in series, perhaps aggravating a problem or intensifying a confrontation each time, pushing the issue ever further toward catastrophe. Or, conversely, something turns things around, an emotional reconciliation, an outside intervention, effecting a change of course. The days of growing up are composed of many series of regular and singular points, gradual developments, but also mutant instants and reversals—sometimes as egregious as a brutal or wrongful punishment or sexual assault, but also including strange phrases or gestures or looks, a scene of breakup and fighting between parents, an adult tantrum witnessed by a child—that change the tenor of relations between parent (or authority) and child. These instants are not necessarily remembered as such, but may instead be internalized as a kind of frozen core, and *repeated* in the etymological sense of a *research* on the part of the child to learn their meaning or to recover a prior happiness that seems lost, without having gained much in knowledge or understanding. In these researches and repetitions consists the real but unconscious learning process of a child, where it learns in particular about *jouissance*, licit and illicit satisfaction, and how to get it (or to protect against the *jouissance* of the Other), how to accrue esteem for victories and evade detection and capture for infractions, how to lie or falsely accuse, how to play innocent or fake remorse—all the tricks of what may turn into narcissistic and cynical complacency or a quest for satisfaction at the margins of permissibility and legality, or else may turn into homicidal and suicidal desperation or escalate into spontaneous revolt against a social order that is felt to be oppressive and condemned as unjust, when it is not merely abused for its leniency and manipulated for corruptibility.

This potential corruptibility of the family, its law, and their institutional extensions and avatars has its source in both paternal and maternal complicity, where blindness and imbecility sometimes mix indistinguishably with conspiracy. But the desire of the child breaks its own path into the "forests of symbols/That observe him with familiar looks" (Baudelaire). Some of its researches lead it to question the rules governing aggression and the eroticism that is internal to it. A true *act* can appear only against the background of the norm it exceeds, the custom or pact it violates, or the signifying or symbolic order it abrogates. A "passage to the act" (*passage à l'acte*) shuts off communication and takes aim at the signifier of the law it intends to outrage or destroy, whereas "acting out" is intelligible as a symptom in the context of transference or a familial situation where it makes sense as the reproduction or reenactment of a repressed, traumatic scene, and a research in search of a satisfactory meaning to human action and passion. The body or the act itself becomes symbolic, symptomatic, conveying a message to or from an unconscious Other supposed to know or retain this meaning. A line of direct communication is opened across time and repressed memory through a series of traumatic moments that

established a symptomatic act or recurring dream as a failed or inadequate response, misinformed and misunderstood. Interpretation
retroactively establishes an untraceable origin for the blanks, repressions, and senseless remnants of an undecipherable secret writing of the
body. At this level, being "bad" or "acting up" is designed to capture
the attention of the parental or symbolic Other.

The imperceptible transition that makes a passage to the act, on
the other hand, exhibits a potentially unmanageable aggression that, in
its beginnings in misbehaving, tantrums, lies, and minor thefts, may
function as transgressive appeal to the Other or call for intervention,
but eventually it aims at structurally perverting the pact with the Other,
the social contract, or dissolving it altogether, disabling the constitutive
function of the word, and thus preparing the destruction of the symbolic order itself. Acting out communicates a message (of trauma or
dissatisfaction), *passage à l'acte* channels and releases a drive directed
at the order of things. They are related in that both rupture the ordinary
train of events, but the symbolic *acte manqué* introduces into the
semiotic-institutional machine a lapsus or malfunction that the other
act turns into a kind of perverse counterinstitution operating within the
official one, unless it spins out of control and into self-destruction, or
forms itself into a "war machine" with the aim of destroying the institution and its signifiers.[5]

Sade brought out the logic—Hegelian, according to Blanchot,
Kantian for Lacan—of the drive attempting to destroy the moral order
of the universe, instituting the self-destruction of desire as represented
by the father, and destruction of institutional *jouissance* itself as representing maternal reproductive nature. However, a potentially suicidal
aggression is implied by any subject's negative reaction to the *jouissance* of the Other. This is because the Other does not ultimately reside
exterior to the self. Only the law of desire opens the self to the outside.
Thus, a *passage à l'acte* aiming to sever the link with the Other is also
necessarily designed to do violence against the subject, not only by
provoking a punishing superegoic reaction (and the superego really
knows how to violate, in the name of the Other), but by eliminating the
symbolic opening to the desire of the Other that constitutes it as subject. The institutionalization of *jouissance* entails the eradication of
subjectivity and the installment of an ethics of totalitarianism.

In 1994, *Frontline* ran a Canadian documentary about "troubled"
or "problem" children and adolescents, "The Trouble with Evan," that

clarifies the distinction between symbolic act and drive. Evan has already crossed the line from "getting in trouble" and skipping school to acts of theft and setting fires that foreshadow a definite break with civil order. But the real "trouble with Evan," as it turns out, perhaps predictibly, is with the eleven-year-old's abusive and threatening parents. The father (stepfather), especially, curses Evan and threatens him, and both accuse him, sometimes wrongfully, of lying and stealing, and issue harsh and desperate ultimatums. Finally, at his wit's end, the father dissolves all parental relation and implicit contract with Evan, banishing him from the family and announcing that he will be excluded from all functions, including meals. What is evident from this exceptional and troubling documentary (the family permitted a surveillance camera and microphone to be installed in their home) is that what is at stake in Evan's "acting out" and its escalation to *passages à l'acte* is his very membership in society, his participation in a symbolic order and social bond. His acts are designed to test the limits of that order and "family bond" and to provoke an explicit confirmation of his suspicion that he does not belong there (or anywhere). It appears that the parents, perhaps in order to provide an illusory focus to their own problematic lives and destructive relationship (they exist in intensive "co-dependency": since her attempted suicide, he has custody of her two children by a previous marriage, Evan and his younger sister), have targeted Evan and simplified their situation by imagining him to be their real problem. They have somehow chosen him for "sacrifice" and are systematically training him for delinquency and more (he has conscious, express fantasies of killing his stepfather). Finally, in part as a result of the documentary, Evan and his sister were provisionally removed from parental custody to foster homes.

The curses, threats, and insults shouted into Evan's face already strain the limits of the symbolic function and span its threshold to the asocial act. Evan takes the abuse in perfect silence, out of fear and to forestall any escalation to physical attack, but also because the very mediating or tempering function of language has been abridged. Language transforms violence into speech (for example, complaint or accusation), but the drive infuses speech with aggressivity. The notorious "silence of the death drive" indicates a fundamental hostility to speech and its significations on the part of feelings that are blocked and inarticulate or inexpressible, or that (like the death wish against the stepfather) are forbidden and foreclosed from symbolic expression. The father's florid rage and the son's solemn fury (harboring impulses to commit arson and murder) both give evidence of having "had it" (as the father says) with each other and with negotiation as, anticipating assault, each preemptively fantasizes finishing the other off before it's too late.[6] Thus, each receives his own imaginary message from the other in inverted form and reflects the signal back to his adversary. One day the unresolved and potentially deadly contest may be replayed between Evan as adult and a new counterpart, perhaps his own son, whom he will figure threatening him as he was threatened by his detested parent.

The duel between Evan and his stepfather is obviously a relationship that threatens to spin out of control, untempered by any symbolic mediation. It thus brings out a failure of paternal function—one of the most complex concepts of Lacanian theory, and its symbolic nexus. Even Woman is one of the "Names of the Father"; the Name is detached from biological sex and "natural" function.

We know that the Father stands for some mediation between Earth and sky, or between god and nature, a symbolic power consisting in a ritual of separation and communication between the power of nature as incarnated in the human family and tribe, a power of reproduction and physical existence, fertility, embodied in maternal function; and a transcendental power invested in the word, the law, a "transbiological"[7] libido that makes up for the eventual (but immemorial) loss of natural and maternal narcissism. This scene of mediation is replayed every time an infant is inducted into childhood, into the order of social and linguistic interaction. It consists in a deflection of the demand for enjoyment of maternal love, into another kind of pathway, a passage by way of the desire of the Other that is represented by the Father, because fatherhood makes a spontaneous and structural intervention into the relation between mother and child in the human family. This can happen at the moment of birth, when a child is handed to its father for confirmation or symbolic recognition. He intervenes repeatedly to sever their attachment and reground the child's desire (or constitute it for the first time) in the language of the law, universalized as incest prohibition. It is in this way that a space of forbidden fantasy is opened up behind the law against enacting it. At this level, the function of the father is to "rescue" mother and child each from the other and from the Other constituted by maternity itself as a potentially total institution (in the absence of the father) in which every member is at the mercy of the other. No one fully understands this complex language of the law, deployed in a drama in which humans act as living signs. The father does not know all that he does: he stutters, stumbles but learns to "limp," until limping itself and being lame become part of the myth of the father. This slight failure of function makes it possible for desire to find enjoyment in unexpected places, where the father turns a blind eye.[8]

The father who looks the other way upholds the law without seeing its violation. This is already an element of the pact between father and son. Evan, however, is both unsupervised and under constant surveillance, identified as "trouble" and always about to be banished. He is out of control; but mostly he is subject to continual interrogation and accusation. Between Evan and his stepfather, the symbolic relation has reduced itself to an exchange of threats. If a law can be invented or imagined, it can be challenged, trangressed, even abolished. Who first threatened to abolish the law in Evan's case? In any case, there is no telling who is responsible anymore, nor who is calling the shots, for although it is certain that a boy is no physical match for his father, the battle here is fought out on symbolic and linguistic ground where Evan, who is of above-average intelligence, can begin to outmaneuver his father. The father recognizes this, knows he is being mocked and thwarted (while his wife sits silent and confused or joins in yelling), and wants to turn the boy out of doors for good. Their struggle calls the symbolic pact into question, always recurring at its limit where the father is about to put his son out the door or the son about to pick up a weapon against his father. It is clear that the father has lost control of the situation. How did this come about?

Let us posit that the most primordial function of the Father in relation to his son would be to substitute for force and rivalry a word or pact, *to say no to the aggression of the drive*—but first of all, *to his own potential violence against his family* (acting as perverted authoritarian *Urvater* or *père jouisseur*). The law is founded by a word he also stands beneath. Thus, although he embodies the threat of violence (even in the name of the law), he is always at the same time under restraint by his own paternal function, which says no. The father is divided: one part of him is tempted to use force to get satisfaction, retain control, and terrorize others—often in the name of his paternal authority; but the other part speaks from beyond this impulse, in the Name of the Father he is supposed to represent on Earth. On the one hand, he could be the perverse *père jouisseur* or authoritarian sadist who can have his way or pervert the law because he is physically stronger; on the other, he represents the law to which he himself is subject, and is "castrated" by this self-transcendence. At the same time, by restricting his own *jouissance* (and violence) in the name of law, he can allow his child a margin of freedom for self-assertion, even freedom to be "bad." Evan's father is obviously of the humiliated and reactive, authoritarian type, frustrated and enraged by a more fundamental impotence, and he does not even know how to turn a blind eye and limp.

Evan and his father do not simply mirror each other's lack of self-control. In the father, the paternal function has broken down to the point that rage is all that is left to represent the law. Somehow the law has failed while the superego, expanding without limit, acquires reinforcements from the energies it suppresses, like a conquering army conscripting forces from the vanquished population. Or it can become like the Los Angeles police force beating Rodney King in the name of the law while, according to its rules of engagement and pacification, representing him to be "in control" (that their violence is really just his violence put in check, and if he stops moving they will stop "restraining" him). When he plays dead, they kick him and prod him, provoking a reaction. It is this violence in the name of the law and provocation of rebellion that exemplifies the potential viciousness of a superego in which the drive to repress and punish becomes indistinguishable from sheer aggression.

There is a zone of indiscernibility between surplus repression of transgressive drive and a *passage à l'acte* by the superego itself representing the law—"as misunderstood" (Lacan). Within this threshold the two, as rivals for power, become interchangeable. Consider the dynamics of the vigilante posse or its extension into a mob. The Rosemont massacre, Florida, 1924: a white posse, hunting a black man accused of raping a white woman, turned into a lynch mob, which then rioted and burned its way through a "colored" town, killing some forty people. This violence was enacted in retribution, in the name of vengeance. The superego's command, *Jouis!*, becomes a perverted law: "We want justice!" becomes "String 'em up!" This murderous aggression in the name of the law incarnates a perverse or group-psychotic *jouissance* of the Other.

The true purpose of punishment is only partly correction. It is *jouissance* in an aggression turned against those who are accused or convicted of violating norms or laws of the community. When asked sixty years later why he thought the mob went on such a rampage of burning and killing that night (it turned out that the perpetrator was probably an escaped convict, not the man they went after), one eyewitness answered: "It was just satisfaction, I guess."[9]

Satisfaction in the name of the Other (in this case, the sanctity of Woman's chastity is evoked implicitly), a ritual of *jouissance, jouissance of the Other*. Between acting perversely in the name of the law and acting to deny or destroy the law, there is only a reversal of symbolic identity. That is one of the Sadean arguments for anarchy. The perverse appeal to the Other's *jouissance* implies a knowledge of "natural right" as obstructed by "arbitrary" law. It also means a mastery of the signifiers and discourse of the Other adequate for rhetorically manipulating subjects who are not under direct command. The dialectic of revolution might be seen in the passage from perverse knowledge to the destruction of the signifier of that law without foundation (a cycle that continues to regenerate itself).

On the other hand, any appeal to what is right is an invocation of the Other as *opening to an ethical relation*. This opening to the desire of the Other is precisely what is symbolized by the arbitrariness—or, really, the contingency—of the signifier. And precisely because of the virtual arbitrariness concealed by the historical contingency of "phallic law," this law without foundation, eradicated during revolution, becomes an ethics that evolves freely in search of its own foundation. Of course, revolutionaries tend to react to perceived injustice, which contains a radically symbolic moment, by an eruption of aggression whose aim is overdetermined by the history of social relations, for example, between police and community. The "L.A. Riot" of 1992— the largest and most intense eruption of suppressed aggression in U.S. history since the 1960s—broke out the moment the jury returned a not-guilty verdict exculpating the officers who brutalized Rodney King. It is this obscure dimension of judgment that introduces a wild card into the play of social forces. In fact, the problem of justice is inseparable from that of the *jouissance* it judges and evaluates.

The passage to the act is by no means a return to the wild or savage state. Whether it is the violence of police or prison guards or a mob coming unleashed from the paternal law in the name of right, or even a criminal infraction, the outburst is aimed first at the rule of law insofar as the rule or its enforcement is felt to be unfair, misrepresenting the true Law—until the validity of any law, and Law itself, is questioned and denied. The vigilante mob cannot wait for justice that is too slow and passionless and may even let the guilty go free on a technicality or for insufficient evidence. "We know better!" The rioting mob too perceives injustice in the byzantine mannerisms of the court system (or in the distribution of justice and rights) and decides to settle matters in its own way. In this regard, lynch mob and riot mob are indistinguishable: both have abrogated the paternal function that says no to its own immediate gratification by aggression and stands for the passage through the desire of the Other. Both enact the *jouissance* of the Other in their drive for just satisfaction. They can touch off a revolt, or become a revolution.[10]

Another part of paternal function, then—one that is shared by the maternal—is to distribute the rewards of symbolic recognition, the lawful enjoyment of satisfaction (what is part of "phallic" *jouissance*). It is thus also to restrain the actual father (and then son) incarnating the symbolic function from enjoying unbridled power. This function of self-restraint implies a respect for the desire of the Other (for example, his wife or son). But the family's procedures of evaluation and distribution, like those of its institutional avatars, may be perceived as lame, or systematically unfair and prejudiced. Then the paternal function itself may come into question in a revolutionary way, or be skipped altogether as unnecessary in a perversional leap to immediate social gratification.

Narcissistic Satisfaction in the Father's Failure

The problem of justice today (as ever) is just the problem of what to do about *jouissance*. In *Civilization and Its Discontents*, Freud reminds his civilized contemporaries that they are all getting sick of it—that is, of not getting any, or not enough, or not the right quality or intensity of satisfaction. And sick of the Other, whose "behavior" (*jouissance*) is getting out of control. In undergoing civilization, the drives have been so constrained and domesticated that the main enjoyment is achieved in moral "reaction formations" directed at ferreting out and suppressing the real (forbidden) Thing wherever it appears, with aesthetic practice dispersing the remnants of intensity into symbolic sublimations. In 1930, the moral war of extermination against "savage" drives seems at least theoretically completed, yet not only is uneasiness and dissatisfaction growing in spite of increased leisures and amenities, but the capacity for genocide and self-destruction is evolving to alarming proportions.

What is the relation between the suppression of a supposed "natural" spontaneous aggression and the ever more gruesome eruptions of a collective death drive? Is aggression a drive unto itself or a component of the libidinal drives?

Lacan advanced comprehension of the drive's narcissistic modeling by exhibiting an ego reflected into its image and placing this double at the illusory focal point of the object (so that self-aggression and murder can become confused in the image-object), and by showing the ego-object sown together evolving with the subject in a chamber of fantasy, seeking a treasure trove guarded by a signifier-dragon of Death, a disguised castration scene folded into a pocket of consciousness of a subject rendered thereby "aspheric."[11] In effect, the object of the drive being the lost treasure of primary narcissism (or primal libido, instinct of immortality driven unconscious, into fantasy), its perverse or revolutionary aim is erasure of a transcendental Signifier guarding the gateway of passage to the womb and unconsciousness (of death), thus preventing closure of the ego within a sphere of imaginary satisfaction. In practice, perversion would aim to silence any call to the father to defend against the *jouissance* of the Other, and to deny that our speech, and existence as speaking beings, implies such a passage through the indeterminacy of ethical relation. This aim of liberation from the Signifier holding the subject open to the desire of the Other can manifest itself by an obsession with rivals for prestige or reward, or by possession of a jealously guarded object fantasized to exude the power of salvation. As Freud said, neurotics prefer the "cure by love" to analysis; but where there is no satisfaction to be had, many prefer a cure by hate. The object of the drive becomes the oblivion to be had by the erasure of *Dasein*.

The signifiers of indeterminacy—of death and fatherhood—hold the subject open to the Other and desire. Thus, rivalry for possession and aggressive drive, but also the maternal matrix of institutions that channel this *jouissance* and redirect these "powers of abuse," can become mediated by recognition and respect of the Other's desire. The word (*parole*) symbolized by the Name of the Father incarnates this respect. Like perversion and racism, discipline and criminality are codesigned to prove this passage through symbolic recognition of desire unnecessary. They achieve this proof by violating the Other in a ritual mimicking erasure of the paternal signifier, as reminder of the default of the Other (the castration of the mother), which they refuse to transmute into recognition of the Other's desire.

Giving rigor to the "borderline" diagnosis, Lacan's topology of asphericity—the impossibility of the libido-object's being incorporated within the subject to complete it (as in love)—clarifies the function of the paternal signifier as guardian against incest and abusive *jouissance*. In effect, the borderline must fix the object somehow on the periphery between interior and exterior, and can neither take it in to be loved, thus risking internal damage (being hurt or "poisoned"), nor let it escape. The imperative is not to destroy but to control the other that was imagined to make the subject complete but now threatens to manifest a real desire or to escape. The object must be kept at a safe distance so as not to usurp the subject's personality and self-identity. The function of the Father is to represent another kind of distance, the psychic balance of desire and respect that precisely permits intimacy. It is true that this desire is mediated by the signifier of death and transcendent Law, but this is because the ethics of desire demands that its law be enforced to the limit (where the law is surpassed only by intellectual love).[12] Racism and institutional perversion accentuate the temptation in love or in parental narcissism to shape the other into a misrecognized double of oneself used to sustain the passion of ignorance and to blot out the reality of a limited existence. The other, outside the law, becomes a savior or, when the organization of narcissistic *jouissance* breaks down and the cry for inquest and judgment is heard, a scapegoat.

In his early studies of paranoid acts of "self-punishment"—especially the Aimée case, in which a fan stalked and knife-attacked a star actress when her "complaints" went unanswered—Lacan focused on the "systematic *méconnaissance*" that makes the subject mistake the turmoil of her own soul for an effect of the other's persecution. The ego, after all, is an imaginary function established through identification, a process of miming and masking. Consequently, the resulting identity is alienable—in fact, is alienation in its essence. Why should an enthusiastic and adoring fan not demand some satisfaction, some *recognition* in return, from her idol who would not be what she is today if it weren't for her special admirer? In the film *King of Comedy*, late-night talk star "Jerry" is kidnapped by his two greatest admirers. One wants to *be* (replace) Jerry; the other apparently wants to *have* (sexually possess) him. After all, what is the harm when it's all a joke? And who does the Jerry identity really belong to anyway? When we say that the borderline lacks boundaries or confuses himself with his objects, we are assuming the stable subsistence of a fixed term of self-identity—which is exactly what our very process of commodity development, career modulation, and self-marketing have abolished (even as myth). Identity goes into modulation, continual metamorphosis, perpetually spinning at the edge of control.

Hence, again the significance of the Name of the Father is asserted, as corollary to the distributive function of apportioning *jouissance* on behalf of a symbolic community (whose respect the leader enjoys), here guaranteeing a fixed point of reference in assigning a name and identity that otherwise threaten to dissolve into FBI and credit files, or resolve into genetic printouts. Abrogation of that authority of word and name unleashes the Aimées and other imaginary clones into their acts. The late-late adolescent who wants to be Jerry, Rupert Pupkin, has entirely imaginarized the symbolic function. His actual identity has become a function of the fantasy life he plays out and earnestly practices in his basement, over the noise of his mother's calling, which fails to rupture his dream-interview scenes fitted out with cardboard figures. The *passage à l'acte* displaces the existing order of identities to install him in the symbolic position he has imagined and trained for and that he feels is ready-made for him. It is not primarily a case of emulative rivalry but points to the missing symbolic function of distributing earned and lawful *jouissance*. Rupert has not the slightest regard for the system of actual legal identities authorizing some to enjoy special fruits of privilege and power. He knows that he can very well substitute for the other and claim his identity by usurping his personality and role. The three women in his life (there are no male friends, only his imaginary alter ego, Jerry)—his mother, his accomplice, and his quasi girlfriend—all have some interest in tolerating his pretenses and delusions (of which they seem more or less aware). The fourth woman he encounters incarnates the law. She is one of Jerry's producers, who listens to Rupert's pitch to be a guest on the show and politely rejects his tape promoting his "act," then throws him out when he becomes a nuisance. Her rejection—a clear message from the symbolic Other—hardly fazes him; it only hardens his resolve to enact the kidnapping scenario. Finally, when he meets the FBI to negotiate the ransom for Jerry, his demand is to replace Jerry on the show that night if they ever want to see the host star alive again. How can they refuse? Their hands are tied by the law of the signifier (in a comic version of self-suppression of paternal violence) that forbids them to sacrifice the public they are supposed to defend in order to nab or punish even a capital offender.

As for Jerry, it seems that Rupert does not know what to make of him. It has never occurred to him that Jerry as a person could be deserving of respect because all his adolescent life has been spent imagining *himself* to be Jerry. The fact is that the function of the Father—to mediate the passage into action—could not possibly be performed by anyone in the film except Rupert himself, but his will to *jouissance* is powerful enough to overcome any scruples he might have about his own dishonesty and disrespect. Abrogation of the word is accented by the act of taping Jerry's mouth shut. The failure of the paternal function thus verges on "foreclosure" (Lacan's term for a kind of prior annulment), whence it yields to the mirror play of confidence games and a cacophony of false claims and psychotic pretensions.[13]

The paternal function is not an act of force or power, nor an intimidation, nor reverence of the lesser for the greater or divine power. In the absence of theocratic mediation, the man of violence or warrior is either bound by the power of capital (bonds he may break and master in turn, in a fascist or war economy) or undergoes self-restraint. Power can be restricted only by a greater power, force yields only to greater force. But the symbolic force of the paternal "no" is of another order.

Destruction of the Symbolic Family as Unconscious Metaphysics of Perversion

The relation between Judaism and Christianity continually reenacts a drama structured by the family dynamics of perversion, revolution, and the signifier of the father's law. Its obscure and obscene denouement, the most horrifying crime and *passage à l'acte* in human history, was named the Holocaust, signifying a burnt offering sacrificed to divinity. Lacan likens the Holocaust to a sacrifice, but the question is, sacrifice of what and for what purpose? From our perspective, it would be a mistake merely to identify the "Jew" with the Lacanian *objet a*—as Lacan appears to do.[14] Of course, if the paradigm of sacrifice is correct, the victims of the Holocaust do embody the offering of *jouissance* (embodied in the *objet a*) to the Other, the "dark god" of the Nazi imaginary. However, at the extreme limit of a true dialectic of *jouissance*, it is the paternal function itself, represented by the Jews, the people of the law of the father, that is the real target of Nazi rage. Its aim is to erase the memory of the signifier along with the paternal law symbolizing self-restraint, which is the true enemy and the obstacle to Nazi wilding and superegoic nonstop *jouissance*. Thus, the Holocaust is a perverse *imaginary* fulfillment of the *symbolic* murder of the Father initiated during the Enlightenment. The institution of the death camps effects a bizarre fusion of perverse discipline with the infantile father of rage, the two bonded in denial of symbolic fatherhood with its law of desire opening the subject to the Other.

For the Western and Christian imagination, the Jewish people represent the Law. They are chosen by God to hear the Word, but what they hear and understand is Law. Yet, what is law to us today? Is the law of the father even understood? It is well known that the Akedah of Abraham symbolically eliminates human sacrifice from the ancient world and institutes the law of the covenant, the symbolic pact with the Other. But what does this mean in terms of desire and *jouissance*? God calls to Abraham and commands him to offer his son as a burnt offering. But the hand of the father is halted, in the act of immolating his son, by the voice of the angel of the Lord. A sacrifice is offered to satisfy the demand of the Other, of divinity. It is not the human lust for violence that is in question but the divine demand for satisfaction. When Abraham is restrained by the voice of God, it is the divine superego holding back its own command to *jouir*. God's desire can no longer be satisfied by human sacrifice. His desire becomes that of an Other that cannot be known through divination or revealed through a demand for *jouissance*. The desire of the Other, and the Other itself, now emerges as pure lack. Of course, what supplies the understanding of this desire is knowledge of God's will in the form of law. There is a covenant. God will "multiply the seed" of Abraham "as the stars of the heaven" for having heeded his command to sacrifice his only son. The desire of the father is pronounced in this covenant; Abraham is determined to be the "father of many nations"—that is his desire *as father*, as his wife's is to bear children. Thus, the human anxiety about death and contingency becomes alleviated by the promise of futurity. This future is not genetic or personal, it is symbolic and tribal. By keeping the law and the covenant, the people are creating a symbolic transcendence, a transmortal, transcendental function. The law itself incarnates immortality, being the only hypostasis, the only certain revelation of divinity (God's direct communication to the prophets is never overheard and verified). The people must keep themselves together as a human family by keeping the law of God represented by the father. But this law, in becoming a prohibition against serving the *jouissance* of the Other with human sacrifice, now potentially becomes a law respecting desire—that of the human friend and stranger as well as God's—as something Other.

Of course, the way is now prepared as well for law to be interiorized in subjectivity as responsibility and guilt, a relation of severity with oneself. This relation, diagnosed by Freud as a malaise of culture, must be tempered by the paternal function in order for the superego (the *jouissance* of the Other) not to become aggravated by the dissatisfaction of an ego tormented by guilty impulses feeding on moral repression. What is crucial in this regard is that in the relation with oneself, too, desire shows itself as a search for satisfaction that implies a sustained self-questioning irreducible to the interrogations of a guilty conscience.

Thus, we perceive a further complication and difficulty. If the ethical function of the father is to refrain from violating his family, does not the new internalized superego, instantiating the missing *jouissance* of the Other in the command to *jouir*, still feed on the father's self-repression? What is the true difference between the father's self-restraint of his own *jouissance* in refraining from tyrannizing over (violating) his human family, and the superego that feeds off the repressions it exacts from the ego to curb the id, and uses this fuel to torment the father as unable to satisfy the desire of the Other? It is the difference of desire, the *real of desire*. In order to free itself from the *jouissance* of the Other, it is inescapable that the paternal function must "castrate" the superego. Thus, law is the true and originary self-castration. The real struggle is between the law and its own executive agency, the hand of justice with its "terrible swift sword," which turns against the subject when there is nothing else to sacrifice, unless it can understand that the Other is not making a demand for suffering. The superego organizes the *jouissance* of the Other, of the law misunderstood as injunction to punish, to satisfy an Other angered by human trespasses. But the true law refuses to represent the Other as will or demand. Rather, the Name of the Father stands for the *desire* of the Other—not just the father's desire for children to inherit his name, but a desire that is unknown to him; for he is unconscious of its meaning, this discourse of the Other. Thus, he stands for that unconscious knowledge, as he stands for the desire that is not contained or determined by any positive knowledge but creates itself and holds itself open to an Other.

And yet, the logic of perversion seems to dictate the course of history and the creativity of institutions. It is as though the relations between the Christian church and the Jewish Name of the Father had foreshadowed or served as rehearsal for the later displacement of God by the total institution, as though desire were incapable of sustaining itself before the will to know and to control the reproduction of knowledge and its living signs, bodies deployed in the immanent transcendence of power. The perversion of this desire is so easily accomplished (it constitutes the metaphysical logic of history) because learning to enjoy repression is what the superego and its disciplinary avatars are all about, and creativity has never been its forte. Unable to think for itself or to respond to the desire of the Other, it has, however, created for humankind a reactive second nature, consisting in a system of total and familiar institutions that realize a systematic perversion of the law of desire. In the ethical logic of Kant, the internal tension of the process comes to a head in confronting a metaphysic of the will with a dialectic of desire. This logic led Kant to posit a categorical imperative as a purification of the superego function; paradoxically, it would realize the institutionalization of desire by referring itself to no revealed law or will of the Other, no positive prescriptions or injunctions, only a moral law positing nothing beyond its own necessity: let there be a universal legislation on Earth, good for all humankind. The theoretical equivalence of desire and *jouissance* is thereby officially established and can be put into historical practice.

In his own analysis and deduction of the categorical imperative, Kant argues that it merely enunciates a compulsory self-legislation purified of any reference to impulse, pleasure, drive, or nature. But why have any moral imperative? What is wrong with impulse and "pathological" desire? The basic problem is not that these are not moral or good, or that the good is indeterminable, it is (as Spinoza said) that they mean enslavement to passion, sad affects, hatred and ignorance, and a love wallowing in uncured narcissism. The superegoic compulsion to suppress these pathological motifs rationalizes and justifies itself by claiming to purify desire, to realize human freedom by liberating the human subject finally from both the ancient bloodlust and the modern "pathological impulses" with their appeal to nature and natural right. Of course, natural right tends to be open to perverse (today, scientific) representation. However, the Kantian law does not actually rule out natural right, and not because it cannot be defined or discovered with scientific objectivity. But human nature is finally not determinable as an object of possible knowledge, precisely because it folds into itself an ethical relation, a language of call and response to others, and a freedom to express desire and to hear and witness and interpret the desire of the others.

Kant believes that he is instituting this law of pure and free desire with the imperative to *give the law to human nature* (this is the sense of an *allgemeine Gesetzgebung*).[15] However, it is evident, as Lacan showed, that this self-legislation can serve (especially during revolutions, when the rule of law gives way) as license for the superego to command total satisfaction of the moral law, which is not the law of desire that limps, but a demand for compliance. Thus, with the theoretical elimination of the father's law in favor of a pure signifier of obedience (compulsory behavior determined by "rational" deliberation), the way is cleared for ethical programming by a set of bureaucratic rules and functions authorizing an already operational, implicit, and unconscious process of normalization.

Kantian morality sets Reason as the highest arbiter of nature or will. Thus, contrary to Adorno's thesis on Enlightenment, it is not Reason that becomes the instrument of will in Kant. Clearly, will is not in command, for it must submit and conform to its own Good Form—it is a will that always listens to Reason, which *gives the law to the drive* and *subjects the will* as it disciplines human nature. This is called a "self"-legislation, but Reason, represented by a pure signifying function whose content is the drive in action, is the Self in command of the self. It is this splitting of self that Lacan calls a subject, "represented by a signifier." In maintaining this divided structure of "free will" even with the apotheosis of the signifier, Kant thought to maintain and purify the law of desire and subjectivity. But the signifier in its pure positivity (Reason) commanding the will is not the desiring law, it is a superego that has installed itself as rational morality inside the command and control function determining the subject in its acts. It is true that the categorical imperative maintains the indeterminacy of true desire by eliminating any "phenomenal" content to the law and becoming a pure form of expression in the imperative mode (freedom as rational self-determination). But it sacrifices the essential, the *opening to the Other* in which desire consists.[16] In the cause of justice (the rational distribution of rewards and punishments), and with the intention of eliminating unfair *jouissance* and dissatisfaction (symbolized by the patriarchal regime of inequality), Kant rationally justifies the institutionalization of the superego as differential will determining the behavior of the ego-individual.

As the perverse or revolutionary dialectic progresses, the signifying memory of *jouissance*, as represented by the institution of inequality symbolized by the Name of the Father, and then, in its turn, by the reproductive body of maternal institutions, becomes the object of transgressive or destructive drive. To understand this dialectic, it is necessary to realize that the Other is split within itself. Let us say that in the Western tradition one part of the Other is represented by God the Father, and the other part by Satan, God's ego or alter ego. God's (alter) ego is the personification of his pride and jealousy, his mirror double. Satan is God's "temptation," the jealous paranoia of the ancient Father of *jouissance* (number One)—who reappears continually as a superegoic emanation that taunts and pushes God and goads him to passage into action. As tempter, the satanic God demanded from Abraham the sacrifice of Isaac. It drove God to take away all happiness from Job, to destroy his life in order to test his loyalty.

What, then, motivates God to limit his own satisfaction? What brings it about (and this is the ultimate significance of law) that God himself is subordinate to the law that castrates even him and keeps him from achieving total satisfaction? For this is the significance of the famous arbitrations the Jews carry on with their God. Abraham negotiates the number of righteous men required to spare Sodom from destruction: "but Abraham stood yet before the Lord.... Shall not the Judge of all the earth do right?" (Gen. 18: 22–25). God himself is in principle subject to a right and a wrong that can be enunciated but not objectified. He becomes subject to the principle of moral Reason. But isn't the last temptation of God precisely to enforce this principle itself without limit? To destroy humanity because he is jealous, to destroy nature because it is too productive and creates something beyond good and evil? Finally, to destroy the signifier of right and wrong and achieve peace at last, in a final and total oblivion?

As a passage into action, *total jouissance* would consist in erasing all memory and history, achieving true and absolute unconsciousness. It means destruction of the signifier as memory exterior to consciousness—or interiorized as self-consciousness—and mind, and brain. Total *jouissance* means going (totally) unconscious. *Law is the signifier that prohibits the totalization of jouissance*; hence the act becomes the enemy of law, as represented by the Name of the Father, and its *jouis-sance* is the erasure of signifying memory. A *passage à l'acte* is an act that violates the social pact and tends toward destruction of memory or life or, at the limit, totally destroying all memory of life itself. Yet, it derives its force from the human subject's urge to recover an innocence imagined lost to law and reason, to self-consciousness and awareness of the inevitability of death.

What is it that moves God to stop the *jouissance* of the Other? The history of civilization reaches back beyond memory to a mythic threshold, where patriarchal order is instituted by the repression of chthonic or subterranean powers—whose return as the repressed furies of the Mother made them dreadful for the ancient patriarchs to contemplate. After the removal of the law of the father, it is the suppressed forces of femininity that break through the maternal reproductive-disciplinary regime as it comes into question in its turn.[17] These forces are now growing and expressing themselves, but what do they "signify"? Is it the emergence of an Other *jouissance*, no longer the *jouissance* of the Other, but "the love of the Other"?[18]

What would be the position of the father in this event? The father is not just a function representing law and self-restraint. Only the father—because of his affinity with violence and law—can give to his daughter a *sign of love*, or a signifier not of law or *jouissance* but of love.[19] The gift of this sign is his act of paternity that links father and daughter, and is no longer a function, nor perhaps even a signifier, but a gift of "love without limit" (Lacan), outside the law. It is the index or intuition, perhaps, of an *amor intellectualis*, outside the bounding dialectic of law and *jouissance*, a father's Other satisfaction.

Notes

1. Willy Apollon, "Nouveaux visages et nouvelle identité du racisme" (unpublished). In what follows, this and other essays by Apollon provided theoretical orientation and guidance toward understanding the problem of the desire and *jouissance* of the Other.
2. The perversion and extirpation of maternity following the beheading of the father is a necessary consequence of the dialectic of Sadean revolution. The father's humiliation is followed by a violation of the mother in an eruption of the long-suppressed primal father of terror who now triumphantly reasserts the law of *jouissance*, in the form of a command to rape and murder. See Maurice Blanchot's essay on Sade in *Philosophy in the Bedroom* (New York: Grove Press, 1965) and Pierre Klossowski, *Sade mon prochain* (Paris: Seuil, 1967).
3. See Jacques Lacan, *L'éthique de la psychanalyse* (Paris: Seuil, 1986), 243–56.

4. See Willy Apollon, Danielle Bergeron, and Lucie Cantin, *Traiter la psychose* (Quebec: Groupe interdisciplinaire Freudien de recherches et d'interventions cliniques, 1990).

5. See Gilles Deleuze and Félix Guattari, *A Thousand Plateaus: Capitalism and Schizophrenia*, trans. Brian Massumi (Minneapolis: University of Minnesota Press, 1987).

6. Compare the defense in the Menendez case, parodied (as "imperfect self-defense") by Mark Leyner in the *New Republic*, March 1994.

7. Jacques Lacan, *Les quatre concepts fondamentaux de la psychanalyse* (Paris: Seuil, 1973), 224.

8. Michel Sylvestre, *Demain la psychanalyse* (Paris: Navarin, 1987).

9. From *60 Minutes*, a CBS news magazine, first broadcast 1984; rebroadcast 1994.

10. In the 1980s, the failure of social justice to distribute *jouissance* in fairness and without hypocrisy was symbolized by the injunction to "just say no" (to drugs and sex) that issued from the mouth of the first lady of a president who represented "deregulation" of the capitalist vector of superexploitation. Nike ("victory"), knowing the true score, implicitly endorsed the latter with its motto: "Just do it!"

11. On the *asphère*, see Jacques Lacan, "L'Étourdit," *Scilicet* 4 (1973): 5–52.

12. Lacan, *Les quatre concepts*, 247–48.

13. Here would be the place to open a discussion with the theses of Thomas Szasz. Unfortunately, Szasz weakens his otherwise forceful critique of the "insanity" defense by failing to distinquish fakery from psychosis and by glossing over the problems of belief, delusion, and self-deception, as though these were irrelevant to the question of responsibility. See Thomas Szasz, *Insanity* (New York: John Wiley and Sons, 1990).

14. In *Les quatre concepts fondamentaux*, 246–47. I have written on some aspects of this problem in "Jesus Christ, Holocaust: Fabulation of the Jews in Christian and Nazi History," *Copyright* 1 (1987).

15. Here I am conceding somewhat the Hegelian interpretation of legislation as a negative dialectic and education as "eradicating nature" in the child. The categorical imperative commands, "Always act in such a way that the maxim of your will could also serve as the principle of a universal legislation." It is on the way to becoming indistinguishable from the "moral" imperative of capital: always pay your debts (in a timely fashion). However, the first responsibility (and ethics) of freedom is still to create, to help fashion a rational society, capable of becoming free.

16. Kant attempted to make up for this short-circuiting of desire by deducing a law of respect ("always treat the other, the human person, as an end, not as a means"). But because engagement with the other's desire is omitted and cannot be legislated anyway, this formal respect sacrifices unpredictability and any sense of play or creativity, hardening into correct behavior and good manners.

17. Such a breakthrough or breakout of uncontrolled femininity threatened to overwhelm the moral resources of the French Revolution. See Lynn Hunt, *The Family Romance of the French Revolution* (Berkeley: University of California Press, 1992).

18. See Lucie Cantin, "Femininity: From Passion to an Ethics of the Impossible," *Topoi* 12:2 (1993): 127–36. Of Teresa of Avila, Cantin writes: "What was meaningless takes its significance in love. All the manifestations of jouissance are, in a way, signs from God, which guarantee the linking of jouissance to the signifier of the love of the Other for her. . . . It is the truth of that love that is being made visible in her body in the form of raptures and ecstasies" (134).

19. Willy Apollon, "Four Seasons in Femininity or *Four Men in a Woman's Life*," *Topoi* 12:2 (1993): 101–15.

Master Betty, Bettymania

THAT QUEER STAGE OF YOUTH

Julie Carlson

An empire occupied by a boy of thirteen!
The history of the world furnishes not a similar example.
— *Courier*, December 3, 1804

William Henry West Betty (1791–1874)—variously known as Master Betty, the Infant Roscius, the Young Roscius—took the London stage by storm in December 1804 at the age of thirteen. This "child of nature" and "wonder of the age," who earned more during his first season on the stage than star patent theater actors earned during their entire careers, provides an unprecedented look at the queering of Shakespeare, the stage, and youth in early nineteenth-century England and discourses of Romanticism.[1] Apparently, everyone got into the act. Both men and women were transported by his appearance even as they ruined theirs to attain seats at his sellout performances;[2] William Pitt allegedly adjourned the House of Commons so that ministers could see Master Betty as Hamlet;[3] the king and queen as well as "persons of fashion" everywhere sought audiences with him;[4] even "Buonaparte and the war" were "eclipsed" in and by press accounts of him.[5] Betty's phenomenal success turns on his representations of male tragic heroes, especially Shakespeare's, in all the beauty and naturalness of youth, and thus invites reflection on the polymorphous and pedophilic appeal of theater. The brevity of his success—two seasons on the London stage— suggests how quickly publics turn on actors when the sexuality of youth becomes public rather than remaining latent. The Master Betty phenomenon, then, constitutes an early-nineteenth-century instance of the secrets of identity and its politics now being "outed" by theorists of queer performativity. Not exactly "drag" as we know it—or the drag that early-nineteenth-century London theater is reputed to be—the Master Betty phenomenon clearly "works through the hyperbolic" to render visible what counts as nature.[6]

It is perverse to invoke English Romantic discourse on theater to reflect more broadly on contemporary accounts of queer performativity. Among other reasons, English Romanticism has long been seen as "undramatic" and "antitheatrical" precisely because it privileges interiority, sincerity, development, organicism. Romantic subjectivity, the argument goes, takes an inward turn; as a consequence, acting, in whatever sphere, threatens the potentiality ascribed to "character" and the "sluggishness" being promoted as English character in this age.[7] But we need only invoke Jonathan Dollimore's formulation of the perverse dynamic to detect within such oppositions the proximity of the theatrical to the intuitive.[8] Or, from within the period, we need only invoke the indisputable master of character, Shakespeare, and the controversy surrounding the "master-mistress" of his passions, to bring into focus the perverse dynamic of Romantic closet drama. The privileged site of Romantic interiority, designed to cordon off publicity, materiality, visibility, collectivity, the closet and its dramas allows imaginative men to keep their fantasies, and particularly their native genius, to themselves. Taking the lead of Peter Stallybrass, we can reflect more comprehensively on the peculiar charge of the Romantic closet. Emerging fresh from Edmund Malone's reissue of the 1640 edition of the sonnets, which restores the chronological order of 1609 to the sonnets and thus a homosexual desire to the bard, the native genius of England assumes his historical character in the early nineteenth century "as a potential sodomite."[9]

Reflection on the queering of Shakespeare in the Romantic age and particularly on the generic and aesthetic distinctions enlisted to manage such unsettling revelations of character should give pause to contemporary theorists of queer performativity. We may still need to interrogate rather than assume the proposition that "theater" and its correlatives— theatricality, performance, drag, acting out—provide a less essentializing and more subversive picture of identity than does "reading" and the genres associated with it. At the least, we need to distinguish more precisely the ontological from the psychosocial and psychosexual effects of constructions of identity in theater. By focusing on early-nineteenth-century theater, I mean to pursue this question by linking together what have hitherto remained divergent areas of inquiry in the project to rethink homosexualities. To the extent that queer theorists embrace the model of theater, they ignore the important stages of the early nineteenth century (as do most scholars of theater). To the extent that they focus on the early nineteenth century in efforts to recover alternative categories of sexuality now overridden by the homo/hetero divide, they align such "proto-forms" —and particularly that of the masturbator— with "novelistic point of view."[10] These pre-texts, of both sexual identity and dramatic practice, challenge the penchant to oppose reading to theatricalizing and heteronormalizing to queering identities. Reflection on the sensations of the early-nineteenth-century closet, apparently still available to us, and those of Master Betty and masturbation, which we have ostensibly outgrown, suggest that there are novel and regressive lessons to be gained when queer studies attends to Romantic theater.

Acting Out in English Romanticism

Acting

> What would appear mad or ludicrous in a book, [when]
> presented to the senses under the form of reality and with the
> truth of nature, supplies a species of actual experience.[11]

In what follows, I wish to track some interconnections between two trajectories of Romantic acting out: theories of acting embedded in discussions of dramatic illusion, imitation, and closeting; and notions of "acting out" as perceptible in discussions of "youth." Investigating the former category complicates late-twentieth-century understandings of the closet and the reliance by queer theorists on the nature of imitating and copying in efforts to reconceive homosexuality.[12] Investigating the latter raises the stakes in contemporary projects to maintain "difference" in groups. The Romantic "youth" already carries with it associations later named and at times pathologized as "adolescent" by psychoanalysis: autoeroticism, homosexualities, latency, groups. What interests me in this partial genealogy of queer performativity are the ways that "youth" is managed like "acting" in this age. Both are characterized by latency—though in this period theater takes the lead in ascribing that quality to youth. Both demand the closet at the same time that they command the house, and both are mastered by Shakespeare. In fact, bardolatry mirrors the idolatries of the stage of youth in this age. Shakespeare is offered as the chief guide to character precisely as the delineation of his character makes him unfit company for youth.

The equation between "closeting" and "homosexual" identity would not be the first to spring to mind in early-nineteenth-century England (though it would *not* not spring to mind either, as the case of Shakespeare indicates). More likely, the space into which one would be understood to go if one "came out" of the early-nineteenth-century closet is theater. Because of the indissociability of the closet and theater in that age and the overridden nature of that connection now, Romantic formulations of the closet disclose a slightly different epistemology than that articulated by Eve Kosofsky Sedgwick. Not that the pairings and the epistemological assumptions underlying the pairings secrecy/disclosure and private/public do not apply to Romantic closet/theater, nor that such pairings are not already invested in "knowing," and surveilling, "proper" sexual activity or even in producing a heightened interest in homosex.[13] But the knowledge—and particularly the "privileges of unknowing"—associated with closet/theater are not the same as that attributed to closet/sex; for Romantic "knowing" in theater is an "open secret" and a disavowal: the ability to know one thing and feel another. Dramatic illusion turns on the mind's capacity to turn off its powers of discrimination in order to reactivate them at a deeper, less conscious level. Consequently, this structure of "unknowing" called feeling subtends far more than it subverts nature.

Another impediment to the exposure, by Judith Butler, of heterosexuality as an "incessant and *panicked* imitation of its own naturalized idealization" is the tendency to use "imitation" and "copy" interchangeably, as if they provided equal assaults on originality.[14] Such a conflation ignores a more nuanced and pernicious understanding, embedded in Romantic articulations of mimetic practice, of how the normative appropriates deviance *through* imitation. As opposed to the copy, imitation aids in the naturalization process because it shows spectators how to "know" but not "feel" difference. As Coleridge puts it, "imitation, as opposed to copying, consists either in the interfusion of the SAME throughout the radically DIFFERENT, or of the different throughout a base radically the same."[15] Moreover, this distinction pertains to both the making and the reception of art. In the case of production, because imitation acknowledges the "total difference" in the medium and materials used for art, whereas the "copy" aims to disguise the distinction, imitation achieves the effect of "nature," whereas "copy," by attempting to duplicate it, fails both as nature and as art. Whether a viewer acknowledges difference affects reception as well. The state of mind produced by a "good imitation" is one that proceeds from "diversity toward unity and/or similarity" and thus effects both pleasure and peace. The state of mind produced by a good copy is the reverse—the movement from similarity to difference arouses disgust.

A long history of homosexual panic and homophobic violence unfolds from this distinction: imitation is living, productive, organic, pleasurable; copy is dead, unproductive, mechanical, unpleasurable. My point is neither that we should respect this distinction nor that nothing is accomplished by seeing heterosexuality and homosexuality as copies of a copy. It is, first, that we should apprehend the Romantic recognition of the homogenizing effects of imitation when we promote the theatrical paradigm and, second, that we should avoid the tendency to associate mimesis with realism. The latter mistake, in my view, enables the confidence placed in "hyperbole" and "parody" generally—and in drag, cross-dressing, transvestism more specifically—as strategies for subverting gendered and sexual identity. One more advantage provided by a focus on Romantic theater is that no one—except the canonical Romantic poets themselves—would accuse this stage of realism. Romantic formulations of the "semblance" of theater, the "illusion" of acting, grant more accurate depictions of the mind's ability to "half create what we half perceive"; for the "distinct" end of the stage is to "imitat[e] Reality (Objects, Actions, or Passions) under a Semblance of *Reality*."[16]

The proximity of reality to semblance in theater guarantees it an immediacy not obtained by reading and constitutes the "grand Privilege of a great Actor above a great Poet."[17] But the immediacy of its nature also constitutes the peculiar danger of theater. Indeed, the difficulty of attaining semblance in a medium so tied to reality is one reason Romantic drama so often ends up in the closet. But this does not mean that theater and closet are wholly separate spheres. Romantic theories of acting emphasize form over content in their cultivation of the spectator's capacity to see semblance in what is actually alive. Not only does this vision challenge the realism—and the identity politics—associated with visibility, but what aids this aesthetic project is precisely what queer theorists now promote as the subversive potential of theater. Oscar Wilde, in *The Portrait of Mr. W. H.*, articulates the strategy most concisely, but the argument—and the controversy that prompts it— stems from the Romantic period:

> To say that only a woman can portray the passions of a woman, and that therefore no boy can play Rosalind, is to rob the art of acting of all claim to objectivity, and to assign to the mere accident of sex what properly belongs to imaginative insight and creative energy.... The very difference of sex between the player and the part he represented must also, as Professor Ward points out, have constituted "one more demand upon the imaginative capacities of the spectators," and must have kept them from that over-realistic identification of the actor with his role, which is one of the weak points in modern theatrical criticism.[18]

A second weak point in postmodern performativity follows: when boys playing girls is both drag and high drama, something less essential makes the difference.

Acting Out

> The little Actor cons another part;
>   ... As if his whole vocation
> Were endless imitation.
>   —William Wordsworth,
>   "Ode: Intimations of Immortality"

Managing difference makes youth like acting in this age. For both, imitation is the chief means to their ends and a description of their chief end: movement from dissimilitude to similitude or unity. The end of unity applies equally to the development of individual and national character. Youth, and its theater, is the process of becoming a group. Wordsworth's *The Prelude* serves as the canonical English text in its emphasis not simply on the growth but on the interpenetration of a poet-patriot's mind. Enabling this development are the many "Characters" of Shakespeare published in this period geared toward the education and civic education of youth. Simply as title, Wordsworth's *Prelude* names the Shakespearean story of youth: potentiality—what we now also call latency. Considered in relation to its composition history, *The Prelude* demystifies "development" in a mode we tend to associate with Coleridge, where potential is the whole story; for *The Prelude* is prelude to *The Recluse*, a philosophical poem meant to amend the public mind and still waiting to be written. This too is part of the genius of youth: the "genius" is organicism, where "youth" functions as a stage. And this stage is revealing precisely in its capacity to be perverted by what is proximate: development is arrested; ideas never get "actualized." More to the point, the Romantic stage of theater and youth is undone by its defining feature: a semblance of reality.

The queerest part of the illusion revealed as delusion by the stage of youth is the naturalness of heterosexual attraction. In our day, the work of Laurence Rickels goes the furthest in articulating the mismanagement of youth from the perspective of psychoanalysis: adolescence is homosex because anticouple and pro-group.[19] Discourse on "Shakespeare" in the Romantic age offers some similar insights from the perspective of theater. It faces (if only to efface) Shakespeare's alleged hostility to women as recorded implicitly in his plays or explicitly in his sonnets, and positions him either with the groupies of theater or the group-of-one in the closet.[20] I return us to Romantic form(ul)ations of youth in order to grant theater the lead over psychoanalysis in proposing a less regressive conception of latency. I do so also to shift the terms of analysis by foregrounding nonsexual aspects of the "queerness" of youth. Like Sedgwick's recovery of pre-"sexual identity as we know it," Romantic "youth" restores a less constrained "adolescence"—a category itself being installed at roughly the same time as the "hetero-homo" divide.[21] As the case of Master Betty suggests—as usual, in exaggerated fashion— "youth" in this period covers a wide span of time and identifications. This thirteen-year-old male is termed a "youth," a "boy," a "child," an "infant," whose presence speaks to something in virtually everyone. Yet, to recover the relaxation of boundaries in early-nineteenth-century English conceptualizations of identity and sexuality is not to attain more progressive understandings either. In this case, psychoanalysis resumes precedence in its articulation of the sobering realities of group psychology that attain high visibility in the theater and youth of any period.

Master Betty represents a particularly striking instance of the interconnections I am proposing among youth, theater, and queer sexualities, but the stage is set for him by theoretical links forged between theater and youth in Romantic discourse, not simply in the convertibility of the metaphor of "management" to manuals of childhood development and to critical strictures on actors—though drama and theater criticism do figure importantly as conduct books for youth that, moreover, make "appearance" evidence of "character."[22] The interrelation is more essential; for the state of mind achieved by dramatic illusion—

"suspension of disbelief"—is ascribed by Coleridge to the "nature and beauty of youth," which is the "ability to know what is right in the abstract," to "body it forth" in "beautiful Forms," and to "project this phantom-world into the world of Reality, like a catoptrical mirror. Say rather, to make ideas & realities stand side by side, the one as vivid as the other."[23] Working the other side of the mirror, stage illusion is what returns the adult to the child. "Now what Pictures are to little Children, Stage-Illusion is to Men, provided they retain any part of the Child's sensibility."[24] By suspending the "calculating faculty," stage illusion ignores the distinction between past and present, absence and presence. The "child's sensibility" reinhabits the grown-up, but under certain conditions.

This nonrational and nondevelopmental view of the psyche is what allows theater to achieve its transporting effects. It unfixes viewers from the here and now of personal identity and social policy, and transports them to an ideal future and an idealized past. This is what writers such as Burke mean when they consider theater a "better school of moral sentiment than churches" in a revolutionary age. The cultural "conservatory" of "natural human impulses," theater restores viewers to a more "intuitive" condition and keeps them from being "graduated in the school of the rights of men."[25] Such a tradition-based project is one reason present-day cultural critics should think twice about championing the "natural" subversiveness of theater. To be "beside oneself" is an uncanny way of being one's former selves. Yet, the Romantic promotion of theater as nature conservancy does wonders for "the child"—at least for our view of the Romantic child, who regains a more complicated psychology of innocence.[26] There would be no reason to reactivate one's inner child if that child is a sheer blank. To revive the child's sensibility—whether in the person or the nation—is to appeal to habit, tradition, familiarity, prejudice. What moves it depends on its unconscious history, what it re-members is captured in and by affect. In this regard, the Romantic child is less a blank slate than a sedimented slate. To speak to its nature through theater is to trigger those habits of aggression from its mirror stage.

In the case of theater, then, that "child" who is father of the man is discovered not on the stage but recovered by it. The alleged unsuitability of theater to unfold character over time is why the novel is associated with psychological development. But the effect of double consciousness achieved by theater makes it more effective than novels in revealing the adult as haunted by the child; and the principal means by which this special effect is attained underscores the most perverse component of theater: illusion of visibility; for stage practice depends simultaneously on seeing what is (not) there and not seeing what is (not) there: not just in the conventional senses of not seeing the actor in order to see the character or not seeing the character in order to see one's own ideal character, but also in seeing through actions to the "germ" of character implicit in such acts and thereby intuiting the prehistory of each character according to the germ of one's own. The latency of vision in theater—where one can see oneself in everything and recapture stages of one's former self—is a source of profound viewing pleasure. Among other things, it revives archaic pleasures and perversities, where the father becomes fathered by the child.

Latent in Youth: Bettymania

> Everybody here is mad about this Boy Actor.
> —Charles James Fox in a letter to Lord Holland,
>   December 17, 1804

The object of near-universal appeal, Master Betty provides an object lesson in the latency of vision in theater and its prime subject, youth. The "prepossessing" nature of his beauty yields an audience—not to say a nation—possessed. Press accounts of him, and especially those many "Authentic Lives" hot off the presses and written to fan as much as "gratify the increasing curiosity [some introductions say "thirst"] of the Public on this interesting subject," prepare the way for Master Betty's triumphal entry on the London stage.[27] Even before his debut in London, Playfair avers, he was the most famous person in Britain. Such releases recover some remarkable insights into the production of a star and, in this case, a teen idol adored by all ages and sexes. Here we can only focus on two mandatory tricks of viewing: how to see sameness in difference; how seeing becomes believing in groups.

These two processes of vision require each other not only because Master Betty is a child playing a man. Master Betty only makes it to London because his authentic memoirs endlessly rehearse the public's nightly conversion to him—first in Ireland, then Scotland, then the provinces of England.[28] The same process unfolds in the London papers, especially the *Courier*, where the debate rages between a "WW" and "Philo Roscius."[29] From the start, his career was dogged by detractors, who worried less that the emperor had no clothes than that he had too many. This boy of thirteen who commands an empire has no character, no interior life, no heart. This child of nature who rivals Shakespeare in powers of intuition is a "puppet," a "pupil," a genius at "stage business." For a while, such detraction only fueled his success, not simply by generating publicity, but by producing those defenses that allow publics to (more than) half create what they half perceive— another instance where psychoanalytic insights take their cue from theater. The "authentic" narratives both of Master Betty's character and of the public's conversion to him reveal the secret psychology and secret society of youth. With Betty, these involve gender ambiguity and the polymorphous erotics of latency; with the public, a group psychology that eschews difference within and without.

The debate in the *Courier* boils down to an evaluation of the nature and stages of man: whether a youth can know or naturally embody things beyond his years;[30] whether audiences can see something other than a boy of thirteen in a boy of thirteen;[31] whether in this youth audiences see what "is" or what is in process; whether they see in youth what they are, were, or want to become. The answers provided to such questions indicate why we should approach "imitation" and its excesses with skepticism. Believers find "nature" in virtually anything: artifice, study, the preternatural, the mechanical, even unevenness.[32] The paradox of acting—that nature is evoked and human nature displayed through assuming fictive identities—is heightened by the beauty of youth. After all, youth is becoming. Gender ambiguity strengthens this appeal.[33] Not only is Master Betty's beauty so "feminine" that at one point his father is forced to publish a copy of the entry of his son's name in a baptismal register to squelch the rumor that he "was of the feminine gender, and arrived to a period of life beyond what even the law would deem infancy," but the primal scene of Master Betty's conversion to acting turns on maternal identifications.[34] Not surprisingly, they are double: his biological mother, from whom—all the stories go— he "is indebted for the origin of his penchant for the stage"; and the reigning queen mother of the stage, Sarah Siddons, who played the lead female in the play that changed Master Betty's life. "Master Betty talked of nothing but Elvira; he spouted the speeches of Elvira, and his passion for the stage became every hour more vehement and uncontrollable."[35]

The polymorphous nature of this appeal goes a long way toward explaining the popularity of this youth. In front of the catoptrical mirror of youth, what Rickels calls the "dream screen" of adolescence, Master Betty commands identifications—and enormous profits—while uncovering this secret of viewing in theater: seeing is disavowing and is informed by the child. But, because detractors were saying (and seeing) this from the start, it does not account for what brought the dream screen down. Here the Master Betty phenemenon reveals this problem with latency: not just that in it perverse tendencies are out, but that there are some "realities" that illusion won't bear. Nor will groups, which is why the closet is not so opposed to theater as it seems and why the in-group of Romanticism is closeted. With Master Betty, as "latency" becomes visibly, not simply phantasmatically, coupled with polymorphous sexuality, audiences take less pleasure in this child and their transport. What worked for a time to keep his sex appeal invisible was focus on his "chasteness" onstage and his juvenility off.[36] Virtually all accounts of his performances agree that Master Betty was unconvincing in depictions of heterosexual passion, whereas he came into his own, so to speak, in scenes with his mother (better yet, in deathbed scenes with his mother). The sexuality latent in such impassioned scenes between a stand-in man and his surrogate mother undoubtedly would have raised the issue sooner or later. But before it did, his body started to act up by producing a symptom of latency, his hoarse voice and cough.

This symptom sends a mixed message, reactions to which testify to the queer latency of sexuality. On the one hand, audiences view his hoarse voice as a sign of nature: "he is about that time of life in which the voice begins to lose that shrillness that belongs to boys, and to assume the deeper tone which is the property of a man" (*Courier*, December 5, 1804). On the other hand, it signals various perversities. Concern over the unhealthy activity of this youth—"his being languid from too great fatigue and exertion"—sounds like those warnings against masturbation that enjoin youth to store up rather than spend vital energies. His visible enervation combines with a discernible narcissism that makes his self-possession appear all too self-contained. "Never did I see more coldness and artifice" (*Courier*, December 7, 1804). But, if Master Betty forfeits some public sympathy over his absence of sympathy onstage, this is nothing compared to the outcry against Mr. Betty. Press accounts transform the appearance of self-abuse into the reality of child abuse by a moneygrubbing, pimpish, and inhuman father. Censure of the father was so strong that at one point proceedings were under way to place Master Betty under the protection of the Court of Chancery and, barring this, under a series of surrogate fathers: Prince William Frederick of Gloucester, the Duke of Clarence, the Prince of Wales, Fox.[37]

The willingness of such men to offer Master Betty their services is where the latent sexuality turns homosexual. Naturally, hints of this tendency are there from the start. As Playfair—who on this question does not always live up to his name—notes, "Master Betty's vulgar following appears to have been largely male. At his opening performance the men outnumbered the women by an estimated 20 to one" (*The Prodigy*, 82). But when this tendency becomes a matter of permanent record, the homosociality that underwrites Master Betty's success turns homophobic. We read this in various offhand but snide remarks, such as this one from the *Times*: "Master Betty's success is very naturally the cause of much envy and heart-breaking amongst the Master Polly's and Master Jenny's of Bondstreet and Cheapside, who in all their attempts to distinguish their pretty persons and effeminate airs, have only Miscarried" (December 5, 1804). But the scandal surrounding the firing of the tutor, Mr. Hough, brings the perversity too close to home. Hough himself threatens to go public with "An Appeal—Hough versus Betty, senior, to the judgment and candour of an impartial British Public . . . in which will be introduced a curious and truly original Correspondence, previous and subsequent to Master Betty's first appearance on the stage" (Playfair, *The Prodigy*, 129). This "truly original correspondence" no doubt had something to say about the copy that was his master's nature: at the least, that he, Hough, was the brains of the whole operation and that Master Betty had been trained, schooled, packaged, managed. But there were apparently other forms of correspondence that even Hough was unwilling to reveal (for, as Playfair speculates, given that Hough was silenced for only fifty guineas a year, he must have been in a weak bargaining position [ibid., 22]). A scurrilous pamphlet gets to the bottom of things. Addressed to Master Betty in the form of a mock application for the vacant post as his tutor, one "Peter Pangloss" presents his qualifications: "For I've a wondrous rod in pickle/Your pretty little Bum to tickle."[38]

As queer theorists have been showing for a while now, a little homoeroticism goes a long way toward shoring up heteronormativity. The latter reality will not bear uncloseted homosexuality because illusion, like youth, depends on the pregnancy of latency. When discourse regarding Betty names sodomy or pederasty too directly, the "wonder of the age" is on the wane. But latency does not reproduce "pregnancy as we know it," either. Master Betty's appeal is strengthened, not threatened, by his appearing "incommoded" by women. "He extended his arms from one of her shoulders to the other, but he never touched her" (*Courier*, December 3, 1804). What clinches his being sent to play in the provinces, it appears, is neither his bad copy of heterosexuality nor his too-good imitation of homosociality, but the copycat phenomenon he provoked: "some twenty or thirty young wonders, or infant prodigies, under the title of Infant Billington, seven years old Roscius and Billington, Infant Columbine, Ormskirk Roscius, Young Orpheus, Infant Vestris, Infant Clown, Comic Roscius, Infant Degville, Infant Hercules, and Infant Candlesnuffer."[39]

Such a series of replicants gives the lie to the "genius" that discerning audiences believed they had seen. It recaptures less the child's sensibility than it renders the adult as teen. Scales fall from eyes that find themselves mesmerized, mechanized, dupes of fashion. Adult spectators regain their independence by withdrawing to the closet, where they resume the fantasy of creativity and generativity. This state is achieved through the great "I AM" of imagination, that by definition surpasses the fancies of fashion and restores originality. Although this is not the same difference as being reduced to replicants by replicants, it replicates a similar canceling of difference. This proximity of the closet to theater exchanges groupies for a group-of-one who is no less enamored of reproduction. It also heightens the gender asymmetry of illusion; for the most damaging replica to our child of nature is a certain Miss Mudie, who goes down in history as ending the Master Betty phenomenon. John Kemble—who, with his sister, had retired from the stage in protest during the year of Betty's fame—engaged her to appear at Covent Garden just three weeks before Betty was due back in London. In the event, she gets hissed off the stage for, in her case, one sees that illusion is clearly delusion: "What shook the stage and made the people stare?/*The infant's early breast and woman-air*" (quoted in Playfair, *The Prodigy*, 136; emphasis in original). Only a Master Betty, as long as he remains a master and masterable, embodies latency or makes a child the father of the man. Only a certain (anti)body of men can embody the "germ" of character that is allegedly the same in everyone. These are intimations indeed.

Notes

1. For information on Master Betty's salary, both before his London debut (in theaters in Ireland, Scotland, and northern England) and on the terms of his engagement by Drury Lane and Covent Garden, see Giles Playfair, *The Prodigy: A Study of the Strange Life of Master Betty* (London: Secker and Warburg, 1967), 48–58, 63–67.

2. Assurances like the following accompany all newspaper accounts of Master Betty's first (as well as subsequent) performance: "In the full knowledge of the serious accidents and confusion which have taken place in several towns in which this Phenomenon has appeared, a provident arrangement has been made for the safety and protection of his Majesty's Subjects.... Thus the lives and properties of the Public will be happily protected, and he or she who happens to be too late, may easily retire with purse untouched and bones unbroken" (*Courier*, November 28, 1804). Apparently, such promises of precaution were kept, though with limited effect: "[The Managers] knew that the House would be besieged.... they provided a select number of peace officers inside, and they procured a strong detachment of guards outside.... In the pit many gentlemen fainted, and were dragged, seemingly lifeless, up into the boxes.... Frequently we heard screams from those who were overcome by the heat" (*Courier*, December 3, 1804). See also *Times*, December 14, 1804, for his debut at Covent Garden.

3. The adjournment occurred on March 14, 1805 (on the "evidence" for this event, see Playfair, *The Prodigy*, 10). Already at the end of January, Master Betty made his own appearance in the House of Lords, and on February 7 in the House of Commons, where, according to the *Times*, "his entree was marked by very warm congratulations, not only from the spectators, but also from several of the performers. He seemed to be more at home here than when in the Upper House, as the *Dramatis Personae* were nearer his own level, being all of them not so much originals as representatives" (February 9, 1805).

4. "His Royal Highness the Prince of Wales was in his private box with a select party.... The lower boxes were filled with persons of fashion" (*Times*, December 5, 1804). "Both the lower and first tier of boxes were taken in the name of Ladies of the first fashion" (*Times*, December 7, 1804).

5. "Every thought and wish were directed to the young boy: business engagements, and amusements seemed to be at a stand; he alone occupied the public attention, and the war and Bonaparte were for a time unheeded and forgotten" (*Courier* December 3, 1804). See also *Faulkner's Dublin Journal*: "Criticism and panegyrics upon the Young Roscius, as he is called, exclude almost every other matter from the columns of the London newspapers. Buonaparte, and his Invasion, and his Coronation, are all alike forgotten and disregarded" (quoted in Playfair, *The Prodigy*, 36).

6. I am citing Judith Butler's definition of drag in "Critically Queer," *GLQ: A Journal of Lesbian and Gay Studies* 1:1 (1993): 27. Implicit in my account of the Master Betty phenomenon is an expanded notion of drag that includes categories other than gender in the narrative of normative development.

7. I deal with these issues at greater length in *In the Theatre of Romanticism: Coleridge, Nationalism, Women* (Cambridge: Cambridge University Press, 1994).

8. "The perverse dynamic signifies that fearful interconnectedness whereby the antithetical inheres within, and is partly produced by, what it opposes" (Jonathan Dollimore, *Sexual Dissidence: Augustine to Wilde, Freud to Foucault* [Oxford: Clarendon Press, 1991], 33).

9. Peter Stallybrass, "Editing as Cultural Formation: The Sexing of Shakespeare's Sonnets," *Modern Language Quarterly* 54:1 (March 1993): 91–104.

10. Eve Kosofsky Sedgwick articulates this argument most concisely in "Jane Austen and the Masturbating Girl," *Critical Inquiry* 17:4 (summer 1991): 818–37, reprinted in *Tendencies* (Durham, N.C.: Duke University Press, 1993), 109–29.

11. Samuel Taylor Coleridge, *Lectures 1808–19: On Literature*, 2 vols., ed. Reginald A. Foakes; vol. 5 in *The Collected Works of Samuel Taylor Coleridge*, Bollingen Series 75 (Princeton, N.J.: Princeton University Press, 1986), 1:429.

12. See especially Judith Butler, "Imitation and Gender Insubordination," and Carole-Anne Tyler, "Boys Will Be Girls: The Politics of Gay Drag," in Diana Fuss, ed., *inside/out* (New York and London: Routledge, 1991), 13–31, 32–70.

13. Indeed, Sedgwick specifies the "period initiated by Romanticism" as accomplishing the linkage of "cognition itself, sexuality itself, and transgression" (Eve Kosofsky Sedgwick, *Epistemology of the Closet* [Berkeley: University of California Press, 1990], 73).

14. Butler, "Imitation and Gender Insubordination," 23.

15. *Biographia Literaria*, 2 vols., ed. James Engell and Walter Jackson Bate; vol. 7 of *The Collected Works of Samuel Taylor Coleridge*, Bollingen Series 75 (Princeton, N.J.: Princeton University Press, 1983), 2:72.

16. Coleridge, *Lectures 1808–19: On Literature*, 1:133; emphasis in original.

17. Ibid., 1:429.

18. Oscar Wilde, *The Portrait of Mr. W. H.*, vol. 6 in *The Complete Works of Oscar Wilde*, ed. Richard Butler Glaenzer and Dr. Clifford Smith (Garden City: Doubleday, Page and Company, 1923), 250–51.

19. See especially Laurence A. Rickels, *The Case of California* (Baltimore: Johns Hopkins University Press, 1991), and "Psy Fi Explorations of Out Space: On Werther's Special Effects," in Alice Kuzniar, ed., *Outing Goethe and His Age* (Stanford, Calif.: Stanford University Press, 1996).

20. "Shakespeare wrote for men only but Beaumont and Fletcher or rather the gentle Fletcher for women" (Coleridge, *Lectures 1808–19: On Literature*, 1:297–98); "Collins encouraged the common error on this subject by saying—'But stronger Shakespeare felt for man alone'" (*Characters of Shakespeare's Plays*, vol.1 of *The Collected Works of William Hazlitt in Twelve Volumes*, ed. A. R. Waller and Arnold Glover [London: J. M. Dent and Company, 1902], 252). "Group-of-one" is Rickels's phrase.

21. The work of G. Stanley Hall is usually credited with generating the discourse on adolescence; (see his *Adolescence: Its Psychology and Its Relations to Physiology, Anthropology, Sociology, Sex, Crime, Religion, and Education*, 2 vols. (New York: D. Appleton and Company, 1905).

22. On the prevalence of management as the "standard by which parents measured their activities and their position relative to the child," see James R. Kincaid, *Child Loving: The Erotic Child and Victorian Culture* (New York and London: Routledge, 1992), 85–88. More generally, I am indebted to Kincaid's book for its insights into pedophilia and the necessary fantasies of childhood innocence.

23. Samuel Taylor Coleridge, *Collected Letters of Samuel Taylor Coleridge*, 6 vols., ed. Earl Leslie Griggs (Oxford: Clarendon Press, 1956–71), 2:1000.

24. With this relevant distinction: "except that in the latter instance, this suspension of the Act of Comparison, which permits this sort of negative Belief, is somewhat more assisted by the Will, than in that of the Child respecting a Picture" (Coleridge, *Lectures 1808–19: On Literature*, 1:135). The contribution of the will to illusion (and adulthood) needs to be taken into account when proposing the "perversions" of theater.

25. Edmund Burke, *Reflections on the Revolution in France* (Garden City, N.Y.: Anchor Books, 1973), 94–95.

26. On the Romantic child, see Peter Coveney, *The Image of Childhood: The Individual and Society: A Study of the Theme in English Literature* (New York: Penguin, 1967); J. P. Ward, "'Came from yon fountain': Wordsworth's Influence on Victorian Educators," *Victorian Studies* 29 (1986): 405–36.

27. J. Merritt, *Memoirs of the Life of William Henry West Betty, Known by the Name of the Young Roscius, with a General Estimate of His Talents, and a Critique on His Principal Characters* (Liverpool: J. Wright, 1804). There were at least five lengthy memoirs in circulation when Master Betty made his debut in London, but, in case London audiences had not seen them, shortened versions of them accompanied press accounts of his initial performances (see, for example, *Times*, December 3, 1804). As Playfair notes, by August 8, 1804, Master Betty had "become news for *The Times*; it carried a report from Edinburgh with the hardly tentative conclusion, 'Mozart, the great composer, was a similar example of premature genius'" (*The Prodigy*, 43).

28. As George Davies Harley puts it, "Doubting was the order of the day; recantation that of the night" (*Memoirs of the Young Roscius: An Authentic Biographical Sketch of the Life, Education, and Personal Character, of Wm Henry West Betty, the Celebrated Young Roscius* [Sheffield: T. Gillet, 2d ed. 1804], 56). Much of the point of these "authentic" memoirs is to detail the process by which a public and public persons become converts.

29. See especially *Courier* December 7, 10, and 17, 1804; see also "To the Editor" of the *Times*, December 14, 1804, where a "Mitio" engages in a defense of Master Betty against "WW" without even having "seen this theatrical prodigy."

30. This debate is revealing about what "passions" are deemed appropriate for a child/youth. "Perhaps, however, it would be too much to expect that a boy of thirteen should have any accurate ideas of passions, to which he must hitherto have been a stranger. Of love, of pride, of anger, of revenge, he can know nothing. Filial tenderness is the strongest feeling such a boy can have, and in the scenes with his mother he was wonderfully impressive" (*Courier*, December 3, 1804).

31. "Are these the qualities of a boy actor? Are these the proofs of his being great only because he is 13? They are precisely the proofs that his genius has stepped beyond his age, and it has advanced to manhood, if not to maturity" (*Courier*, December 3, 1804).

32. Philo Roscius mounts this defense against WW: "The Writer of these letters still considers the boy as having been tutored, because his performance of particular scenes was unequal and inferior to his performance of other scenes; but was the greatest genius that ever lived at all times equal? Is not this inequality to be found in Shakespeare, in Dryden, and in many, if not all authors? Was Garrick at all times equal?" (*Courier*, December 17, 1804).

33. Playfair notes how makeup and costume were "evidently used to accentuate his young and girlish beauty." Moreover, "An Old Actress" recounts how offstage Master Betty looks more like a "female in male costume" (*The Prodigy*, 77).

34. Ibid., 40.

35. The first quote is from *The Wonderful Theatrical Progress of W. Hen. West Betty, the Infant Roscius, in Ireland, Scotland, and Various Parts of England, also at the Theatres Royal Covent Garden and Drury Lane with an Accurate Sketch of His Life, by an Impartial Observer* (London: Barnard and Suitzer, 1805), 4; the second from Merritt, *Memoirs of the Life of William Henry West Betty*, 22. Moreover, the

narrative of Betty's conversion to acting casts him as a true adolescent: "From that moment, his fate was decided" (that moment being his attendance at his first play, Sheridan's adaptation [*Pizarro*] of Kotzebue's *Der Spanier im Peru*, at the age of ten). "When he came home, he told his father with a look of such enthusiasm and a voice so pathetic, 'I shall die if you do not permit me to be a player'" (ibid., 21).

36. Many accounts detail Master Betty's "boyish pranks" offstage; the "fact" that during the interval between the first scene of *Barbarossa* and his entrance onstage, Master Betty, "instead of being employed as the other performers were, in reading his part, amused himself in playing numerous boyish tricks with" Mr. Knight, becomes the matter of some press debate over what this signifies about whether his acting is the product of rote or nature (see especially *Courier* December 7, 1804; the *Times*, December 14, 1804).

37. See Playfair for the negotiations, particularly by Professor Robison, on Master Betty's behalf (*The Prodigy*, 59–61, 83–85. Apparently, the Lord Chancellor's offer was declined "because of the boy's mistaken belief that it would entail his being separated from his parents" (83).

38. Peter Pangloss Esq. L.L.D. and A.S.S., *The Young Rosciad, an Admonitory Poem, Well-Seasoned with Attic Salt, cum Notis Variorum* (London: W. Gordon, 1805).

39. Allardyce Nicoll, *Early Nineteenth Century Drama 1800–1850*, vol. 4 in *A History of the English Drama 1660–1900* (Cambridge: Cambridge University Press, 1955), 20.

Willfulness–*Eigensinn*

Elisabeth Weber

> Once upon a time, there was a willful [*eigensinniges*] child, which
> would not do what its mother wanted. The dear Lord, therefore,
> did not look kindly upon the child and let it become sick. No
> doctor could help it, and soon it lay on its deathbed. After it had
> been lowered into its grave and covered over with earth, its little
> arm suddenly reemerged and reached up, and when they put it
> back in and scattered fresh earth on it, it was no use: the little arm
> kept coming out. So the child's mother had to go to the grave
> herself and beat the little arm with a switch, and as soon as she
> had done so, the arm pulled back in, and the child had finally
> found peace below the earth.[1]

Although this, the shortest of Grimm's fairy tales, can no longer be
found in fairy-tale collections for children, in the nineteenth century
it was one of the standard tales served up, with their pleasant and
unpleasant surprises, to numerous generations of children in the Ger-
man-speaking world.[2] The Brothers Grimm regarded their fairy-tale
collection, as they write in their preface to the second edition of 1822
(the first comprehensive edition), as an "educational book" (*Erziehungs-
buch*), which as such was naturally intended for children (Grimm 1819–
1822, 1:vii–ix; cf. Grimm [1819] 1949/1988, 30–31):

> For such an [educational book] we are looking not for such purity
> as is achieved by the fearful expulsion of all that refers to certain
> conditions and situations that occur in everyday life, and that can
> and should by no means remain concealed. . . . We are looking for
> purity in the truth and in the straightforward story which harbors
> no wrong. In doing so, we carefully deleted from this new edition
> every expression unsuitable for children. Should it nevertheless be
> objected that parents are embarrassed by something or other, or
> find it offensive, such that they wouldn't quite want to pass the

> book into the hands of children, this concern may be warranted
> in individual cases, which can thus easily be chosen by them;
> however, on the whole—that is, for a healthy constitution—there
> is certainly no need for it. Nothing can better defend us in this
> than nature itself, which has allowed just these flowers and leaves
> to grow in this color and form. Whoever does not find them
> salutary according to his special needs cannot demand that they
> therefore be colored and carved otherwise. Or, to put it another
> way, rain and dew descend as a benefaction for everything on
> earth. Whoever dares not place his plants into them because they
> are too sensitive and might be damaged, . . . cannot demand that
> rain and dew should therefore cease.

These fairy tales, then, pose no danger to a "healthy constitution"; they are "straightforward" and do not "harbor" any "wrong." Those expressions unsuitable for children have been "carefully deleted." Nature itself guarantees that these stories are like rain and dew, flowers and leaves.

In the context of pedagogical reform that predominated in the early nineteenth century and, as Friedrich Kittler shows in *Aufschreibesysteme* (*Discourse Networks*), assigned to mothers the key role in socialization and acquisition of literacy, the story of the willful child might be read as a reactionary anachronism from earlier days. Typical of this context is the view, held by pedagogical reformers such as Pestalozzi and Stephani, that the medium of the mother's voice and mouth guarantees the painless acquisition of literacy by linking it directly to maternal love (Kittler 1985: 33/27).

> [Thus,] the mother's mouth redeems the children from the book.
> In place of letters, they are given sounds. . . . Out of the phonetic
> experiment emerges a psychology or psychagogy which makes
> writing totally consumable. . . . Later in their lives, when the
> children look at books, they will not see letters, but, with an
> overpowering longing, will hear a voice from between the lines.
> And what this voice does is unheard of: it doesn't say a word,
> let alone utter a sentence. . . . It does not speak, but rather makes
> speak. (Ibid., 40/34–35)

Jacob and Wilhelm Grimm also learned to read this way (ibid., 58/52). What, then, prompted them to include in their fairy tale and educational book a story such as that of the willful child, whose image of motherhood seems to be at odds with the educational ideals of their day?

In keeping with the spirit of the time, the above-mentioned preface takes "literally the leaf/sheet metonymy of ancient rhetoric"[3] and puts into play a "primordial writing [*Urschrift*] as the genesis of writing out of nature." The "impossible—that letters should appear in the realm of nature—becomes an actual event." What Kittler has demonstrated in another context can be observed here as well: *Urschrift*, primordial writing, is assigned exactly the same place "in the field of writing" as that inhabited by "the maternal voice as natural origin in the field of reading and speech" (ibid., 92/86).

Although this maternal voice never comes up in the story of the willful child, "primordial writing as the genesis of writing out of nature" is mentioned not only in the preface but also in the "Annotations to Individual Fairy Tales" (*Anmerkungen zu den einzelnen Märchen*) prepared by Jacob and Wilhelm Grimm for their first comprehensive edition of 1822:

> The hand growing out of the grave is a widespread superstition
> and is attributed not only to thieves, but also to violators of for-
> bidden trees [gebannt, i.e., declared to be holy and inviolable][4]
> and to patricides. . . . It is a mere transformation of this idea
> when flowers or inscribed pieces of paper grow out of the mound
> and mouth of the buried, indicating their guilt or innocence.
> There is also a legend and belief that the hand of one who has
> struck his parents grows out of the earth. (Grimm 1819–1822:
> 3:205–6)[5]

Hands, flowers, scraps of paper with writing on them: all appear here to function in the same way as signs, and this function is attributed to One Nature, as though they all possessed the same degree of naturalness. Signs and writing pass judgment over guilt and innocence, and these verdicts that sprout from the earth are immediately interpretable. In passing, as if it were a matter of course, willfulness, a relatively unspecific term, is reinterpreted explicitly as theft, violation of sacred trees, insulting one's parents, and even patricide. In short, willfulness comes to connote the worst of crimes.

Now, according to the preface, everything depends on the "proper use" (*rechter Gebrauch*) of these fairy tales, and such appropriate use will turn up "no evil," but will instead reveal, as a charming saying goes, "testimony of our heart." The text continues: "Children interpret fearlessly into the stars, while others, by popular belief, thereby offend the angels." Children also interpret words without fear, and they do so less by searching for a hidden meaning than simply by reading or hearing what is said. What is said is that willfulness is tantamount to crime, punishable by death, and not only by death, but by the impossibility of dying. What is said, too, is that "peace below the earth" is a reward, a reward, that is, for overcoming and renouncing willfulness, finally—below the earth—after the harshest of punishments. This is precisely the willfulness (*Eigensinn*) of which every child knows what it affirms: a will of one's own (*einen eigenen Sinn*), a wish, a desire that as such is already—and wrongly so—interpreted as the transgression of a prohibition. That such a transgression is punishable comes as no surprise. This punishment is as banal and inevitable as a child's guilt, which is always already established before any prohibition. What interests me here, however, is not this punishment but the fact that willfulness and the repression of willfulness *do not end* with the child's death. It is only through chastisement in and after death—chastisement by the mother (this is crucial)—only by chastisement of the dead child, if not of death itself, that both willfulness and its repression are exhausted.

What appeared in the mother's behavior to be an archaic remnant from times long past might turn out to indicate an antagonism that can never be mediated—not even by a reformed pedagogy: This is the conflict between, on the one hand, an "inner sense [*Sinn*] called the Mother's voice" (Kittler 1985: 35/29), which originates in nature and which lends to words an intelligible meaning and to subjects a soul,[6] and, on the other hand, a willfulness (*Eigensinn*) that, in contrast to such presumed inwardness, is necessarily outward in its orientation: a willfulness that resists any hermeneutic and that does not respond to the mother or to nature, to the demand to be understood and obeyed. This willfulness does not respond, then, with any kind of meaning or sense (*Sinn*) (whether acquired by learning or by empathy) or with any understanding, but simply, in an incorrigible tautology, opposes to mother or to nature nothing other than itself. Willfulness opposes the imperative of the production of sense with the bare fact of its occurrence. Thus, *Sinn* stands opposed to *Eigensinn*; the child's endless love for the mother, which produces itself anew in every future act of reading, stands opposed to the desire of the other; and the soul stands opposed to the affirmation of sexual difference.[7]

Thus, children are told, simple death can be squandered—by willfulness, for example. Good children will thus receive, as their ultimate reward, a simple death, one that will not need to be complicated and doubled by chastisement. This is, in fact, what is at issue here: the doubling of death, death within death.

It is significant that in the story of the willful child there is no third authority or agency; the dear Lord is just the double of the agency of the mother. Each outbids the other—the dear Lord by punishing willfulness while the child is alive, the mother by doing so postmortem. No father, no brothers or sisters appear; only the silent duel between the mother and the child, of which we do not even know whether it is a boy or a girl. The father's absence corresponds to the link that Jacob and Wilhelm Grimm establish in their annotation between the hand that reaches out from the earth and patricide. The father is indeed an empty space, but why? As the result of what sort of disappearance, if not of murder?

Would this fairy tale not be unthinkable with a different distribution of roles, one that cast a gender-determinate child opposite its father? Would it not also be unthinkable with another woman in one of the two main roles? The silent duel enacted here defines a context in which it is not possible to count to three.

To be able to count to three is, according to Lacan, the condition of the opening of the symbolic order, that is, the space of desire. And to be able to count to three is, for Freud, one of the conditions of the joke. Freud found some of the most successful jokes to be those in which someone makes fun of his own nature, makes himself the object of the joke, this being a conspicuous feature of Jewish jokes: "Incidentally, I do not know whether there are many other instances of a people making fun to such a degree of its own character" (Freud [1905] 1960: 112).

Such self-distancing, in reserving a space for a third person, explicitly recognizes this third agency, and thus another law, when the object of the joke is not only the person himself or herself, but also the signifier that supplies his or her proper name. Take, for instance, the famous joke about Katzmann, who emigrates to France and, fed up with this name that betrays his origins, decides to change it by way of translation: *Katz*, "cat," becomes *chat*; *Mann*, "man," becomes *l'homme*: from then on, his name is—*Chalom*.

> In order to better hide his (perhaps) Jewish origins, poorly
> covered by a German signifier, he transposes this signifier into
> another language and falls right back into his language of origin
> which is suddenly exposed, into his "true" language of origin

which he doubtless doesn't even speak, but which itself speaks
him, follows him, precedes him. . . . The Other, the Unconscious,
is here, in this hollow, in this empty space around which several
languages circle. (Sibony 1983: 58–59)

One could hardly be further from the indispensable third element
of the symbolic order such as can be found in the joke than in the story
of the willful child, in which no empty space can open up to the play of
signifiers, the play of a language that both speaks the subject and speaks
about the subject, long before this subject expresses itself in it. The
question of how one can speak a foreign language without having a
language of one's own[8] is answered here: this foreign language speaks
us before we speak it. The Jewish jokes cited by Freud recognize this,
the impact or effect of the Other as the locus of language. Seen in this
way, any talk of words having the meaning or sense given them by
nature becomes literally senseless. If a language is regarded as one's
own, as one's mother, as one's mother tongue, this is at the expense of
forgetting the locus of language, which is radically elsewhere, emerging
on another scene.

In the silent duel of the story of the willful child, in which there
is no opening up to a third agency, the child (which is here neither girl
nor boy) cannot evade the maternal agency, because this agency sus-
pends even the ultimate law, the law of that unattainable other — death.
The chastisement or persecution even in death takes place in the name
of the mother, in the name of nature, and in the name of the dear Lord.
It is directed against a willfulness (*Eigensinn*), against a sensuality
(*Sinnlichkeit*) that insists on the only possession that claims nothing of
its own: separation; a sensuality that insists on a spatial and temporal
interim, interval, or in-between (*Zwischen-Raum, Zwischen-Zeit*). The
willful child's mother closes this interval, the emptiness of the in-
between. She does not *speak*, and she repudiates the discourse of the
Other (Kittler 1985: 40/35) as the agency of the symbolic order that
allows an irreducible Other to break into the order of the mirror image
and of resemblance. In the Grimm story, the mother annuls the agency
of the law, of the third party, of the name, and replaces it with her own
law, which establishes and guarantees the absence of the third agency,
once and for all, and even in death.

The chastisement even in death annuls the empty in-between; it
annuls death just as it annuls language, the law, and desire. Death is

closed off by an inability to die, the punishment for willfulness. This death within death aims at the final eradication of willfulness, which never claims anything of its own, but affirms sensuality and the desire of separation, keeping its distance from any commonality or community with Mother Nature.

Now, every child knows the impossibility of its own innocence. Every child knows that the name of the willful child is its own name. It will try therefore to preserve willfulness but to undermine the chastisement, to make it impossible, that is, to break the maternal law. Above all, however, it will attempt to forget the scene, the image of punishment, and not only to repress the threat of death as much as the punishment in death, but, in view of the overwhelming nature of this threat, to shut the dead willful child whose name is its own in a secret tomb, in a crypt. And with the child, it will enclose the "words buried alive" that name the unspeakable prohibition, but that nevertheless have "the value of positive existence," because the prohibition was transgressed *before* the desire (whose fulfillment meant the transgression of the prohibition) was repressed (hence the child's harsh punishment) (Abraham and Torok 1987: 256/160).

It has already been pointed out that the mother's punishment surpasses even that of "the Other," of the divine agency, thus annulling the very divinity of this agency. Here, only the mother is omnipotent: she disposes even over death. She alone claims to be the child's law, meaning precisely that she recognizes no other law—indeed, she does not even recognize *that* there is law. Above all, the seeming asexuality of the child, the speechlessness of the scene, and the intervention of the dear Lord suggest that everything on the child's body that is reminiscent of

> the paternal contribution is denied and annulled [by the mother];
> and first and foremost, all that can serve as a reminder that [the
> child] is the fruit of a sexual union, that, as a sexed being, [it] is
> also the son [or the daughter] of the father. It is here that the
> foreclosure of the Name of the Father has its point of origin.[9]

And not only this. The demand addressed to the willful child is that it be not willful (*eigensinnig*), but rather, as the child of its mother, of one mind (*eines Sinnes*) with her: of one mind in every sense (*Sinn*), that is to say, also of one body with her. The child's resistance to this results in the mother's radical expulsion of the child, which robs it not only of its life, but also of death.[10] From this it follows that the child must not

exist as willful (*eigensinniges*), as its own (*eigenes*) subject that is separate from the mother. In other words, this means that the mother has
been unable to grant the child a body independent of herself. This
granting, however, is indispensable, indispensable according to a temporality that gives rise to the need for it even *before* a child can hear it:
before its birth. If a mother turns out to be incapable of according to her
child, even before its birth, an "imaginary body" independent of herself, a body that is of course completely distinct from the real fetus and
separate from her own body, but that will "give [the child] that point of
reference *outside* of [itself]" and "will permit [it]" to experience itself
"as 'other' than that state of coenesthesia" with the mother, "which is
experienced in an immanence at times anxious and at times compla-
cent" (De Waelhens 1972: 45/61; emphasis added), this is one of the
possible causes for the occurrence of psychosis. "Even before the separation of the two beings has taken place in the real, the infant already
exists as *one* and as *an other*, opening a way for the possible play of
identifications and recognitions—first on the part of the mother, and
then for both the mother and the child" (ibid., 45/62).

If the child is condemned to be of one mind and of one body with
its mother, then it will never be able to experience the imagined unity of
its body. "Therefore, there is little or no possibility for the future 'subject' to posit some 'elsewhere' beyond its chaotic immanence, which
would serve as the signifier of the unity it must still conquer" (ibid.,
49/65–66). In order to win the—always imaginary—"unity," a radical
Elsewhere is required, or, in Lacan's terms, a radical excentricity.

The stubborn willfulness of the child may now be illuminated as
an attempt to elude an absolute immanence, that is, ultimately, the fragmentation of psychosis. The mother's punishment is explained in this
light as the extreme reaction to the willfulness of an Other who resists
her law and whose resistance she can only understand as an illegitimate
rebellion, just as if a part of her own body had suddenly become
autonomous and, because it had determinedly eluded her control, had
been rejected and expelled.

As to the children who might hear this story and understand it
perfectly, it cannot be excluded that one or another of them will, in the
face of these threats, attempt to enclose the willful child in its vault
along with all its wishes, affirmations, and demands, and, along with
the words of its desire, which "have been struck by a catastrophe,
causing them to be withdrawn from circulation" (Abraham and Torok

1987: 256/160). But it is from out of this crypt that the words, the willful child, the willfulness of the child will continue their subversive activity. Against this subversive activity, however, the psychic agencies whose equilibrium is threatened by it will set up a defense, most effectively by way of paranoid projections. These projections might seek (and find) surrogates for the buried third agency and might expose them, as supposed persecutors, to ruthless persecution. It is just this mechanism—a persecution of the Other, motivated and nourished inter alia by paranoid projections, even into death—that Horkheimer and Adorno discerned in anti-Semitism.[11] Without claiming that it is possible to draw a straight, direct, historical line here, one should nevertheless keep in mind that from Luther to Hegel a certain Jewish willfulness—including the biblical characterization of Israel as "a stiff-necked people"[12] and the exegesis of Scripture and its meaning—has been rendered as impenitence, pride, coldness, lying, perversion, hatred, madness.[13] And it is certainly worth thinking about the fact that it was always only a short step to accusations of the bloodiest of crimes, and that in 1543 Luther was already recommending to the "rulers" (*Unsern Ober Herrn*) the burning down of synagogues and forced labor as drastic measures against the Jews, without, however, allowing himself to hope that this "would help." "If this does not help," not "this," and not the "merciless beating" (*Dreynschlagen*, exemplified by none other than Moses) that he also recommends, "we must drive them out like mad dogs" (Luther [1543] 1920: 541–42/292).

Katzmann, however, who, while crossing through the languages that cross him, cannot shed the language and the law of the Other; Katzmann, into whose senses and (to borrow from Paul Celan) into whose heart "living nothingness" (*das lebendige Nichts*) was inscribed, and who affirms the willfulness, the *Eigensinn*, the peculiar sense, *den eigenen Sinn*, of this living nothingness even against his will—this Katzmann would be hunted down in our century even in the remotest corners of Europe, and even his death was to be killed off.

Translated by Dana Hollander

Notes

This essay was first published as "Eigensinn," in Dietmar Kamper, Ulrich Sonnemann, and Rudolf Heinz, eds., *Wahnwelten im Zusammenstoß. Die Psychose als Spiegel der Zeit* (Berlin: Akademie Verlag, 1993). This essay first appeared in translation, under the title "Willfulness,"in *Semiotics 90/91*, ed. John Deely and Terry Prewitt (Lanham and London: University Press of America, 1993): 231–36.

1. "Das eigensinnige Kind," in Grimm [1819] 1949/1988, 564. Translation adapted from *The Complete Fairy Tales of the Brothers Grimm*, trans. Jack Zipes (Toronto and New York: Bantam Books, 1987), 422. Cf. a different translation in *The Complete Brothers Grimm Fairy Tales*, ed. Lily Owens (New York: Chatham River Press, 1981), 662. Note that these two translators do specify the gender of the willful child, and that they come to different conclusions.

2. Oskar Negt and Alexander Kluge devote a chapter to this fairy tale in *Geschichte und Eigensinn* (Frankfurt am Main: Zweitausendeins, 1981).

3. "... die alte Rhetorenmetonymie Blatt/Blatt": In German, *Blatt* means "leaf" and "sheet of paper."

4. Jacob and Wilhelm Grimm's *Deutsches Wörterbuch*, vol. 1, column 1116, quotes Friedrich Schiller, *Wilhelm Tell*: "... die bäume seien / gebannt, sagt er, und wer die schädige, / dem wachse seine hand heraus zum grabe."

5. As early as 1522, a *Meisterlied* by Hans Sachs explains: "reckt der tote Jüngling in Ingolstadt, der einst seine Mutter mißhandelt hatte, die Hand aus dem Grabe, bis jene auf den Rat der Doktoren und Geistlichen die Hand mit einer Rute blutig schlägt" (Bolte and Polívka 1963: 550).

6. Cf. Kittler 1985: 17/11: "[Faust] wants, not to leave thirst and desire open, as do philologists and rhetoricians, but to quench them so thoroughly that they are extinguished. The name of the death of desire, however, is soul."

7. Cf. Lacan 1975: 78: "Le *Horsexe*, voilà l'homme sur quoi l'âme spécula." Translated in Juliet Mitchell and Jacqueline Rose, eds., trans. Jacqueline Rose, *Feminine Sexuality: Jacques Lacan and the École Freudienne* (New York and London: W. W. Norton, 1983), 55: "The outside sex [*Horsexe*], such is mankind on whom the soul did speculate."

8. This is how Bernhard Siegert describes Kafka's relationship to Yiddish and German (Siegert 1990: 232).

9. Piera Aulagnier-Spairani, "Remarques sur la structure psychotique," *La Psychanalyse* 8 (1964): 54–55 (cited in De Waelhens 1972: 48/64).

10. The Brothers Grimm themselves mention an alternative—which is here impossible: In a Serbo-Croatian version of the belief "that the hand of one who has struck his parents grows out of the earth," the "hand [reaching] out of the grave" "is pulled back as soon as the mother withdraws her curse and kisses the hand" (Bolte and Polívka 1963: 550–51).

11. Max Horkheimer and Theodor Adorno, "Elemente des Antisemitismus," in *Dialektik der Aufklärung. Philosophische Fragmente* (Frankfurt am Main: Fischer, 1981). in "Elements of Anti-Semitism," in *Dialectic of Enlightenment*, trans. John Cumming (New York: Continuum, 1988).

12. See, for instance, Exod. 32:9 in Martin Buber's and Franz Rosenzweig's translation: "ein Volk hart von Nacken" (*Die fünf Bücher der Weisung* [Heidelberg: Lambert Schneider, 1954], 243).

13. See, for example, Martin Luther [1543] 1920, 427/149, 435/159, 483/218, etc.; G. W. F. Hegel [1798–1800] 1986, for example, 287/195. See also Pierre Legendre, "'Les Juifs se livrent à des interprétations insensées.' Expertise d'un texte," in Adélie and Jean-Jacques Rassial, eds., *La Psychanalyse est-elle une histoire juive?* (Paris: Seuil, 1981), 93–113.

Bibliography

English translations have been cited where available, and modified in the text as necessary.

Abraham, Nicolas, and Maria Torok. 1987. *L'Écorce et le noyau*. 2d ed. Paris: Flammarion. *The Shell and the Kernel: Renewals of Psychoanalysis*. Vol.1. Ed. and trans. Nicholas T. Rand. Chicago and London: University of Chicago Press, 1994.

Bolte, Johannes, and Georg Polívka, eds. 1963. *Anmerkungen zu den Kinder- und Hausmärchen der Brüder Grimm*. 2d ed., vol. 2. Hildesheim: Georg Olms.

De Waelhens, Alphonse. 1972. *La Psychose. Essai d'interprétation analytique et existentiale*, Louvain: Éditions Nauwelaerts. *Schizophrenia: A Philosophical Reflection on Lacan's Structuralist Interpretation*. Trans. W. Ver Eecke. Pittsburgh: Duquesne University Press, 1978.

Freud, Sigmund. [1905] 1960. "Jokes and Their Relation to the Unconscious." Trans. and ed. James Strachey, in collaboration with Anna Freud. In *The Standard Edition of the Complete Psychological Works of Sigmund Freud*. Vol. 8. London: Hogarth Press.

Grimm, Jacob and Wilhelm. [1819] 1949/1988. *Kinder- und Hausmärchen*. Munich: Winkler.

———. 1819–1822. *Kinder- und Hausmärchen*. Gesammelt durch die Brüder Grimm. 2d ed., 3 vols. Berlin: G. Reimer.

Hegel, G. W. F. [1798–1800] 1986. "Der Geist des Christentums und sein Schicksal." In *Werke*, vol.1, *Frühe Schriften*, ed. Eva Moldenhauer and Karl Markus Michel. Frankfurt am Main: Suhrkamp Verlag. "The Spirit of Christianity and Its Fate." Trans. T. M. Knox. In *Early Theological Writings*. Chicago: University of Chicago Press, 1948.

Horkheimer, Max, and Theodor Adorno, "Elemente des Antisemitismus," in *Dialektik der Aufklärung. Philosophische Fragmente* (Frankfurt am Main: Fischer, 1981). Published in English as "Elements of Anti-Semitism," in *Dialectic of Enlightenment*, trans. John Cumming (New York: Continuum, 1988).

Kittler, Friedrich. 1985. *Aufschreibesysteme 1800/1900*. Munich: Fink. *Discourse Networks 1800/1900*. Trans. Michael Metteer with Chris Cullens. Stanford, Calif.: Stanford University Press, 1990.

Lacan, Jacques. 1975. *Le Séminaire*, Book 20, *Encore*. Paris: Seuil.

Luther, Martin. [1543] 1920. "Von den Juden und ihren Lügen." In *Werke, Kritische Gesamtausgabe*, vol. 53. Weimar: Hermann Böhlaus Nachfolger. "On the Jews and Their Lies." Trans. Martin H. Bertram, in *Luther's Works*, ed. Helmut T. Lehmann, vol. 47, *The Christian in Society*, ed. Franklin Sherman. Philadelphia: Fortress Press, 1971.

Sibony, Daniel. 1983. *La Juive. Une transmission d'inconscient*. Paris: Bernard Grasset.

Siegert, Bernhard. 1990. "Kartographien der Zerstreuung. *Jargon* und die Schrift der jüdischen Tradierungsbewegung bei Kafka." In Wolf Kittler and Gerhard Neumann, eds., *Franz Kafka: Schriftverkehr*. Freiburg: Rombach, 222–47.

Of Wall, Sign, Screen, and Split

THE WALL AS NATIONAL MASS SYMBOL OF THE GERMANS

Klaus Theweleit

The mass symbol of the Germans was the army. But the army was always more than the army: it was the marching forest. In no modern country worldwide has the feeling for the forest remained so alive as in Germany. The rigidity and parallel lines of the erect trees, their density and sheer number, fill the heart of the German with a profound and secret joy. To this day he seeks out the forest in which his ancestors lived and feels himself one with the trees.

Their cleanliness and stark separation from one another, the emphasis on verticality, distinguishes this forest from the tropical jungle where creeping vines grow together in every direction....

The individual tree, however, is larger than the single human, and grows ever more redoubtable with age. Its steadfastness has much of the same virtue of the warrior. In a forest in which trees of many of the same species are found, the bark of the trees, which may at first seem like armor, in fact resembles the uniforms of an army regiment. Army and forest were for the German, without his being aware of it, in every way merged together. What might appear to others stark and bleak in the army has for the German the life and radiance of the forest. There he had no fear; he felt protected, one of all these others. The abruptness and straightness of the trees he accepted as his code of conduct.

The young boy who was driven out of the narrow confines of the home into the forest, in order, so he believed, to dream and to be alone, thus experienced in advance his ultimate entry into the army. In the forest, the others already stood in readiness, those who were loyal, true, and upright, just as he should be, one just like the other, because each one grows straight up, and yet quite different in height and strength. One should not underestimate the effect of this early forest romanticism on the German. He absorbed it through scores of songs and poems, and the forest that appeared in them was often named "German."

The Englishman liked to imagine himself *on the ocean*, the German enjoyed seeing himself *in the forest*; it would be difficult to express the differences in their national feeling more concisely.[1]

Whether that still resonates now, all the way to the millennium, is a question of only secondary interest. The aging of texts has less to do with their contents than with their mediatic materiality. And as media, Elias Canetti's texts are rather like word baths—invigorating ones—one swims in them and becomes water oneself, that is, thought; perhaps Canetti would no longer say "forest" today; but it would still remain valid that the "national mass symbol" lives on in affects.

These are only apparently contradictory complexes of feeling that Canetti saw as connected with the individual German's entry into the collective body of the forest: on the one side "joy"/"feeling oneself at one"/"experiencing acceptance," and on the other side "separateness"/"cleanliness"/"protection." A combination of effusiveness and a certain protective function ("the armor of the tree bark") adds up to "power" and "life": the German entering the forest was composed in equal parts, according to this account, of emotion and SS body training.

> The direction in which it pulls a person's eyes is that of its own transformation: the forest grows inexorably upward. The sameness of the trunks is approximate, even that reflects more the sameness of direction. Whoever goes into the forest feels sheltered; he is not at the highest point where it continues to grow, nor at the place of its greatest density. Precisely this density is the protection it gives, and the protection lies above. Thus, the forest became the original mode for reverence. It compels man to look upward, grateful for the protection lain over him. Looking up many trunks becomes a looking upward as such. The forest prefigures the church experience, the standing before God amid pillars and buttresses. Its most regular and therefore perfect expression is the dome of the cathedral, with all the trunks woven into an ultimate and inseparable unity.[2]

With the effusion of becoming one and the goal-oriented clarity of self-protection comes a third experience, a church feeling: the greater body in which the individual German oriented his existence in national-symbolic terms was therefore a cathedral: Greater Germany.

A cathedral, a dome—let us say, the sky over Berlin at the fall of the Wall, at the singing of Beethoven/Schiller, joy, the feeling of unity, the cathedralesque—all divine sparks present in excess; but more on this later.

The psychophysical process involved in the individual's joining a national mass symbol is the production of the wholeness of the person. The German, says Canetti, achieved wholeness through absorption into a greater whole: the army. The German was a soldier. The body of the army thus became the superbody of every individual German; the boundaries of the male body and of the military body were on the outside absolutely identical. That is the reason why individual Germans left over from that time still react with such sensitivity whenever anyone calls into question the narrative of the "absolute cleanliness" of the Nazi army in World War II. They don't just feel that way—they are personally attacked; they exist still, even now, not as individual persons, but rather perpetually as part of this greater unity: the army must remain clean, must have remained clean, otherwise their own bodies would lie there as severed body parts, as fragmenting bodies in the dirt.

In letters to the editor to this day, therefore, no rapes were ever committed by German soldiers' bodies, the army never killed any Russians (save in the honest battle of the forest against the steppe), and it had never, in all the occupied territories under military command, had anything to do with the deportation of the Jews ... What does the forest know of the train—or of the desert? Surely, nothing at all.

The perpetual effectiveness of national mass symbols in some bodies is readily legible in these reactions, and also in the way they appear: namely, as body armor, modeled in these cases on the bark of trees.

Requiem for One Still Living

Now, since the 1970s, during the transition the Germans underwent from Nazi history to pardoned, post-Nazi history, which was also a transition from a political to an ecological history, much evil has befallen the German forest: among other things, the forest died. And it wasn't only that the connection between forest and army had been forced apart by the Allies: the forest succumbed to acid rain, coal dust, auto exhaust, ozone hole, bark-boring beetles. In short, the forest grew ill—triumph gave way to infirmity. Rarely has one seen a national mass symbol decay so pitiably and heartrendingly—its leaves withered, its power surrendered, utterly broken. Forests may in fact still survive, in the realm of the real, but not so *the Forest* in the reality of national mass symbols. The Forest that had provided protection now became a

patient in need of protection: the army, so that it might be spared a similar fate, had to distance itself from this dying.

When I first had the opportunity to travel to America in the late
1980s, so as to convince myself of the other than mythological existence of the continent, I found that all real Americans, at least those
interested in Europe, were in agreement on the issue of the forest:
"When I was in Europe last year, when I was in Germany, everything
was totally green"—said with hearty laughter—"Germany is *nothing
but* forest," they said, "except for a few cities—and you talk about
Waldsterben" (they all knew the German word). If some parts really are
dying, they said, "those are particular monocultures, especially those of
the conifer family; they always die after eighty to a hundred years—
that's normal—check when the trees were planted, you'll see..."

For them, the "dying forest" was very clearly a German national
mass fantasy.

What was I supposed to say? "The newspapers in Germany maintain that Americans are not interested in ecology," I said. Laughter
again: "Smell the difference," they said. The absent stench of gasoline
in large U.S. cities decided the matter easily in their favor—in which
country ecology was carried out more with symbols and where it was
conducted with catalytic converters.

"Then reforest! Rethink your forest management practices, if the
monocultures are dying. Ahh, but you would rather sit around and
speculate about the body politic..." The German, even as an ecologist,
becomes identified as a perpetual man of the woods, a forest person,
however, who presides over the death of the forest. And of course the
dying of the forest played such a tremendous role in Germany precisely
because more than just the green of the trees was dying.

> The trees have finally given up
> Paper tigers slide through the forests,
> Disguised as recyclers ...

Thus the opening of a poem from the early 1980s by the now deceased
Wolfgang Neuss. The forest, he determined, still exists in the first place
as a source of pulp, as a natural resource for newspapers.

National mass symbols not only have a unifying function; they
also hold a power of purification for those who join their cult. The
acceptance that the members experience is one of being taken up into a
big clean body. The formulation "the poisoned forest" already indicates

the extent to which the forest can no longer carry out that function of purification associated with national mass symbolism. Accordingly, the discussion about environmental pollution in the Federal Republic of Germany was an assemblage of real fears and findings and the linguistic-argumentary confusion that characterizes the public sphere in instances of uncertainty or with major shifts in the greater psychic atmospheric conditions of nations with a heavily media-influenced public.

The forest/the waste/the poison, especially the poisons in foods, are of course real existing problems, but they become translated, through newspaper and television, against the background desire of the individual body for redemptive absorption into the purifying Greater Body, almost automatically into concepts of the politics of belonging and isolation. These come to fruition in Germany, then as now, as a politics of cleanliness.

In the dying of the forest, in waste, in the poisoning of the environment was thus a portion of perpetuation of fantasies of the clean, radically isolated but included German body, as well as a portion of the search for renewal and security with regard to the national mass symbol.

The Body Is the Battlefield

Feelings of accord and belonging, the so-called construction of identity, always start playing out on the skin. Identity in the infant develops as a bodily feeling: according to the degrees of closeness and rejection felt through that body, and through the bodies that hold and nourish him, or do not hold and do not nourish him. If they push him away, let him starve, waste away in the cold, in fits of screaming, in diffuse pain and disorganized motor activity, he develops perhaps only rudimentary perceptions of a sense of correspondence with himself. One must be taken up, taken into, and animated by another body in order at some point to become an individual separated body that can get along without the means of incorporation of and violence against others. Every young child must be stimulated and animated through touching, attention, feeding, warm beds, beautiful tones, through language, mild air, surrounding water, or through cuddly stuffed animals. At the same time, the child gets drained of liveliness, hindered in the development of its energies, through punishments, condemnation, stretches of cold and hunger, threats from siblings, through icy silent treatments and many other forms of neglect—in extreme cases, robbed of life itself, simply killed off. That is to say, the child inhabits both a sensitive and an anesthetized body.

"Identity": I am in accordance with another body. With the ability for greater differentiation of bodies and objects in the infant—the ability to evaluate various bodies emotionally, the ability to generate the "No" position—there slowly grows a kernel that can be called "I." At the same time, the human body moves in a rhythmic alternation between the feeling of correspondence and a sense of rejection.

Where the primary correspondence with other bodies, where the early kernels of identity through symbiosis with nurturing, protecting, holding bodies were missing, identity—which is produced out of one's own "self-lived" history—can develop only with great difficulty. The body that remains *foreign to itself* is then shunted toward forms of identity outside itself: toward social identities, identities thrust upon him, according to whose norms and structures he can learn to "behave."

What Canetti calls the mass symbols of nations are precisely such offers of imposition and imposture, such offers of help for the massively produced individuals with bodies that have not yet been fully born. The process of the experience of acceptance has, against this background, a dangerous verso: each act of being accepted ("I belong to …") corresponds on the other side to a splitting off ("I don't belong to …"; or "That person/those people don't belong to …").

National mass symbols thus also provide information about the degree of psychic splitting dominant in the individual bodies belonging to a "nation," about the degree of their feelings of irreality, and that means in turn about the degree of their specific madness or sanity in relation to the national standard of insanity that surrounds them.

In relation to its masses, all nations display something like a standard of insanity, whose rising or fall is physically perceivable to everyone in the country, on the one hand as an emotional charging that compels them to perform certain actions, and on the other as a constant source of danger; their evaluation of the source determines their own proximity or distance to the mass actions of the body politic. (Emigration might be interpreted as the consequence of a consistently high threshold of insanity in a people.)

Split: a few people will recall that Germany, until recently, was not simply a divided country but a split country; in Germany, this is being forgotten or split off with great dispatch.

A split, however, does not begin by going through a country but by passing through people, through each individual person.

Through every body there runs a split, at the very least along this line of differentiation: a strong fluctuation between degrees of activity and numbness in the limbs, fluctuation in various realms of function and perception, and in motor and emotional abilities. In the attempts of our bodies to enliven themselves, or to deaden themselves, to make freer those zones of occupation, to turn defensive reactions into sensitive ones, to make out of those areas ruled by repetition compulsion and compulsion to work areas that get rid of the imbedded thorns of coercive forces by making connections with other people—in all these efforts, I see attempts at a second, a third, a fourth birth, attempts by the body not yet completely born to give birth to itself again, to become more real, or, as functional components of social machinery, more unfeeling, but also thereby more real.

In Germany between 1870 and 1945, there lay the task, especially in the military, to give birth anew through drills and marches to bodies of individual men. They were outfitted with a muscular and behavioral identity, and thus became other Germans and otherly German than they had been before the military. There is no more precise identification of the symbol craved by their bodies than the army/the forest.

In comparable ways, factories, sports associations, and youth groups intervened in bodies. Architecture adds on to the bodily boundaries, through the interior walls of apartments ... the beds. Whoever grows up outdoors under an open sky and in wide-open places, to him the sky becomes part of his bodily boundary; to the mountain man the mountains, to the typist the ceiling or the cone cast by the lamp's illumination.

Bodies do not end where we, with our eyes, perceive that they end. They pass over into other bodies, they construct themselves with the aid of auxiliary bodies, they transform themselves into part bodies of the various mass formations in which they act. In some branches of psychoanalysis there is a concept of body imago: this is the body representation that every individual person has of his or her own body. It can include the body parts of other people and, just as easily, exclude certain of its own body parts; it can join with city borders, national borders, with forests, oceans, the desert—with anything at all that is demarcated by borders.

The topos of "the city or state as a human body with head, limbs, and a stomach, which has been infecting political theory since ancient times" (as Karl Markus Michel formulates it) is based on the existence of the body imago. The ethnologist Mary Douglas has described how, particularly in cultures with little differentiation in infrastructure, in so-called primitive societies, the compulsion to equate bodily boundaries with the borders of their land is accepted as natural. Violations of those geographic borders are experienced as woundings of the body itself and are answered in kind: with panic and then with war.

Bodies in Pieces

Germany after World War I must in this respect have been a very primitive nation, at least the salient majority. The correspondence of the individual body with the body of Germany in the folksy propaganda of the Nazis was, in any case, total. There is scarcely a text on the situation of "Germany" in this period—hardly a report, a biography, a novel, a political pamphlet—that would not have portrayed the conquered German nations as a dismembered body: Upper Silesia had been "severed off" ... North Schleswig ... the Saar region: the "amputated" limbs and members of the Great German Body. The "corridor" ... a cut through German flesh with a Polish knife ... the most painful wounding ... the Baltic states: a piece torn out of the shoulder of the German giant ... the haunches harassed by Belgians ... the French tear away at the loins ... the Poles dance on his back ... the butchers of entente had arrived with a cleaver ... black occupying forces on the Rhine and Moselle, filled with cannibalistic desire ... the termites of Versailles, unscrupulously democratic ... gnawing away, lips smacking, at the great white German body that a cowardly stab in the back (Jewish weaklings and women on strike on the home front) had laid low ... to feed the vultures of dismemberment.

The members and limbs were to be reattached, bodily integrity restored. That is the fundamental affective position of the nationalistic politics of the *Volk* throughout the twentieth century. Hitler was the conscious executor of this state of mind.

The movements advertised a return home, back into the Reich; all the plebiscites conducted in the "cutoff" territories, all annexations were carried out as the fantastic restoration of the body of Germany made whole and healthy again. Hitler was the healer, to whom one shouted "Heil Hitler," which contains in the same "hail" greeting the injunction to "heal," a very precise greeting. The body stood larger and more powerful than it had been and was to grow more and more as a form of restitution for the dismemberment that had taken place: Austria was to be annexed to the body, sutured onto it, and then on to the East: Bohemia, Czechoslovakia, Poland . . . corporeal protectorates, ruled by "Defense Squadrons" . . . Germany begins its defensive war . . . the body of Greater Germany was unstoppable in its healing growth, the forest set itself in motion and took off . . . thus, the individual body, one's own body, became ever greater, ever more powerful, unwoundable, together with the individual Greater German soldierly oak, a rock of one burgeoning body.

A millionfold fantasy of indestructibility was thus sent off into World War II. Since the time of Genghis Khan's Indians on their pony rockets never had so many invincible soldiers stamped their marching feet upon the earth—invincible as end result of having been put back together again. Some, it had to be admitted, later on could not meet the requirements and took the correction of their miscalculation through Major Generals and grenades . . . an unpleasant chapter . . . the Germans don't like to think about it . . . the Germans did not like to think about it . . . (not as long as they were the losers) . . . they had the conquering tree inside their bodies . . .

Two Bodies, One Soul

The nature of Germany's dismemberment that ensued with the end of World War II as the punishment for its insatiable master-race body took quite a different form, one considerably better suited to the German body image. No longer were limbs clipped off piecemeal here and there, but great, clean cuts were made by surgeons of another kind. Sectors . . . zones . . . ultimately there remained two large formations, subordinated to the two major political power blocks. This was far more tolerable and more favorable for development than the many small "senseless" cuts following World War I.

I tried to underscore this a few years ago in a footnote I added to the book *Reagan's America* by Lloyd de Mause, which Jürgen Freund and I translated into German. The footnote took its lead from de Mause's view that the older, more backward psychic classes of a society have no objection to the sacrifice of the young men of their country in wartime—in Canetti's words: the elders transform themselves into survivors, and transform the young men into the dead—that the psy-chic class of "survivors" gladly sees this sacrifice and uses it as balm for feelings of guilt harbored as a result of its generation's excesses and transgressions. The text of the note, written in 1984, reads as follows:

> Precisely for this reason, the West Germans are the psychological victors of the Second World War (as has often been noted with astonishment): they had succeeded in putting behind them the greatest festival of slaughter: the Jews were gone, the communists gone, the workers' movement broken, the sexual revolt of the twenties snuffed out, with "strength through joy," full speed ahead into the Adenauer era, in their back twenty million Russian war dead (most of whom were not killed on the battlefield but were murdered as civilians), but the army had remained, as we all know, clean, and whole generations of their own young people, to please the gods, littered the battlefields and rotted—the sacrifice in the First World War had in this respect completely failed: it had not eliminated but had rather unleashed sexuality, communism, and Jewish libertinage. Only the Second World War was truly satisfying and opened up future perspectives. And for that reason, solely for that reason, was the psychic energy so abundantly available for the postwar reconstruction, which could proceed so undisturbed by all the murders precisely because that had been its precondition—the sacrifice had been successful, and everything evil was on the other side, over there, in the other state. Never in the history of the world had there been a cleaner state-entity than the Federal Republic of Germany after 1949.
>
> The famous detergents that figured in debates for and against the new state stood for something real, the total detergent blood, the blood of those sacrificed in the Second World War. The white tablecloths, with which the tables were covered and history covered up, were won from that blood, and for that reason the few remaining members of the Communist Party in the 1950s had to disappear back into prisons or into oblivion or, their identities changed, into the leadership of the German Social Democratic Party, because they were the spot of blood on the neatly set tables, on which the cadavers of the sacrificed were eaten in the ritual of the so-called wave of feeding. It could be proven statistically: the number of broiled chickens that were consumed in Jahn's "Wienerwald" fast-food chain up to the middle of the 1960s should roughly equal the number of humans killed in the Second World War. It seems less appropriate to discover an inability of the Germans after the war (the inability to mourn, for example) than to stress their abilities, their amazing ability to make the very best of awful situations: it was the first great satisfaction, on this

order of magnitude, of their desire for murder and sacrifice (all under the cover of the necessity of the healing war) that made it possible to set about the task of reconstruction in the 1950s in such a cheerful manner and to set a course, undisturbed, into the liberated land of uninhibited philistine bliss. And the Sinti and Roma, for example, have the same circumstance to thank for their perpetual registration and harassment; they are the leftovers from the concentration camps, ghosts sprung from the lists of those to be sacrificed. The blood stain doesn't stop seeping through somewhere. But even the beneficial effect of the sacrifice is still without end. Secure in the reputation as the worst murderers in history and as members of the cleanest state-entity, Germans still behave with relative reassurance, everything under control, or "Roger," as schoolchildren say these days. Triumph of the older psycho classes.

I wrote that in 1984 for West German citizens. Like another good split-off and splitting West German who didn't really care much for the East because of its world-famous uncommunism, I had not considered the East Germans.

Meanwhile, the Wall is gone, and the sharp division of Germany, as far as the structure of the state is concerned, has been dissolved. If anything made sense in what I had written about the function of the Wall in 1984, then the falling away of the Wall must have produced massive displacements in the psychic security system of the Germans.

One seldom gets such a chance to assess speculative pronouncements on "history"; usually, it simply turns out that one was in error and that history had, once again, done what it usually does, namely, play a trick on you; but here it seemed to me that I had not been so far off the mark.

Since then, it occurs to me, even more so than in 1984, that the Wall was a security bulwark for the psychological perversions not only of the West Germans, but of the East Germans as well; that the Wall was not simply an East German prison wall, but also a deeply mutual East–West coproduction, necessary for both sides for the splitting off of that which had been so deeply repressed. In a first construction of the Wall, in the hectic building efforts of restoration in the West, it was not Hitler but rather the connection between the citizens of the Federal Republic and Nazism that was being walled up and away; the German Democratic Republic could offer no corresponding structure in opposition; so it answered (under pressure from the Soviet Union) with its wall, *the* Wall, which prevented the citizens of the Democratic Republic from defecting into that false construction of walls. In the course of the years that followed, the Wall was beloved outright by the West Germans (although officially under censure) as guarantor of the fantasy of their own well-being, of the evil of the others, and of their own redemption from history: I believe that, in the 1970s and 1980s, the Wall became a new national mass symbol in Canetti's sense: the Wall was heir to the forest. The German (of either state) did not run to the army to experience the absorption into the collective Greater Body; he built himself up brand-new as a purified body, split off through the Wall from history, the body of a new historical epoch of nonwar, of the stalemate between the power blocks, a stalemate whose signal visible expression was the Wall.

Precursors in this function were the "Siegfried Line" of World War I and the "Atlantic Wall" of World War II, which was supposed to wall off magically the ocean itself and America, which lay beyond it. The divisive wall also appears in another catchphrase of the fifties: someone should be "lined up against the wall." Everything in sympathy with things Russian fell under this categorical imperative.

In the Federal Republic, history disappeared behind false marble facades, in a world of beautiful commodities, in the body of the department-store cathedrals.

In a structurally parallel manner, the Democratic Republic used the Wall for its cut with the Hitler history. As a state of obligatory antifascism, it had similarly done away with Nazism without ever having come to terms with what had happened. The Democratic Republic too had landed in a sort of fantastic paradise; on one side, America delivered one from one's own history; on the other side, the Soviet Union—together, the two world war victors gave the individual German body absolution.

The Falling Away of "Over There"

The splitting off of what happened in one's own history was the true soul, the heart, of both Germanys. "Over there" was valid on both this and on the other side of the Wall. The "good" thing was precisely that one was not "over there," that is, on the side of one's greatest evil (either communism or capitalism); the Wall guaranteed the type of redemption best suited for either side.

"Please keep an eye on the fate of the word *drüben* [over there]," I was advised in 1990, after the fall of the Wall, by a Jewish American woman, one of the many daughters of exiles at American universities who are interested in German history. Even from that distance, the word to her seemed to be *the* linguistic hallmark of the German postwar period: "Why don't you go over there"—that was in fact the West German motto for almost forty years; just as "over there" was the central fantasy in the East right through the end of the division, as in the lines: "Wo die Westzitronen blühen / da-hien, möchte ich ziehn" (There where the western lemons bloom, thither would I go).

Thus, one wall with two "over there's. "This national mass symbol, the wall, did not disappear as quickly as did the one of stone, which found its way into houses: a *pars pro toto* souvenir in all Berlin households; it could not disappear that quickly, because psychic displacements follow laws other than those dictated by television interventions, at a different tempo than broadcast tempo or the tempo of demolition.

If the Wall was part of a comprehensive system of security set up against "history"—against all sorts of covered-up anxieties that the German societies carry around with them: against "communism," against "capitalism," against anarchy, against one's own accountability for the murder of the Jews—then all these exclusions had to come out in the light of day with the fall of the Wall, in a form different from the previous one of splitting. And they did exactly that, and with great celerity. The so-called shift to the right in Germany seems to me to be the becoming visible of a potential for violence that was there all along, but covered up, successfully hidden with the help of the "brothers and sisters" over there, with the help of the fantasy about the cleanliness of one's own state image, and in the West with the added help of the continually increasing gross national product.

National symbols, mass symbols, function in times of peace as big containers for the poison and the insanity of a whole people; the West Germans deposited monstrous amounts of their toxicity under the Wall; thanks to the curtain, the iron one, the insanity threshold was kept at a relatively low level.

That one could say something similar about the German Democratic Republic is clear to me in the way, among other things, that Wolf Biermann continued unflappably, for several years, singing the song about the "better half," the half that had deported him, a man with a "double woe": the Democratic Republic as the "in principle" better

Germany, even for one of its sharpest critics (at least until he finally recanted that sentence in all its versions). Even in the Democratic Republic the wall container was set up for the huge quantity of national toxins that had to be dumped somewhere: the guilt for the imprisonment belonged to capitalism ... they lived behind a wall that the enemy had forced them to build. One went to the secret police as to the confessional: the sins of the neighbors, those who sympathized with the other side over there. Tilman Moser writes that, for the unofficial collaborator, the secret-police agent often had a therapist's function: drain off the poison, restore stability; join the greater whole. The secret police files ... a wall the length of the Great Wall of China. The secret police as the great open container for "fascism," with unlimited powers of comprehension: "Hitler—not here!" ... And there's work here too ... in the West, unemployment is ever on the rise ... and to the left, there are those students ... (even when their status as leftists had to be twisted around to fit the idea of the left that suited the Democratic Republic). All that was not simply nothing: it functioned in fact for an astonishingly long time and appeared halfway palatable to many citizens of the German Democratic Republic.

After the fall of the Wall, after the falling away of the great toxic waste container, there appeared first of all the open hatred of foreigners (which the Democratic Republic had officially forbidden and which the Federal Republic had channeled with the help of the other side over there and through the possibilities opened up by an extended tourist industry; there appeared again the ugly residues of undigested history, anti-Semitism and the hatred of the unloved sibling nations, a sudden right radicalism as a counterreaction to state-issued antifascism. There appeared in the West the tendency to judge without mercy (a consequence of the undigested history in the Federal Republic of the Nazi "People's Court"), and there appeared in the East the Western pathway to happiness: the stampede into the department stores and auto dealerships ... everything that had been covered over now burst forth ... The Empire Strikes Back ... the empire of the evil locked away in the body ... here too not created anew: it had merely been buried beneath the Wall.

Revenge and Reunification

As cynical Westerner, who could do just fine "without" the Democratic Republic, I am belatedly grateful to the Wall because of its function as security system controlling the worst traits of the Germans. For forty years it was possible to live in Germany—on the condition of the existence of two German states—as if there were peace. At the moment of "unity," I feared that this peace might vanish; beyond the one truly happy moment, when the Wall fell, I never celebrated German unity again, not for a second, but rather experienced it as the opening celebration of possible future wars in which Germans would participate, the preparations for which are currently on the agenda of German politics.

Unification has "happened," but it also didn't happen: especially not in the economy, and economic unification will not happen for some time; this is only partly because of the former economic system of the Democratic Republic, which was seen as too decrepit for any reasonable prospect of its restoration, and only partly because of the Mafia-like activities of the State Trust set up for the privatization of the former East German economy. The delay in economic unification is also the result of the un-Caesarean conduct by the West, if we are willing to accept Caesar as a representative of the historical principle of political gentleness, of *clementia*: the West takes revenge on the East; it takes revenge for the removal of the beautiful splitting device. It is not by accident that communism is down today; every teacher believes the phrases about the Eastern bloc that for forty years he told his students ... After all, we have proof ... "socialism cannot work, because human nature is against it." "Private property and a free market economy" have been Darwinistically affirmed, with banners flapping, by nature as by history, conceived now as economic law of nature. First of all, the people from the East, who stupidly resisted for so long, have to fall to their knees; first of all, they must realize just what kind of crap they fabricated over there (behind the Wall); not in order that they "comprehend" anything, but to make sure that the Westerner can profit from his victory (after all, it took forty years of hard labor to deprive oneself of the blessings one could expect of a possible socialism in a rich society). So now the Western state-security type, steeled by renunciation—here it was possible to be a secret-police informer if necessary without the extra effort of denunciation—this Western type thus enjoys his historical moment.

The Germans unified themselves somewhere else entirely: in their national, collective symbol. The Wall is gone ... long live the Wall. In the course of recent years, the Germans from both states have managed to rebuild the wall, the wall on which they depend so much in order to secure the continuation of their modes of thinking and perception. It is not a question of creating "two, three Vietnams," but of creating two, three Walls . . . "Vietnamese out of Germany!" — that was the first. In its so-called politics and policies for foreigners, the unified Germany set out to rebuild the Wall that, up until 1989, cut right through the middle of its body, but this time to secure its outer border: the "secure third countries" (Poland, the Czech Republic, Austria) are once again serving as the belt of stone special-ordered by parliament to fit around the German hips of lard. They form a wall against the East, against the notorious forces of the steppe and of the Caucasus, against "balkanization" as the very embodiment of the Non-German Principle. Again, we have the so-called gypsies, and they belong to Romania, as their name "Roma" indicates and demands; there is, again, the country that has to serve as sacrifice for well-known historical reasons (the only major political figure in Germany who publicly complained about the attitude of the German media toward Serbia as structural perpetuation of anti-Semitism was, at times, Peter Glotz) . . . but, on the other hand, hundreds of thousands of "Germans" living along the Volga and in Siebenbürgen have to live . . . a German passport awaits each one of them within one week . . . after all, most of them are ultraconservatives; please stand on the right side of the Wall; a good trading policy for the strengthening of the Christian Democratic national team.

Wall, Shield

The wall that is created by individual Germans at the new borders of country and body is more modern, more technological in design: it is a wall made by electronics. Currently, it is being tested most palpably in Bavaria and in other German border jungles: an electronic barrier in the hands of the German border control against illegal entry of black Moors across "green borders"; whether or not that will work: the belief generated by German TV that such a strategic defense initiative (SDI) shield can in principle deter every unauthorized foreign foot from stepping onto German soil and into the German living room is fatally sufficient for restructuring the "wall in the head" (as German newspapers love to call it): the wall as a kind of Nibelungen-electronic shield. Protective shield citizens, the German flag draped around the body just as the national soccer players display it on their jerseys: a wall (barely camouflaged as jagged wave) of a world—excluding black, red, and gold, running around the body.

The wall as *shield*: this word brings us close to the truth, namely, to the guilt that is kept on the other side of the wall by force and power. Fending off guilt consumes all the force and power the Germans can muster. The Germans from both states are absolutely determined to continue living in a state of historical innocence, even if it takes becoming a neo-Nazi. Even that extinguishes guilt: Hitler was just another mugger with a club; is that really so horrible, after all? And now: put the wall and shield around the historical preserves!

The unbelievable gall of a chancellor who dared to demand the grace of innocence even already for the first post-Nazi generation just forty years after the Nazi slogan could be heard all across Germany—that the Jews had to atone "up to the thousandth member" (that is, up to the end of all generations)—appears as believable, of course (it goes without saying), to all wall Germans.

The splitting off of Nazi history away from the feelings of the people was the emotional core of the Federal Republic's formation; this annihilation of history repeats itself with full force directed now against the German Democratic Republic.

Every Easterner (every artist over there) who ever entered the inner core of secret-police headquarters is now apprehended as a Nazi collaborator; in addition, we have the antijugglers who say: Let's forget it! We have to be able to forgive. Both attitudes sweep the history that was—for example, the history of the actual resistance to East German despotism—right under the rug, just as the real resistance raised up against the Nazis was made to disappear in the commotion around the self-presentation by certain members of the Christian Democratic Union as resistance fighters too.

What really was—just has to be split off. The German body cannot stand to be in proximity even to the least significant historical truth; this is because of the enormous amount of guilt this body nevertheless senses very well. Shield against guilt: electronic as well as law-giving wall.

The governing Christian Democrats would like to maintain this wall and reinvent it as a wall of blood: the core substance of the Nazis, the inherited German blood, will continue to decide which body can legitimately claim the right to call itself "German"—and which one cannot.

Screen Cover

The electronic shield does not only have the shape of the border light barrier; I also see it shining where the German directs his gaze nightly during his evening political devotions: on the TV screen.

In the so-called news coverage of the Gulf War, we saw for the first time in all clarity how the TV screen can be used as an SDI shield against all perception of reality. There, more than anywhere else, it could be proven. But that was already the whole difference from every-day TV: the calculated irreality, which runs across the screens as news every night, not only generates the permanent effect of abyssal disin-formation, it works beyond that to produce precisely that effect which the photographing Gulf War missiles produced by their strikes on tar-get: namely, the transfer of the phantasm of invulnerability onto the TV viewer. The screen works upon the viewer's firm belief that the world does not exist beyond the TV image—except for when he travels in the summer.

Behind the TV screen, the viewer himself remains invisible, all guilt is beyond all walls, all that is golden remains in one's living room, and the German turns into Alberich, invisible under his magic cap. Invisible, sheltered behind the Wall; not wanting to share "the trea-sure," not with one's own East, not at all with "foreigners"; making contact with the world via a beam of transmission. Once again, the Germans have unified in a Nibelungen-like mass symbol—and that is a dangerous symptom. Nowadays, they don't refer to the master race; they are content with being "another race," German simply ... of another bloodline.

In 1985, Wolfgang Neuss, while joking about the then at times publicly articulate hope for a cancellation of Germany's divided state, managed to come up with the following profound and prophetic for-mulation: he called it the desire for a "reunification of the two halves of the aspirin tablet [*Spalttablette*]." That is precisely the madness: the wish to reunify the line of splitting into halves impressed upon the aspirin tablet. One cannot reunify that which splits, it remains a split tablet, only bigger; aspirin with the split down the middle to the second power: that's the Greater Germany nowadays; split-off tablet behind the wall that splits off: "nobody sees us"; "we see everything" ... and what does the German do when he—split off from everything—is not seen by anybody while he sees everything: he begins to feel responsible.

The responsibility, say, for a military pacification of Bosnia (at the moment when it seemed least likely to achieve anything worthwhile); at least a German colonization of Somalia under UN blue helmets. I am reminded of Jean-Luc Godard, who said about Bertolt Brecht's plays that Brecht could only be "performed in Somalia, and precisely in German." So the German army had to go to Somalia in order to prepare for that one. (A failure for Brecht, to be sure.)

The German discourse about military responsibility for the fate of Yugoslavia's remainder, the fate of Somalia, or whatever might have moved into their place in the meantime—a responsibility that the world expects us to bear—can only be understood as a product of splitting off: the splitting off from everything that the people of other countries and nations really expect from Germany (first of all, that German soldiers stay at home).

Splittings: We are invisible . . . we do not exist . . . just as Hitler never existed (behind those walls made of German forest and the German army) . . . and if we do exist, we are good . . . "no other country accepts as many foreigners as Germany" . . . yes, but also no other country sends so many away again.

The decision about who will or will not be persecuted elsewhere is up to the German bureaucracy that assesses the situation: in June 1993, the German government and the opposition party published a list of countries in which (they claim) political persecution "does not take place." Seated safely behind the wall, the screen, surveilling everything, the electronically guided fingers make contact with global situations. "To mix one's fingers in the affairs of other people" is the longstanding favorite pastime not only of German journalism . . . each lead article is a prescriptive catechism for indigenous and foreign citizens . . . elsewhere, with powerful weapons, raped women are rescued . . . massacred Muslims . . . but they do not have to come over here; rather, we should possibly go over there with the German army (purified by the donning of those magic caps) . . . that is what the heart of the TV-watching, walled-in, invulnerable, and intrusive German truly desires; and if we cannot yet use the army, then we should at least be able to add oil to the flames, as was the case with Foreign Minister Dietrich Genscher's (oh so friendly) recognition of Croatia. Just as is the case with all mass symbols of nations, what is hidden here is the phantasm of ominipotence that can be translated into action.

The most invisible of all the Alberichs crouching behind the wall that already always existed, the SDI-trained German army, slowly attains something like a social reality in the process ... in Germany you never see soldiers ... aside from those drunks riding the trains on weekends ... they are sitting in the split ... just like the soldiers of the German Democratic Republic who sat "behind the Wall" with their rifles ready to fire ... Split specialists in uniform—and perhaps also, all of a sudden, headache specialists in a newly splitting Europe.

The so-called Military Protection Agency (Militärischer Abschirm-dienst) complements the German wall fantasy step by step, making preparations for a military protection that nevertheless advances.

With the blessings of the highest command: on July 4, 1993, we find in the paper *Welt am Sonntag* the notice that Chancellor Helmut Kohl was not planning to participate in the celebrations commemorating the fiftieth anniversary of the landing of Allied forces on the beaches of Normandy. The Press Secretary: "Do you really believe the chancellor would contemplate attending the celebration of an event in which German soldiers suffered defeat?" Up until then, I had assumed that the victory over Hitler's troops in June 1944 marked (at least officially) the laying of the foundation of the current German state. But that is no longer the case. (It later turned out that it was the Allies who had not wanted Kohl to take part. Vogel was just mentioning the chancellor's absence in passing.)

Warning: the forest as army/the army as forest—in that combination there was also implied the inevitability of defeat, as in the eventual felling of trees. Forest as army was possessed by something unreal, fantastic, if not completely insane: the army/the forest as German mass symbol clearly expresses a sylvan-shaded madness. This insanity has not gone away; rather, it is in the process of being transformed into the next mass symbol, the technologized wall: the electronic screen sickens from its phantasm of invulnerability. At least I doubt whether the Germans will succeed historically with their slogan of certainty, "Whoever watches TV will not die!" Something will come and haunt them behind their TV-SDI.

Shame

In conclusion, two reflections on the dissolution of national mass symbols.

First, shame. The shame lacking in most Germans in regard to the atrocities committed by Nazi Germany guarantees that they do not recognize the past even in its most banal and least important aspects. The Germans, insofar as they want to be subsumed under such a collective naming (and most of them want this, while every halfway reasonable human being, at the latest by the end of adolescence, no longer wishes to belong to any "nation"), do not know what that is: shame. That one should be able to be ashamed for something one did not do oneself, but that was perhaps done by one's parents ... people from town whom one knows or even someone one doesn't know at all ... groups, hordes, mobs of people who acted in the name of Germany, or at least with the consent of large portions of the German people—this feeling is beyond the Germans.

"But why? Why should we be ashamed?"

In the course of time, I have learned that they really don't know what that is ... how it works, "to be ashamed." They are not stubborn, not calculating in this respect. They completely cast it aside. But why me? How could one? But I wasn't even ... The sense of "shame" is simply inaccessible to them—something very beautiful that they therefore lack, but they don't know it.

Only the one who can feel "shame" for the things that he has done, for things that were done in his proximity, for things that humankind has done, has access to his own history, his own corporeal history, his own political history, and gets access therefore to the history of others. Whoever does not know this feeling (it involves a dissolution of the body, a meltdown of oneself—the body dissolves in shimmering heat and then reconstructs itself, "purified"), whoever does not know this hallucinatory acknowledgment of the beauty of the existence of others, before whose beauty one feels shame, will be barred, without half a chance or hope, from the perception of the mode of existence of other human beings.

By explicitly refusing to be ashamed about the crimes that were committed in the name of Germany up through 1945, most Germans today show that they are as uninterested in getting to know this history as they are in what their own current history could be. Bernhard Vesper called these instransigent resisters of their own humanization on all fronts "vegetables."

Today, most Germans think that the shameless slogan "I have nothing against the Turks" represents the ultimate imperative of tolerance and worldly openness. They do not know that it is a racist pronouncement because they cannot feel it. Every sensitive human feels shame when he hears such a statement. Whoever can say it has no idea why he should be ashamed. "But didn't I say: I have nothing against the Turks? Isn't that enough? I also have nothing against women or communists."

Man, stop it. But man doesn't stop. Man neither recognizes his racism nor the shamelessness that rises up and says: "Man, I think you're actually really terrific." This is because of the lack of reasonable limits (skin instead of walls) between them. What is still not, now as before, a reliable given in Germany are the most simple forms of restraint, characterized by the political concept of "nonintervention" in the affairs of one's neighbors. Parents, teachers, friends, lovers, children, neighbors, and so on, hardly have any inhibitions about the no-fuss intervention, about the interference in another life with prescription, constraint, opinion, and hints—hints are a big hit in Germany. The people have not grown apart very well. They form a cozy nexus in their knots of family, siblings, friends, and lovers, in the knots of club, pub, apartment such that they know the expansion of their own space as little as the place where the other person begins; they do not experience it as something real, they live in great part in a feeling of permanent irreality. The interferences that come from behind the "wall" are their differentiation aid; they are a mode of guarantee of the other's existence, but a very bad guarantee, a barbaric one at that. The members of a nation that is actually proud of belonging to an "old culture" are extremely underdeveloped in psychophysiological terms. Before they can make the rest of the world pleased about anything "German," they must have become what they are not—individuals: singular beings, separated from other individuals: without an eye on some nebulous mixing. But only very few desire this. It is also not demanded by any public institution of importance right now in Germany.

Unity and Justice and ...

Second, the law. The insensitivity of Germans vis-à-vis their horrible self-righteousness is a condensation of Germany's relation to history. Not just the fact that in the German administration of justice, in the institutional body of a bureaucracy of justice, hardly any significant cleanup of the Nazi elements took place after 1945; in the same way, it has been kept out of individual bodies. Otherwise there would have emerged a high degree of sensitivity regarding the stance of "being right," of being in the right, that builds up a wall between those deserving to live and those condemned to die. With the gesture of "being in the right," Poland was attacked in 1939 and then the rest of Europe, in particular the Bolshevik Soviet Union. With the gesture of being absolutely in the right, Germany went through with the attempt to exterminate the Jews. To that end, there weren't only laws to obey or executive orders to follow, the whole compulsion to do one's duty, but rather an extended canon of civilian, everyday self-righteous modes of argumentation for the sake of legitimizing one's actions and opinions: a complicity of being in the right among Germans. The violation of rights during World War II did not only take place in the name of a law posited by the state, but also with the support of a personal canon of justice shared by many: subjectively, we did the right thing, we were not conscious of doing any wrong, and so on.

That's good, if that's the way it was then a massive mistrust of being right, of the very form of existence of being in the right, should have emerged, namely when this attitude had proved not to exclude but rather to include the most horrible acts of injustice and crime.

What is the case, however, is that in every family feud, in every political discussion, in every economic debate, in sports, in the war zone of intimate relations, and without inhibition against the children, the position of being right celebrates undiminished victories; war is waged, tricks, cheating, deceptions performed with proofs and counter-proofs, arguments and counterarguments; love is recalled, demanded back; the way things are gets twisted around until they fit, until one finds oneself in the unassailable position of being right, in this tackiest of all petty thief positions, for what is easier in the world of causality than discovery and presentation of reasons: reasons for this, reasons for that, proofs, so-called facts? All this we know, already at our mother's breast, is pure power game. The "facts" are hopelessly off the mark when it is access to the "Real" that is wanted; there are fewer and fewer "facts"; they exist only as material for the arbitrary and flexible manip-ulation of legitimations, statistics, and devices of illumination. What a fact is, is determined by some bureaucratic agency, a company, an insti-tution, or whoever or whatever happens to be in power to do so. In emergency cases, the military has the last word, and otherwise we are constantly being told what's what by all sorts of judges and authorities. Who wants to rely on such a thing when a human relation is at stake, a relation to the dead or to the truth of a relationship? Unfortunately, the answer is: everybody, almost everybody. Every discourse, be it private or public, even the discourse of the left, even the green-ecological ones, refers to and legitimizes itself in reference to a discourse of what is legally right. To this day, they don't notice that that's a discourse, all right, specifically an unjust one.

To formulate it in terms of the discourse of drug abuse, which alone seems adequate when dealing with a certain usage of national mass symbols: the Germans had an overdose of nationalism, Prussian nationalism, imperial chauvinism, Nazi superhuman Germanness; they became world champions in German hard work, discipline, won a few European championships in German tourism, gold medals in German economic superiority, gold medals in German industriousness, and with all this they received the secure conviction that it all was a reward given out by "History" for being "German." But the Germans are in need of recovery treatment, several rehab treatments, and a decades-long maintenance of sobriety and abstinence.

This abstinence was indeed achieved in many quarters; but the events in recent years have, to a great extent, reversed this progress.

Right now, the most wall-headed position in Germany is the total editing out of the different starting points of the two Germanys following World War II: financial and economic and political support of the Western part by the Americans on the one hand, and on the other hand the entire lack of support, and that means the application of the Morgenthau Plan, the complete dismantling of the German Democratic Republic's industrial capability by the Soviet Union. Today, West Germans stubbornly insist that the proven economic superiority of the Federal Republic over the Democratic Republic was a product of their industriousness. They do not acknowledge the support they received, and thus need give thanks to nobody for anything. They did it all on their own, alone behind their view of the wall (and yet they would not have been able to reunify in 1990 without the consent of the Allies—which, unhappily, they received). Alone, behind their wall, on which they now stand and bear the burden of responsibility. What they urgently need is someone who could take the burden from them. Even hordes of elephantine political councils could not carry it.

The Double Wall

A question at the end: Can a construction like "the Wall," which is so negatively cathected in the public sphere, function at all as a national mass symbol?

My answer is no—unless the splitting of the Wall itself were already in two places at once: one visible wall (with "death strip," fatal border patrols), which is negatively cathected; a second, invisible wall (wall as protective shield, splitting off magic), which is positively cathected. The foreclosure of the Wall by the official German political establishment even seems to be the condition for its functioning as a secret container of poisonous waste. Its public usage as auxiliary splitting device would have caused the Germans to appear "shameless," and thus would have generated precisely the feeling that the wall served to exclude.

The fantastic electronic SDI shield is also subject to this double coding. As barrier for the sheer exclusion of other people, it is an embarrassment; but it is simply terrific as an electronic locating device that has brought the forest paths under high-tech contol commensurate with the progress of engineering.

The multiple coding of all that is essentially German was, among other things, a specialty of the Nazis; in the 1930s, for example, it served as a way for all the engineers to get into Nazism. It was impossible to lure them with a "blood-and-soil" rhetoric; that was the formula prescribed for the normal nontechnical racist. For the high-tech members of the master race, there was the apotheosis of technological achievement (the exact counterpart of the blood-and-soil rhetoric), there was the "German inventive genius" leading the way in whatever was technically possible in the modern world. The fact that "the machine" was negatively cathected and German sensibility positively did not prevent the exact reversal of this valorization within those spheres dominated by an aristocracy of engineers.

"March separately, strike together" was not for nothing the valid formula for German military strategies since 1870. Split and reunite; double coding; hide/make public.

The hypothesis of John Patillo-Hess that behind the wall shield there lurks a survival of the German army as mass symbol cannot simply be dismissed; the Germans would have then allowed their forest to die in order to preserve the army; the shockingly widespread affirmation among Germans of the historical reemergence of the German army is more that an index for the plausibility of this hypothesis. As the saying goes, "The German army should be as normal as other armies": born again into visibility, electronically reconstituted, separated from the woods by a clean cut. Finally, the Germans will have become modern: from the protection of the woods to the protection under shields of technology—cathedrals of another kind. They already appeared as domes of light above Nazi rallies, walls of light directed against the evil of the world and the cosmos in all its absolute darkness.

Airplanes, however, could not be stopped by this state performance of optical omnipotence. Today, the invisible shield promises better protection. The key phrase of the military after World War I— "As long as we have not lost the war, the war is not over"—found a new basis after 1990 in the breakthrough into the East of concrete. Alberich has come up from his hiding place of roots and concrete; he no longer needs to hide; now the entire "nation" plays magic cap games.

That is true for the entire "Fortress Europe" some conference participants from the "postcommunist" countries throw up for discussion. It is possible that the post-Wall Germans are, in this regard, truly a European avant-garde.

You only die twice. With this book title Konrad Paul Liessmann tried to console himself, us, and the doubly dead Karl Marx. Marx, who died in 1883 and in 1989, can now live in peace as a normal inhabitant of the friendly worlds of libraries. Bayreuth, however, continues its production line; as far as I can see, Wagner's second death is still quite far off.

Translated by Laurence A. Rickels

Notes

1. Elias Canetti, *Masse und Macht* (Frankfurt am Main: Fischer, 1980), 190–91.
2. Ibid., 92–93.

On Watching *Crumb*

Susan Derwin

In the spring of 1996, I organized for the annual meeting of the University of California Psychoanalytic Consortium a screening of *Crumb*, Terry Zwigoff's documentary about the countercultural comic-book artist Robert Crumb. The Consortium represents an interdisciplinary grouping of University of California faculty, including many clinicians, but not excluding colleagues from literature, political science, or history whose investment in psychoanalysis is strictly theoretical. *Crumb*, the subject of the documentary I selected for this professional group, is the creator of such characters as Fritz the Cat and Mr. Natural, as well as the "Keep on Truckin'" cartoon so ubiquitous in the 1960s.

Zwigoff introduces Crumb, his professional reputation, and his family history through a series of interviews and scenes with family members, former girlfriends, comic-strip artists, an editor, an art critic, a journalist, and a gallery owner. We learn that Crumb, his two brothers, and his two sisters (who refused to be interviewed) were raised in the McCarthy era by a father who had fought in World War II and who, afterward, wanted to create a world of predictability, conformity, and control. He was a salesman by profession, and he had written a manual titled *Training People Effectively*. The "training" at home involved regular beatings for the boys, each of whom was a social misfit. Beatrice, Crumb's mother, became addicted in the 1950s to diet pills. In one scene, Charles, Crumb's older brother, reminisces about how his father used to borrow Beatrice's makeup to camouflage the cuts and bruises on his face, the results of her hyped-up tirades. Charles and Robert recall how, in this tense atmosphere, the siblings, led by Charles, formed a society for the creation of comic books. The sons showed themselves to be gifted artists, but only Robert managed eventually to use his art to maintain some kind of connection, both to himself and to the world.

At the time of the filming, Charles was dependent on antidepressants and living a reclusive life with his mother in a shabby fortress of a house in which quilts and sheets were draped over the furniture and the shades were kept drawn over the windows. Charles's artistic development had ended in graphomania; his last work was a book filled completely with minuscule lines that resembled words but were meaningless markings. Maxon, Robert's younger brother, was living by himself in a cheap hotel in San Francisco. The film records him meditating on a homemade bed of nails and practicing intestinal purgation and shows his formalist paintings of female nudes that, as one critic puts it, even a "generous ... apologist for masculine fantasy ... would be pressed to justify."[1]

I felt certain that a group referring to itself as a Psychoanalytic Consortium would be engaged and stimulated by *Crumb*. I had expected that the clinicians would view it as possessing the richness of a satisfying case history, while the humanists would be receptive to the symmetry between the film's subject matter and structure. The reality was otherwise. When the screening was over, the group was silent, the mood was tense. Slowly, a few people began to speak about the film, and they had nothing good to say about it. A graduate student criticized Crumb's art on the grounds that it was sexist. One clinician thought it racist, while another believed that the making of the documentary had probably led to the suicide of Charles, who had most likely killed himself out of shame, after having been so mercilessly exposed in the film. The same person also believed that it would have been preferable if Crumb had not been an artist, if that would have meant that he could have better come to terms with his life. A third clinician felt that the experience of watching the documentary had been simply unbearable, while a fourth suggested that, in the absence of any feeling, Crumb would have been better off killing himself. A lone dissenter eventually came forth, a professor of literature, who saw beauty in the way Crumb's brothers had survived their childhood, notwithstanding the fact that Maxon had accosted women and Charles had committed suicide.

The praise of the brother's lives in aesthetic terms surprised me as much as the repudiations of Crumb's art, his existence, and the film itself. I was baffled by the fact that my predictions about this group's responses had been so inaccurate. With my miscalculations in mind, I watched the film again. This time through I noticed that Zwigoff had included interviews with people who felt about Crumb's artwork very much as we had felt about the film. In other words, he had actually anticipated both our favorable and our negative reactions. The camp of Crumb supporters was headed by critic Robert Hughes, who praised Crumb's work in art-historical terms, comparing his unsettling grotesques to the work of Breughel. Among Crumb's detractors were Trina Robbins, a cartoonist who discussed the unfortunate sexist turn that Crumb's work had taken once he started "vomiting up" his unconscious; Peggy Orenstein, a journalist who related how, as a child, she was traumatized by the monstrous females in Crumb's comics; Deidre English, a magazine editor, who felt that Crumb's work should not be published on the grounds that it was racist and sexist; and, indirectly, Crumb's father, who, according to Crumb, after seeing his work, stopped talking to him.

To the extent that we, as an audience, were rehearsing the responses of Crumb's critics, it felt to me as though we were acting, and acting out psychoanalytically, parts in a film whose script we had never read. This is what one critic was alluding to when he wrote that "Crumb is a rare instance of a film which has no unconscious—it refuses any reading which it does not itself supply, and second-guesses our responses before we can make them."[2]

Indeed, it does seem that Zwigoff included the comments of the "expert talking heads"[3] in order to influence the audience's reaction to his film. I suspect, however, that his perspicacity did not come from a desire to tell the audience how to read the film, but rather how not to read it. I say this because Zwigoff used various forms of irony to offer points of view on the critics themselves. The cartoonist Bill Griffith, for example, spoke about the superficiality of dismissive moralizing readings of Crumb's work. And when Robert Hughes situated Crumb in the tradition of great artists of the abject, Zwigoff deflated Hughes's rhetoric by telling him that Crumb masturbates to his own work, a remark that caused Hughes to stutter into silence.

Zwigoff's irony does not negate the validity of the critics' comments. But it does expose their irrelevance to Zwigoff's own project. This effect is most evident in his treatment of Crumb's supposed sexism. Although English and Robbins make a legitimate case for the work's demeaning representations of women, their perspective seems abstract and academic compared to other women who speak about the way Crumb's drawings have helped ample women to feel "empowered." The effect of including all of this discussion about the virtues and liabilities of Crumb's work is to make each comment seem partial and removed from the work's vitality. As a result, the viewer who aligns himself or herself with any of the critics risks assuming an analogously obtuse position.

This is precisely what happened during the screening. My sense is that I and my colleagues identified with those commenting on Crumb rather than with Crumb himself. And we did this in order to repudiate our identification with Crumb on a deeper level, an identification that, for reasons to be examined, was too disconcerting. In what follows, I will discuss what I see as the relationship between our reactions and Zwigoff's presentation of Robert Crumb.

Zwigoff constructed his documentary in the spirit of Crumb's aversion to the libidinal attraction of power—the power of money, of fame, of Hollywood, of corporate America. He does not translate Crumb's experience into a conventional story that, say, might track a gifted artist's triumph over the travails of his tragic childhood. He stays away from such reassuring fictions and even sheds light on their artificiality. This may explain why he directs his irony at the critics who attempt to define Crumb's work through their different discourses—psychoanalytic, feminist, racial, aesthetic. At least as Zwigoff presents them, these modes of understanding produce predictable narratives out of a body of work that, like its creator, is much too complex and original to be schematized by any system of thought.

I believe that Zwigoff wanted his audience to encounter Robert Crumb on his own terms. In order to achieve this, Zwigoff represents Robert's life and work from the inside out, without the evaluating or judging that can thus be left to the critics. He captures what it is like to be Robert Crumb, and he compels his viewers to enter into Crumb's experience along with him.

The crux of that experience is already announced by the organizing plot of the documentary, namely, Robert's preparations for, and the event of, his move to France with his wife Aline and daughter Sophie. This departure is the corollary of a lifelong psychological practice of Robert's: over and over again the documentary portrays him trying to absent himself emotionally from situations and relationships. This practice is most apparent in the conversations between Robert and his brothers, in which he seems to wall himself off from the experiences his brothers recount to him: Charles discusses his suicide attempts, his dependence on antidepressants, his complete reclusion and detachment from the human race, his antisocial behavior as a youth; Maxon recalls having been the scapegoat of his brothers and sisters and relates the history of his seizures and his sexual assaults on women. Robert hardly contributes more than an occasional laugh or wisecrack to those conversations. It is as if, through silence, he vigilantly attempts to isolate himself from the pain they expose.

The way the three brothers relate their history is as revealing as the actual portrait of the family that emerges. Charles and Maxon talk about their experiences in psychological terms. Charles says of himself, for example, that he emulated his domineering father in his relations with his siblings. He speaks of his injured narcissism, his suicidal tendencies, and the sibling rivalry in the family. The technical language he uses seems to work as a controlling mechanism, structuring, and thereby helping him to manage, his emotions. A comic Charles drew as a young man illustrates the oppressiveness of this relation to language. In the comic, two characters all but disappear beneath the lower horizontal leg of the frame, squeezed out of the limited space by the balloons filled with their dialogue. The way he talks about himself makes you wonder if his eventual suicide wasn't the consequence of his agonizing isolation, from himself as much as from others.

Maxon also analyzes himself from a psychological perspective. He recalls his rage at having been assigned the role of supply boy in the drawing society of the Crumb children and links his seizures to his repressed sexuality. We also learn through Robert that Maxon is jealous of Charles because, according to him, Charles got all of their mother's love.

Robert, by contrast, recalls the violence in his childhood as if he were speaking about another person. For example, he relates an episode that occurred when he was five years old. On Christmas Day, his father broke the boy's collar bone. Robert relates the facts of this trauma and then, as if in lieu of personal response, shifts the discussion to Charles's history of misbehaving.

This practice of speaking about anything but his emotions is endemic to Robert's personality. As long as he is discussing topics other than himself, such as music, or instructing his son in technical points of drawing, or providing social commentary, his wit is sharp and his focus clear-eyed. But when it comes to offering insight into his own psychological makeup or exposing any vulnerability, he is nonplussed. He either does not, cannot, or will not speak about such matters. Early in the film, Zwigoff asks Robert to identify the emotional sources of his work. In response, he shrugs his shoulders and, like a goofy adolescent, answers, "I dunno."

During his conversations with his family, Robert recedes into the background, creating the impression that the other Crumbs have temporarily displaced him from his position as the film's focal point. The title of the film is illustrative in this regard: it does not specify which Crumb the film is about, not because there are multiple subjects in the film (if there were, it would be called "Crumbs") but because Robert is a kind of shadow figure whose affective life is always elsewhere. The emotions of his family stand in for his own interior life, which always seems to be beyond reach.

Robert's appearance also creates the impression that he is present in body alone. On his tall, thin frame he often wears a baggy suit and bowler, an outfit that calls attention to him and disguises him at the same time. Thus costumed, he appears like a Jack Sprat who would be all but invisible were it not for his clothing. His bottle-bottom glasses magnify his eyes to cartoon proportions and add to the effect of camouflage. His wife Aline confirms the impression Crumb gives of wanting to be invisible; she comments, "He's definitely a person who would rather be a brain in a jar than a person in a body. Basically, we both focus on my body sexually. He never takes his shirt off. He just likes to ... not exist."

Ironically, the visibility of Crumb's body is heightened when it becomes the target of aggression, both playful and earnest. In a photo shoot, for example, he assumes a supine position on the floor, pinned beneath the shoes of a line of women. In another scene, Robert reminisces with Kathy Goodell, a former girlfriend, about their ill-fated relationship. Spontaneously, the discussion erupts in testy violence when Kathy kicks Robert in the shins.

If Kathy Goodell wants to make contact with Crumb through violence, Jesse, Crumb's son by a first marriage, wants to touch him through tenderness. He says that sometimes he wants to put his arm around his father, shake his hand, or get close in some way, but that his father can't do these things. In speaking about his father's emotional unavailability in terms of the impossibility of making physical contact with him, Jesse has underscored Robert's ultimate goal: to be beyond reach. Given this, Kathy's gesture of striking out and Jesse's wish to touch his father suggest that they both experience Robert's elusiveness as a form of aggression.

Not surprisingly, the relationships that Robert sustains are based on a mutuality of disconnection. When asked how she feels about his extramarital affairs, Aline quips, "I go out with other men." In another scene, Sophie is sitting on Robert's lap and Robert gives her a kiss on the cheek that she promptly wipes off, a loving gesture of indifference that indicates she is her father's daughter.

The affective life always on the run has a destination, Robert's artwork. Aline makes clear the relationship between Robert's inaccessibility and his art when she says that Robert "depicts his id in its pure form." She recounts how, when they first met, "He . . . never talked. He just drew the whole time. He was . . . catatonic and the only voice he had was his pen."

As the voice of his id, Robert's art is his living language. One of the last scenes in the film stages this function of his art. In an empty room, Robert runs his hand over a blank wall, which is itself evocative of a large canvas. Seen in this way, the wall/canvas appears to be the object that Robert can openly make contact with. The sensuality of the gesture suggests that in his art the connection absent from his relationships materializes.

The two scenes that frame the film bear out the existential significance of his art. The first shows Robert beginning a drawing. The second reveals the completed drawing to be of Robert in bed, pinned there by an invasive, looming camera, the one filming the documentary. The dialogue bubble contains the sentence "I feel nauseous." By positioning these two scenes at the beginning and end, respectively, Zwigoff has created a framing structure that parallels and dramatizes the way drawing holds Robert together. The links between the intervening scenes underscore the existential function of drawing. As one critic has observed of the film's content: "Such diverse material, potentially cluttered and discursive, is henstitched [sic] by Zwigoff and Livingston's [the editor's] rhythmic sense," which creates a film of "unremitting tempo."[4] This rhythmic sense is the filmic counterpart to Robert's own instinct for form, an instinct that is life-saving, as Robert's own words attest: "If I don't draw for a while, I get real depressed and suicidal."

Although Robert says that drawing is the force that keeps him alive, in the next sentence he retracts such a romantic notion. "But I get suicidal when I draw too," he concludes. In keeping with Robert's refusal to espouse psychological truisms about himself, Zwigoff resists "the temptation to treat the relationship between the life and the work as a connect-the-dots exercise."[5] He "doesn't allow the audience (or himself) the illusion that the movie has captured the artist's essence for posterity."[6] Although Zwigoff presents a great deal of material about Crumb's life that can serve as the basis for analyzing the relationship between it and Crumb's art, he avoids making definitive claims about this relationship. This is evident in his presentation of Crumb's drawings of women. Typically, Crumb represents women as larger than life with detachable heads or heads of animals. Zwigoff has included commentary from the cartoonist Trina Robbins and the magazine editor Deidre English, both of whom see Robert's work as sexist, racist, and pornographic. Although he does not directly deny these epithets, Zwigoff provides a context for Crumb's work that may explain its influence in more empathic terms. Crumb himself comments upon what it was like for his father's generation to raise families in the post–World War II era. He points out the connection between the war and that generation's pursuit of stability and conventionality. This account introduces the possibility that the foreboding female figures in Crumb's drawings bespeak his desire to create counterweights and foils to his father, who did not hesitate to use violence to create a "stable" environment at home. The spatial relations between the figures in Crumb's drawings may indicate the extreme anxiety his father's violence produced in Crumb: he often represents women from the perspective of a male figure who, by comparison, is dwarfed. These women may be seen as idealized doubles of the youthful Robert, whose thin body was no match for his father's adult strength.

Although the female figures in Crumb's work loom portentously over the males, the threat they pose is often preempted in the cartoons through a technique of reversal. Thus, the women become the objects, rather than agents, of violence, which is not surprising given Crumb's defenselessness against his father and the rage this defenselessness must have engendered in him. A good example of this technique is a cartoon that so disturbed Crumb he only completed it upon Aline's urging. It depicts a towering woman whose head is shoved into her body so that she can be used indiscriminately as an object of male sexual domination.

What Crumb does not say, but what the documentary and his art show, is the formidable, and one senses controlling, presence of Beatrice Crumb, who, in her corpulence, looks like a figure out of Crumb's drawings. Having survived the death of her husband, whom, we know, she used to beat up, she now lives with Charles and the pet cats. Mother and son refer to them as "the little girls," as if to suggest that the cats are the children of the "couple" Beatrice and Charles. In spite of her initial unwillingness to be filmed, once on screen she does most of the talking. And even when Charles, not she, is being interviewed, she shouts orders from off camera that he promptly follows. One wonders if the three sons' recollections of their violent father functions, at least in part, like a screen memory behind which stands this unspoken maternal force.[7]

Zwigoff's approach to Robert has a great deal in common with Robert's approach to the subjects of his art. In a scene in which Robert instructs his son in drawing techniques, he demonstrates his ability to use his own experience as a key to imagining the state of mind of the figures he draws in order to capture their image. He comments on a photograph of a woman of the nineteenth century in an English asylum, attributing the set of her jaw to her defiance in face of having been forced to sit against her will for the photo. In another scene, in which he is also sketching photos, this time of girls he had a crush on in high school, he mentions that he wishes these girls were with him instead of the camera crew filming him. These two scenes beg to be read in tandem. Taken together, they seem to illustrate how Robert makes use of his current situation as the subject of Zwigoff's documentary to identify with the female inmate of the madhouse. But Zwigoff forestalls such a pat understanding of the relation between Robert's work and art by separating the two scenes by many minutes and intervening scenes. By refraining from placing the scenes in direct sequence, he seems to be reminding the viewer that any conclusion about the connection between the scenes is at best speculative.

Following Crumb's own technique, Zwigoff attempts to shape himself and the film in Robert's image. To do this, he, like Robert, tries to efface himself. He appears to be present only as a disembodied voice that occasionally asks questions from off camera.[8] The one visual reference to him is a small sketch that Robert drew of him in a notebook. By including this drawing, Zwigoff underscores the way he has given up his identity to Robert, his subject, who now literally determines

Zwigoff's own form. Another moment of sympathetic merging occurs when Kathy kicks Robert. In that scene, the camera is thrown off balance, as if in identification with the assaulted Robert. The conversations between Robert and his brothers and mother further suggest how Zwigoff aligns himself with Robert. In them Robert often seems to take over Zwigoff's role as interviewer, in a move that parallels the family's assumption at times of Robert's central role in the film.

We can now understand more fully the implications of the critic's remark that the film has no unconscious. In remaining true to Crumb's experience, Zwigoff does not construct a master narrative that would claim to know any more about Crumb's unconscious than Crumb knows about it himself. At the same time, Zwigoff enables us to recognize Robert's evasiveness as a sign of the presence of an unconscious whose content remains unfathomable.

Given that Zwigoff shapes his documentary after Robert's identity, the question remains: Where is Robert's unconscious if it is not visible in the film itself? We know that in his life, his art is the site of his unconscious. I would suggest that the audience functions in an analogous way: it serves as the repository of Crumb's unconscious. Thus positioned, the audience is asked to hold the repressed affective experience contained by and in Crumb's work, to play host to the id of the Crumb constructed by Zwigoff.

I believe that the reactions of my colleagues were already saying something about the experience that the film had projected onto its audience. With the exception of the person who actually felt how "unbearable" it was to watch the film, they had summoned their master discourses of choice—feminist, psychoanalytic, political, aesthetic—to protect themselves from the impact of the intense affective experience the film had poured into them. They had used their analytic tools to repudiate or praise what they believed to be the cause of their reactions, be it Crumb, his work, the lives of his brothers, or the film as a whole. I believe that this was their way of managing the extreme anxiety the film had stimulated, an anxiety that was as much a part of Robert Crumb's history as of their own. I see now that I, too, had shielded myself from the film's unconscious projections by focusing on the film's form. My admiration was of a piece with my colleagues' praise and derision.

Zwigoff has created a story about what it would be like to be Robert Crumb, the man on the run from his unconscious, his history, the memories stored in his body. In our capacity—or rather, incapac-ity—as an audience to hold Crumb's pain and stay close to its source, we were not so very different from one another, and, in a way, from Crumb, whose evasion of himself and the modern world has given him a place in it.

Notes

1. Michael Eaton, "Drawing It Out," *Sight and Sound* 5:7 (July 1995): 34–35.
2. Ibid.
3. Terrence Rafferty, "Mr. Unnatural," *New Yorker* 71:10 (May 1, 1995): 92.
4. Ibid.
5. Ibid.
6. Donald Phelps, "Crumb of Discomfort," *Film Commentary*, 31:4 (July–August 1995): 84
7. I am indebted to Elisabeth Weber's astute observations about Beatrice Crumb.
8. I do not mean to imply that Zwigoff is not in complete control of the film. On the contrary, he has discussed the extent of his manipulation of the material.

Untitled (group-of-one), Nancy Barton, 1999

Contributors

Peter Canning earned his Ph.D. in comparative literature at Harvard University and has taught at the University of California, Berkeley, and the University of Minnesota. His essays have been published in the journals *Qui Parle*, *SubStance*, *Artforum International*, and *Copyright*, as well as in the volume *Looking after Nietzsche*. A renowned Lacanian theorist, Canning resides and writes in Burbank, California.

Julie Carlson is associate professor of English at the University of California, Santa Barbara. She is the author of *In the Theatre of Romanticism: Coleridge, Nationalism, Women*, and has published numerous articles on English and German Romantic drama and theater.

Susan Derwin is associate professor of German and comparative literature at the University of California, Santa Barbara, where she is chair of the program in comparative literature. Her research interests concern psychoanalytic theory, history of the novel, and Holocaust studies. She is the author of *The Ambivalence of Form: Lukács, Freud, and the Novel*.

Andrew Hewitt is associate professor at the State University of New York at Buffalo, where he chairs the department of comparative literature. He has written extensively on questions of modernism, politics, and sexuality, and is the author of *Fascist Modernism* and *Political Inversions*. He is currently completing a book on dance and the emergence of the modern cultural paradigm.

Gary Indiana is a novelist and playwright who divides his time between New York and Los Angeles. His novels include *Rent Boy*, *Gone Tomorrow*, *Horse Crazy*, and *Resentment: A Comedy*, and he has also published a collection of essays, *Let It Bleed*, and two short-story collections. Among Indiana's plays are the award-winning *Roy Cohn/Jack Smith*, *The Roman Polanski Story*, and *Phantoms of Louisiana*.

Rhonda Lieberman, a recovering theorist, lives in Queens, New York.

Catherine Liu is assistant professor of cultural studies and comparative literature at the University of Minnesota. She recently published her first novel, *Oriental Girls Desire Romance.* Liu is active as an art critic and curator.

Fred Moten is assistant professor of performance studies at New York University. His essays have appeared in *Women in Performance, Semiotics 94,* and the journal *Proliferations.* Moten's book in progress, *Event Music,* addresses reproduction in black aural performance.

John Mowitt is associate professor of cultural studies and comparative literature at the University of Minnesota. He is the author of *Text: The Genealogy of an Antidisciplinary Object,* as well as numerous journal articles.

Laurence A. Rickels is professor of German and comparative literature at the University of California, Santa Barbara, and adjunct professor in the art studio and film studies department. He is not only theorist but also therapist, currently employed at the Westside Neighborhood Medical Clinic in Santa Barbara. He is the author of *The Vampire Lectures* (Minnesota, 1999), *The Case of California, Aberrations of Mourning,* and editor of *Looking after Nietzsche.* A new book, *Nazi Psychoanalysis,* is forthcoming, and he is currently completing an *Occult Quartet* of "vampire screen texts," of which the first, "Take Out," is currently in film production.

Klaus Theweleit is an independent scholar and philosopher in Freiburg, Germany. He is the author of many books, including (in English translation) *Male Fantasies,* volume 1, *Women, Floods, Bodies, History,* volume 2, *Male Bodies: Psychoanalyzing the White Terror,* and *Object-Choice (All You Need Is Love ...: On Mating Strategies and a Fragment of "A Freud Biography").*

Elisabeth Weber is professor of Germanic and comparative literature at the University of California, Santa Barbara. She is currently working on a book-length study of Jacques Lacan's *Ethics of Psychoanalysis.*

Permissions

Elisabeth Weber's piece, "Willfullness—*Eigensinn*," first appeared in translation under the title "Willfulness," in *Semiotics 90/91*, ed. John Deely and Terry Prewitt (Lanham and London: University Press of America, 1993): 231–36. Reprinted with permission.

"Of Wall, Sign, Screen, and Split: The Wall as National Mass Symbol of the Germans," by Klaus Theweleit, is excerpted and translated by Laurence A. Rickels, from *Das Land, das Ausland heißt*, by Klaus Theweleit. Copyright 1995 Deutscher Taschenbuch Verlag, Munich, Germany. Reprinted with permission.